REDEMPTIVE SERVICE

Loving Our Neighbors Well

Lisa P. Stephenson
and Ruthie Wienk

Baker Academic
a division of Baker Publishing Group
Grand Rapids, Michigan

© 2024 by Lisa P. Stephenson and Ruth Wienk

Published by Baker Academic
a division of Baker Publishing Group
Grand Rapids, Michigan
www.bakeracademic.com

Printed in the United States of America

Library of Congress Cataloging-in-Publication Data
Names: Stephenson, Lisa P., author. | Wienk, Ruthie, 1977– author.
Title: Redemptive service : loving our neighbors well / Lisa P. Stephenson and Ruthie Wienk.
Description: Grand Rapids, Michigan : Baker Academic, a division of Baker Publishing Group,
    [2024] | Includes bibliographical references and index.
Identifiers: LCCN 2024004938 | ISBN 9781540965219 (paperback) | ISBN 9781540965691
    (casebound) | ISBN 9781493436941 (ebook) | ISBN 9781493436958 (pdf)
Subjects: LCSH: Social justice—Biblical teaching. | Social justice—Religious aspects—Christianity.
    | Church and social problems.
Classification: LCC BS680.J8 S74 2024 | DDC 261.8—dc23/eng/20240226
LC record available at https://lccn.loc.gov/2024004938

Baker Publishing Group publications use paper produced from sustainable forestry practices and post-consumer waste whenever possible.

24   25   26   27   28   29   30   7   6   5   4   3   2   1

**FOR MY DAUGHTERS,
ABIGAIL AND ISABELLA,**
*may you continue to live your lives
in service to God and neighbors*
—L. P. S.

FOR DR. STEVEN FETTKE,
who taught me how to read the prophets
—R. W.

CONTENTS

ACKNOWLEDGMENTS

Much of the substance of this book emerged from the Benevolence Program at Lee University, in which we are both involved. Over the last several years we have piloted this content through that course and are grateful to the wonderful colleagues who provided invaluable feedback to us as they used the material in their own Benevolence classes. Additionally, we are appreciative to the students we have taught through the years in this class—and other related courses—who helped us further hone our own thoughts on the subject matter.

Many thanks also go to several local organizations and ministries that continually embody redemptive service in Cleveland, Tennessee, and push us to live out the Great Commandment better. Corrine Freeman and Dustin Tommey, your lifelong commitment to this work is a testament to the depths of your faith, and both of us have been enriched by your friendship. While you certainly are not the only ones doing good work in our town, you are the ones we have been fortunate enough to cross paths with and partner with as we all try to love our neighbors well.

We would like to express a special gratitude to our families, who endured with us through the writing process. While the manuscript took longer to produce than anticipated, we especially appreciate the patience and encouragement that our families demonstrated as we worked early mornings, late nights, and a few weekends every now and then. We love you and hope to redeem the time soon.

Finally, we are deeply grateful to the God who calls us to participate in his work of mending creation and who gifts us with skills that work toward that end. May we be ever mindful to faithfully live out what we are encouraging others to embrace.

INTRODUCTION

Appeals for justice and action abound in our society. Technology and social media have made us more aware than ever of the prevalent needs in our world. While it might be easy for us to write a check to a good cause or use our social media profiles to advocate for certain issues, we believe that the Christian faith requires more than that from Christ followers. It is our conviction that service to others—especially the vulnerable, poor, and oppressed—is not optional or marginal to our identity and mission as Christians; rather, it is required and central. If we are truly to be the people of God, the body of Christ, and the community of the Spirit, then pouring out our lives in service to others is essential. Benevolence—which we identify in chapter 1 as "redemptive service"—is not a means to an end (a way to entice others to hear the gospel) but part of the end itself (part of the gospel).

What we hope to establish in this book—especially in part 1—is that concern and care for the marginalized and impoverished is not a secular or foreign ideology that we are attempting to connect to the Christian faith. Rather, this orientation is deeply embedded within the Christian worldview and has grounded Christian faith claims and identity for centuries. It is not new, even if it has been forgotten from time to time. This book is by no means a blanket acceptance of all things "social justice" but a plea to keep your heart and mind open to hearing the biblical texts call us to action. These texts are no siren call but the voice of God attempting to rouse us out of our slumber.[1]

---

1. Nicholas Wolterstorff, "Why Care about Justice?," *Reformed Journal* 36, no. 8 (August 1986): 9–14; Wolterstorff, "The Contours of Justice: An Ancient Call for Shalom," in *God and*

We fully realize that the good news of the gospel cannot be reduced solely to social justice issues, and we are not suggesting they are the whole story.[2] But just because they are not the whole story does not mean they are not an integral part of the story. Many times Christians have failed to attend to this fact. To borrow a music analogy, social justice issues are only one part of the musical score, but this one part often gets drowned out by other portions of the music such that it is not heard at all. Therefore, this book attempts to turn up the volume on this theme so that it may be heard properly alongside the traditionally more dominant ones. And if the social justice score seems too loud, perhaps it is because we are not used to hearing it played!

Our Story

It would be a disservice to the reader not to offer an account of how we came to advocate for the ideas and practices discussed in this book. They certainly did not emerge in a vacuum. Nor were we born with benevolence in our DNA! It is much easier to write about this subject than it is to embody it in one's life. So, while neither of us are under any delusion that we have arrived on this journey of service to others, we are convinced that the vocation of redemptive service is one that Christians must learn to live out in the best way possible. Thus, we offer our own stories of embracing redemptive service to others so that you can learn more about us and why we are writing this book, as well as take comfort in the fact that we have learned by doing. We are still learning and refining our approaches by reflectively engaging in the process of serving others and learning as we go.

My (Lisa's) journey toward redemptive service is fairly unremarkable. I grew up in the South—in the suburbs of Atlanta—in a medium-sized, nondenominational church. I remember my church class periodically visiting nursing homes to bring homemade gifts and cheer to the residents.

the Victim: Theological Reflections on Evil, Victimization, Justice, and Forgiveness, ed. Lisa Barnes Lampman (Grand Rapids: Eerdmans, 1999), 107–30; Samuel L. Adams, "The Justice Imperative in Scripture," Interpretation: A Journal of Bible and Theology 69, no. 4 (2015): 399–414; Roy E. Gane, "Social Justice," in The Oxford Handbook of Biblical Law, ed. Pamela Barmash (Oxford: Oxford University Press, 2019), 19–34; and Mariam Kamell Kovalishyn, "A Biblical Theology of Social Justice," Crux 55, no. 3 (Fall 2019): 30–39.

2. We use the phrase "social justice" because we believe it is a fitting expression that communicates the biblical justice we see in Scripture. See Joe Carter, "The FAQs: What Christians Should Know about Social Justice," Gospel Coalition, August 17, 2018, https://www.thegospel coalition.org/article/faqs-christians-know-social-justice.

Once I was old enough to participate in the youth group, we periodically traveled to downtown Atlanta to serve people experiencing homelessness by engaging in the trifecta of street ministry: singing, preaching, and serving dinner. And every year at Christmas, the church would bus in kids from the downtown area and we would give them presents. While I enjoyed engaging in all of these benevolent activities and knew this was part of what Christ called his followers to do, it was not a main tenet of my spiritual life growing up. My collegiate years did not do much to change this orientation. Again, I was involved in various acts of service to the community from time to time—and even went on a short-term missions trip to Mexico City—but it was not a central focus of my faith or my studies.

It was not until I returned to teach at my alma mater as a college professor that I began to hear and heed the call to redemptive service in a way I had not previously. In the intervening years between my undergraduate graduation and finishing my doctoral degree, the university instituted an eighty-hour service mandate for all students, along with a required one-hour course. This program and course ultimately got me hooked on benevolence but ironically in the role of professor rather than that of student! It was through my involvement as an instructor in this course—and later my role in directing the academic portion of the program—that transformed the way I view service to others. After a decade of leading this program on the university campus, I have come to firmly believe that as Christians we must be attentive to the needs around us and take an active part in mending the brokenness in our world. It is in the context of this journey and from this perspective that I offer my ideas on redemptive service.

Like Lisa, my (Ruthie's) journey to redemptive service involved growing up in church—I was the pastor's daughter—and participating in outreach activities. I remember climbing into a bus with a youth group and driving into low-income urban areas to sing, preach, and perform skits or street theater. I also remember ministries to homeless populations, delivering secondhand clothes, and distributing small Bible tracts that present theology through comics. Additionally, I engaged in short-term missions trips. These experiences all informed my early views of service. However, the idea of transformational redemptive service began when I was in my twenties and starting my professional life.

Fueled by a desire for adventure as much as a desire to engage in benevolent activity, I moved to Khartoum, Sudan, for two years. This served as the beginning of my experience working in and thinking about community development. After leaving Khartoum, I lived and worked in South Korea and Costa Rica for a number of years. In addition to being culturally diverse, these three countries were at various stages of economic and human development. More important than my work, I had the opportunity to develop authentic relationships with locals. I was invited into homes as a friend and shared life with people. In each place, I realized that I had much in common with these new friends. Their families interacted in ways similar to that of my family. They would talk about the importance of work, centrality of housing, dreams, opportunities of education, and limits of health care. And though these people from vastly different social and cultural contexts had similar desires and personal potential, their everyday lived realities and life chances significantly differed from one another.

Seeing both our common humanity and how context limits people's opportunities, I was inspired to return to the US and pursue a doctorate in sociology. Through my studies and research, I have recently been engaging in development work in local communities in the US. So much of what I learned abroad can be put into practice at home. Working to address social ills and connect with people is at the heart of our Christian identity. We are called to care, but how do we care well? That's what I am still trying to figure out.

Overview of the Book

This book is organized into two parts, with the first section presenting the biblical and theological understandings of Christian benevolent activity and the second section presenting practical discussions of service that are grounded in research on what actually promotes justice for the marginalized. This division reflects a logical movement through the issues at hand (answering *why* before *how*), and it corresponds to each author's field of expertise as well. Lisa is a specialist in the area of Bible and theology, and Ruthie is trained as a sociologist who specializes in social stratification and community development. Accordingly, the first part is authored by Lisa and the second by Ruthie.

Part 1 focuses on answering the question of *why* we should serve others. These chapters develop a strong biblical and theological foundation that reveals God's call for Christians to be involved in redemptive service. Chapter 1 begins with distinguishing between "service" and "redemptive service." Because benevolence is not exclusive to Christians, we highlight what is unique about *Christian* service to others. While there are similarities between the benevolent acts of Christians and the benevolent acts of non-Christians, the Christian worldview is different. Therefore, this chapter examines more closely why worldviews are important, what a worldview entails, and what the Christian worldview maintains. From the very beginning God called humanity to serve and steward the world. This calling is not lost because of the fall; instead, because of sin, this calling is transformed into *redemptive* service because it must now participate in the restoration (redemption) of God's creational intent for the world. Chapters 2–5 thus examine how our calling as Christians to be the people of God, the body of Christ, and the community of the Spirit embraces what was initiated at creation by means of the *imago Dei* and informs our work in this world.

Chapters 2 and 3 focus on the Old Testament. Chapter 2 highlights the emergence of the Israelites as the people of God and the laws that governed their communal life. It becomes clear in the story of the exodus that God's redemption of the Israelites encompassed every aspect of life and that God's desire for his people was complete flourishing in this earthly life. Moreover, just as God was attentive to the vulnerable, poor, and oppressed, the Israelites were to be as well. The biblical laws guided the Israelites in how they were to live out their calling as the people of God. Chapter 3 surveys the prophetic texts and explores the significance of the Israelites' failure to act as the people of God. While the prophetic books are not all doom and gloom, the message of judgment is clear and severe, even as there is hope for a renewed future. The prophets help us see the seriousness of our neglect of the vulnerable, poor, and oppressed, as well as the deficiency of our faith without attentiveness to redemptive service.

Chapters 4 and 5 focus on the New Testament. Chapter 4 examines the life and ministry of Jesus Christ, noting that the message he brought was not just the good news of forgiveness of sins and personal salvation but the good news of the kingdom of God and new creation. Integral to the advent of this kingdom is Jesus' own benevolent service for the sake of the world. Jesus is the image of God himself, and as followers of Jesus we are transformed through him so that we become the body of Christ and participate in this mission of service and care for the world as well. To be the body of Christ is to continue Christ's work of ushering in the kingdom of God and bringing God's shalom to fruition. Chapter 5 examines the continuation of this story through the outpouring of the Spirit at Pentecost. In the New Testament, the benevolent vocation of both Jesus and the early church is dependent on the work of the Spirit. The ministry

inaugurated by Jesus is transferred to the church, which is empowered
by the outpouring of the Spirit at Pentecost, just as the Spirit rested on
Jesus. As a community of the Spirit, we are empowered to work toward
the realization of the new creation.

Part 2 shifts the focus from *why* one should serve others to exploring
how one should go about this. While having a heart to serve and being
moved with compassion toward one's neighbor is a beautiful disposition,
it is not enough. In fulfilling the call to love our neighbors as ourselves,
it becomes imperative that we love well. Whether or not we love well is
exemplified in the forms of service that we adopt as we work toward
bringing healing to the brokenness around us. Not all service models are
created equal, and not all of them are appropriate in every situation. This
nexus of *intent* versus *impact* is at the heart of the second half of the book.

Chapter 6 explores various ways people have defined and measured poverty, as well as various explanations that account for why it exists. There
are limits to approaching poverty from a purely economic perspective. A
multifaceted view of poverty includes multiple dimensions of exclusion
and lack, including social, emotional, and spiritual poverty, as well as the
more common understanding of economic poverty. Using this lens, all
of us experience poverty at some point. Being aware of this provides us
with a meaningful foundation for Christian service and interaction with
society. Rather than seeing ourselves as the "haves" and the recipients as
the "have-nots," we are all engaged in mutual learning and help. There
are a variety of reasons persons might be experiencing poverty. To focus
on only one explanation can cause us to misjudge others and fail to participate in any meaningful change.

Chapter 7 focuses on short-term interventions that are commonly called
"relief work," equivalent to giving a hungry person a fish. These interventions often come in the form of food banks, clothing drives, and temporary
shelters for people who experience homelessness. Another major type of
short-term intervention is disaster relief. Short-term interventions that are
beneficial for people empower them and are integrated into a long-term
plan for self-reliance. The chapter builds on the importance of mutual
learning and meaningful connections with others when engaging in redemptive service. Such undertakings are vital components of engagement
with a broken world. The chapter ends with practical suggestions for
service volunteers.

Chapter 8 discusses development, which is equivalent to teaching a
hungry person to fish. We differentiate between economic and human de-

velopment. Development usually entails long-term interventions that seek to build people's capacity. Community development as benevolent Christian activity recognizes the assets of a community. Seeing the strengths of a community of people is a vital part of doing development work. This chapter introduces four principles of development that can be used in evaluating the benefits of different programs.

Chapter 9 presents the concept of advocacy, which in the fishing analogy is equivalent to fixing the pond. Advocacy efforts are a necessary extension of community development. Though each community has unique assets, there is often a gap between what members of a community want to accomplish and what they can accomplish. Usually, this gap is the result of structural limitations that need to be addressed through policy, infrastructure, and other built environment interventions. Advocacy takes a multifaceted approach to understanding social structures and identifies the structural limitations that impact the ability of people to achieve their potential. As with relief and development, the perspectives of communities themselves are prioritized in advocacy campaigns.

Chapter 10 prioritizes people as the heart of any authentic and Christ-centered discussion of relief, development, and advocacy. This chapter encourages looking at a community's social location in order to understand who is included and excluded from planning and policy work. Social location is the system of inequalities that provide advantages for some people and struggles for others. Certain populations are often hidden and missing from community intervention projects, leading to dire consequences for certain members of the population. Understanding social location can highlight who might be missing from common service endeavors.

The conclusion of the book reflects on the intersection of redemptive service and calling. This conclusion presents a threefold distinction for understanding calling (general, missional, and direct) and focuses on one's missional calling and how it relates to redemptive service. Redemptive service is ultimately about connecting our missional calling to the needs of the world and finding ways to use the unique gifts and talents God has given us to make the world a better place. While God is calling all of us as citizens of God's kingdom to work toward the flourishing of all life, including the healing and renewal of creation, how we fulfill this calling individually will depend on who God created us to be. We conclude by highlighting excuses that prevent us from engaging in redemptive service, as we remember that every act of service we perform makes a difference in the kingdom of God and the world.

This book is written to be accessible and interesting to both the academic and lay audience, and it is our hope that any reader will find it insightful and helpful. The chapters are specially designed so that the book can be easily used as a textbook in Christian colleges—particularly those with service-learning emphases—or as a resource for churches. At the end of each chapter we offer discussion questions and a list of further readings in the subject area. These recommendations are not meant as a wholesale endorsement of the resources but are simply suggestions to promote further critical reflection. Moreover, the book is not just a summary of others' views on these issues but our proposal for framing and explaining service to others in light of the Christian worldview. Those looking for critical dialogue and engagement with scholarly sources on the issues will find the more academic discussions and resources in the footnotes.

Potential Responses

When learning about issues of benevolence, two reactions often occur. First, people can be convicted by the realization that their own lives are not fully attuned toward others. We recognize that far too often the character we most resemble is not that of the good Samaritan but rather that of the priest or Levite. Quite frankly, we hope that you do experience this conviction at some point while reading this book, as we did while writing it! As Christians, we should always seek to live a more Christlike life, and we believe that the Spirit can work through such a book to change our ways. Conviction is good! In response to conviction, we don't need to feel ashamed; instead, we can seek to more fully embody the calling God has placed on us to serve others.

Second, once people begin to learn more about the rampant brokenness in the world, they might feel overwhelmed by the enormity of the problems. Rather than motivating us to action, some find that this can lead to feelings of discouragement and depression. If you feel this way at some point while reading this book, you are not alone. However, instead of trying to escape or avoid this gloominess, we encourage you to lean into it. Poverty is uncomfortable. Injustice is uncomfortable. It is an important step in the learning process to understand the magnitude of the brokenness of our world and our own relative limitations. We want to focus not on how to make ourselves feel better but on how to find the courage and strength to continue to run into the tension and the brokenness, looking for ways to make meaningful connections with people and share in the work of relief, development, and advocacy in a manner that will elevate others' dignity. This book is not intended to be a feel-good read—there is a lot of hard work to be done. Rather, this book is meant to be an awakening call that causes us to rise from our slumber and image God in the world around us in meaningful ways by means of our redemptive service.

PART 1

Biblical and Theological Resources for Seeing Our Neighbors

The story of the good Samaritan (Luke 10:25–37) is a commonly cited text when looking for Scripture passages that address service to others. It is frequently offered as a parable primarily about "doing." That is, the narrative compares and contrasts various characters who are given an opportunity to help another person who has been beaten and left for dead. The priest and the Levite choose to ignore the poor man and do nothing. However, the Samaritan stops, bandages the man, and brings him to an inn, where he can receive further care. Jesus concludes the narrative by challenging the expert in the law who had prompted the discussion to "go and do likewise" (10:37). So, this is a parable primarily about *doing* something, right? Well, yes and no! Certainly, a main facet of the narrative is whether one does something for one's neighbors, especially when they are in dire need. However, prior to *doing* is *seeing*.

In reexamining the parable of the good Samaritan, there is a common word that is repeated throughout the narrative for all three of the men who were traveling on the road.[1] When the text introduces the three characters as they encounter the beaten man, it says they each "saw" him. It is a simple word that could be easily overlooked amid other significant details. And yet it is a crucial element for properly understanding the full implications of the story. The priest sees, but he passes by (10:31). The Levite sees, but he also passes by (v. 32). Then the Samaritan also sees, but he does not pass by (v. 33). Rather, he chooses to stop and act.

The Greek wording is identical in all three instances, but the author uses irony to make a point. The text says that the priest and the Levite see the man, yet they do nothing. Given their actions—or lack of—this should cause the reader to wonder whether the priest and Levite truly see the man. Despite the fact that the priest and Levite *look* at the beaten man, they do not actually *see* him. But the Samaritan not only *looks* at the beaten man; he truly *sees* him! How do we know? Because of his actions that follow. While this parable surely emphasizes doing something for others, what we *do* for others is dependent first on how we *see* others. The story of the good Samaritan is as much a parable about *seeing* as it is about *doing*.

The difference between the three encounters is that the first two men perceive the beaten man with their eyes alone, but the Samaritan's vision is accompanied by "compassion" for him (v. 33).[2] What is it about compassion that allowed the Samaritan to truly see the beaten man? Compassion is more than pity or feeling sorry for others. Compassion causes us "to identify with another's situation such that we are prepared to act for his or her benefit."[3] It is a disposition of solidarity: their situation and suffering become our own; their burdens become our burdens. The Samaritan was

---

1. There are many aspects to the narrative that are important to appreciate (e.g., the relationship between the Jews and Samaritans). For further contextual details, see Joel B. Green, *The Gospel of Luke*, New International Commentary on the New Testament (Grand Rapids: Eerdmans, 1997), 424–32; and John Nolland, *Luke 9:21–18:34*, Word Biblical Commentary 35B (Grand Rapids: Zondervan, 1993), 586–98.

2. All three instances in the Gospel of Luke that mention "compassion" are connected with the verb "to see" (cf. Luke 7:13; 10:33; 15:20), in contrast to the other two Synoptic Gospels, which do not always pair "compassion" with the act of seeing (cf. Matt. 15:32; 18:27; 20:34; Mark 1:41; 8:2; 9:22). For Luke, in order to truly see the other, one must see with compassion. Phil C. Zylla explores more fully the intersection between compassion and seeing in his article "Inhabiting Compassion: A Pastoral Theological Paradigm," *HTS Teologiese Studies / Theological Studies* 73, no. 4 (2017): 1–9.

3. Nolland, *Luke 9:21–18:34*, 594.

moved to action by the beaten man's condition and responded accordingly. Of the three travelers passing by, he was the only one who truly *saw*.

Thus, having eyes to see is intimately connected with our love and heart for others, especially those on the margins of society. The first part of the parable of the good Samaritan is about having eyes to see, and so the first part of this book is about seeing. Redemptive service must emerge from a genuine love of our neighbor, not just obligation. And a genuine love of our neighbor best arises when one's service emerges from a Christian worldview, in which we come to a better understanding of our role as human beings in this world and begin to see others the way God sees them.

We are not suggesting that we wait until our heart is perfectly turned toward the other and overflowing with compassion before we begin to serve. If that were the case, most of us would still be on the sidelines! What we are suggesting is that in attending to the actual *practice* of serving others, we should attend to our *perception* of others as well. These two aspects go hand in hand. It is frequently through service to others that we find our hearts are changed in ways we could have never anticipated. So, while the task of the first part of this book is to offer readers ideas and principles that help us see others as God sees them, we fully realize that it is through personally engaging in service (detailed in the second part of the book) that this transformative vision truly takes place. In loving and serving our neighbor, we must have properly formed hearts and practices.

1

Twenty-Twenty Vision

Christian Identity and Mission

Engaging in benevolent service toward others is not an exclusively Christian act. Consider the countless organizations and individuals worldwide who seek to make this world a better place but are either committed to another religion or possess no faith claims whatsoever. An example of this is Malala Yousafzai, a young lady who has devoted her life to ensuring that other females like herself have access to free, safe, and quality education. In January 2008, at eleven years of age, Malala was banned from attending school in her hometown in Pakistan because the Taliban prohibited females from being educated and had burned the girls' schools down. Undeterred, Malala began to speak up on behalf of females and their right to learn. This made her a target of the Taliban, and in October 2012 a masked gunman boarded the bus she was riding and shot her in the head. She survived the attack but had to flee to England. Even still, Malala did not abandon the fight and found a renewed passion and vision to ensure that every female could go to school. She established the Malala Fund, a charity dedicated to giving every young female the opportunity to achieve the future they choose for themselves. In 2014 Malala became the youngest person ever to win the Nobel Peace Prize.[1]

1. "Malala Yousafzai," Nobel Prize (website), accessed May 16, 2022, https://www.nobelprize.org/prizes/peace/2014/yousafzai/facts; Malala Yousafzai, *I Am Malala: The Girl Who Stood Up for Education and Was Shot by the Taliban*, with Christina Lamb (New York: Little, Brown, 2013).

Malala's activism is an amazing example of benevolent service, and yet she is not a Christian but a devout Muslim. That doesn't make her contribution any less significant. But it does raise an important question: What is the difference between benevolent service that non-Christians engage in and service that Christians engage in? Is there a difference? On the one hand, it might seem that there is not much of a distinction at all. Non-Christians and Christians alike feed the poor, house the unhoused, and work for justice. In fact, these two groups can share best practices in the field and even work side-by-side on certain issues. On the other hand, despite similarities, there is fundamentally at least one major distinction between non-Christians and Christians: their worldview. And this difference makes all the difference![2]

In this chapter we unpack the concept of worldview, delineating several elements (stories, answers, and praxis) that make up a worldview. We use these three aspects to explore in further detail the Christian worldview. Only after these two steps are taken can we better understand what is meant by "redemptive service" and why this distinguishes *Christian* service from service offered by those outside the faith. An essential characteristic of the Christian worldview is that we are created in the image of God and, as such, are called to engage in redemptive service to the world. From a Christian perspective, our *identity* as the image of God necessitates that our *mission* is one of service to others.

What Is a Worldview?

Before offering a definition of "worldview" and highlighting its various aspects, let's first consider a helpful illustration from *The Magician's Nephew*—a novel in C. S. Lewis' famous Chronicles of Narnia series.[3]

---

2. The purpose of distinguishing between worldviews is not to preclude Christians from working with those from other faiths. Rather, it is to highlight how one's particular worldview shapes that work. To explore other worldviews—religious and cultural—that compete with the Christian worldview, see David Burnett, *Clash of Worlds* (Nashville: Oliver-Nelson, 1992), 39–118, 168–204; W. Gary Phillips, William E. Brown, and John Stonestreet, *Making Sense of Your World: A Biblical Worldview*, 2nd ed. (Salem, WI: Sheffield, 2008), 19–60; James W. Sire, *The Universe Next Door: A Basic Worldview Catalog*, 6th ed. (Downers Grove, IL: InterVarsity, 2020); Paul G. Hiebert, *Transforming Worldviews: An Anthropological Understanding of How People Change* (Grand Rapids: Baker Academic, 2008), 105–264; and Steve Wilkens and Mark L. Sanford, *Hidden Worldviews: Eight Cultural Stories That Shape Our Lives* (Downers Grove, IL: InterVarsity, 2009).

3. C. S. Lewis, *The Magician's Nephew* (1955; repr., New York: Harper Trophy, 2000). I am indebted to David Naugle who used this same story in the prologue of his book on worldviews, *Worldview: The History of a Concept* (Grand Rapids: Eerdmans, 2002), 1–3.

The overarching story of the book finds two children, Digory and Polly, immersed in an adventure sparked by the finding of magic rings. As the plot unfolds, Digory and Polly accidentally bring the wicked Queen Jadis back from her world of Charn to London. In Digory and Polly's attempt to return Queen Jadis to her world, they accidentally arrive in the land of Narnia. Along with Queen Jadis, several other people accompany Digory and Polly to Narnia as well, including Digory's uncle, Andrew—a shady and selfish character.

At this point in the story, the worldview illustration begins to materialize. When the group reaches Narnia, it is dark, and they find that it is an empty world. However, moments after arriving, they begin to hear a voice singing from a distance. Immediately the blackness is pierced by thousands of points of light as stars, constellations, and planets are created. While the sun begins to rise to bring even more light into the world, the source of the singing is revealed. Aslan the lion emerges. Aslan continues to sing his song, and the creation of Narnia continues to unfold.

Yet not all the parties see and hear the same things. Digory and Polly welcome the voice. The story describes them as drinking in the sound with shining eyes and open mouths of joy. The music is beautiful to their ears, and the emergence of new life is wondrous to behold. As Aslan's song dies down, the creation of the new world culminates in Aslan's speaking Narnia into existence and commanding the animals to speak.[4] Digory and Polly begin to hear the animals conversing with one another in human words, and they begin to talk to the animals as well.

Uncle Andrew's experience of Narnia, however, is quite different from Digory's and Polly's; it is not pleasant at all. The only thing he comes to value in this new world is the commercial possibilities it holds for him because of its youth-enhancing climate and its magical abilities to grow whole objects from merely a small part (like a bar from a lamppost in London is sown into the ground and grows into an entirely new lamppost). When Uncle Andrew begins to hear Aslan's voice, he does not like it. He, too, opens his mouth in response but not with joy; his shoulders stoop, his teeth chatter, and his knees shake. Uncle Andrew wants to escape from the singing. To him Narnia is a terrible, disagreeable world, and Aslan is a brute. Uncle Andrew dislikes Aslan's singing so much that he tries to make himself believe that he can hear only roaring. After a while, that is in fact all he can hear. When Aslan calls Narnia to awaken, the only thing

4. Lewis, *Magician's Nephew*, 108, 126.

Uncle Andrew hears is a snarl. When the animals begin to talk, the only thing Uncle Andrew hears are barkings, growlings, bayings, and howlings.[5]

Why does Uncle Andrew experience Aslan and the founding of Narnia in such a different way from Digory and Polly? Why does he see and hear things contrary to what Digory and Polly see and hear? The narrator of the story answers that what someone hears and sees depends on where a person is standing and what kind of person they are.[6] To Uncle Andrew it is not an enchanting world full of promise and hope but a threatening world full of terrifying creatures. His experience of Narnia is shaped by his worldview, just as Digory and Polly's experience is shaped by their worldview. Worldview is important because it affects the way we see and hear the world. In the case of benevolence, it is central when distinguishing between service and redemptive service.

What is a worldview?[7] Many definitions focus on the second part of the word—world*view*—using the metaphor of sight for their explanation. Worldview is identified as the way one "sees" the world; it is not a literal, physical view but a philosophical perspective. Everyone has a worldview—examined or unexamined, implicit or explicit, simplistic or sophisticated—even though most of the time we take it for granted. Our worldview is like a pair of tinted glasses that we cannot remove. We all wear a pair, and our interpretation of the world is colored by our particular lenses. Most of the time we look *through* our worldview rather than *at* it.[8]

However, this simple analogy should not obscure the power that one's worldview holds. Our worldview is not merely descriptive but prescriptive as well. A worldview is not just a vision *of* life; it is a vision *for* life. One's worldview "provides a model *of the world* which guides its adherents *in the world*. It stipulates how the world ought to be, and it thus advises how its adherents ought to conduct themselves in the world."[9] Consequently,

---

5. Lewis, *Magician's Nephew*, 108–9, 110, 117, 137.

6. Lewis, *Magician's Nephew*, 136.

7. For a detailed account of the historical development of the term, see Naugle, *Worldview*; Hiebert, *Transforming Worldviews*, 13–24; and James W. Sire, *Naming the Elephant: Worldview as a Concept*, 2nd ed. (Downers Grove, IL: InterVarsity, 2015), 23–69.

8. David A. Sherwood, "The Relationship between Beliefs and Values in Social Work Practice: Worldviews Make a Difference," in *Christianity and Social Work: Readings on the Integration of Christian Faith and Social Work Practice*, 6th ed., ed. T. Laine Scales and Michael S. Kelly (Botsford, CT: North American Association of Christians in Social Work, 2020), 83; and James N. Anderson, *What's Your Worldview? An Interactive Approach to Life's Big Questions* (Wheaton: Crossway, 2014), 12–13.

9. Brian J. Walsh and J. Richard Middleton, *The Transforming Vision: Shaping a Christian World View* (Downers Grove, IL: InterVarsity, 1984), 31–32.

while a worldview determines how we see the world (theory), it also affects the way we act in the world (praxis). James N. Anderson sums it up well in saying that a worldview is a "network of ultimate beliefs, assumptions, values, and ideas about the universe and our place in it that shapes how a person understands their life and experiences (and the lives and experiences of others) and how that person acts in response."[10]

To better understand worldviews, let's look at what a worldview provides. First, worldviews provide a *story* through which people view reality. These narratives are offered as a means of making sense of the world. Second, using these narratives, a worldview provides *answers* to the fundamental questions of life. A worldview's narrative offers answers to questions such as,

> Who are we? (The nature, task, and purpose of being human.)
>
> Where are we? (The nature of the reality of the world.)
>
> What is wrong? (How we understand and account for evil and brokenness in the world.)
>
> What is the solution? (The path from brokenness to wholeness.)

Finally, worldviews provide a *praxis*, or way of being, in the world that is necessitated by the other two elements. The question "What is the solution?" necessitates action. In order to work toward the wholeness that is defined by our worldview, we must do something. The real shape of someone's worldview can often be seen in their actions. If you want to know what a person sees, watch how they walk! A person's actions reflect their worldview.[11]

These three elements (story, answers, and praxis) together form a worldview, and we will utilize them throughout this book in the discussion of benevolent service. To better understand how they relate to the Christian worldview, let's examine these three aspects further and demonstrate how each one is embodied within the Christian worldview. Ultimately, they determine how we as Christians think about and engage with the world.

10. James N. Anderson, "What in the World Is a Worldview? Part 4," Crossway, January 31, 2014, https://www.crossway.org/articles/what-it-takes-to-make-a-worldview.

11. N. T. Wright, *Christian Origins and the Question of God*, vol. 1, *The New Testament and the People of God* (Minneapolis: Fortress, 1992), 123–24. In addition to stories, answers, and praxis, Wright also includes symbols as a fourth feature of worldviews. While I concur and would suggest that the image of God, the people of God, the body of Christ, and the community of the Spirit all function as symbols within the Christian worldview, the subject matter at hand is better served by focusing on story, answers, and praxis.

What Is the Christian Worldview?

Story: Plot Analysis[12]

The heart of Christianity is the story that it tells. Proclaimed as good news, the story has been told and retold for generations. Millions have been inspired by its worldview and have devoted themselves to living out its claims. But what precisely is this story about? Is it about Jesus? The church? How to get to heaven? To answer these important questions, it is helpful to take a step back from the content of the story to observe the structure of the narrative and how it functions. Only after the structure is established can we understand how the plot comes together and thus understand what the story is about. By examining the overarching structure first, we are forced to slow down and carefully attend to what is truly happening. New Testament scholar N. T. Wright writes, "Without close attention to the different phases of how the story actually works, the interpreter is almost bound to jump too quickly to this or that (probably wrong) conclusion, particularly when the story in question is over-familiar through frequent retelling."[13] Since the Christian story forms a key element in the construction and perpetuation of the Christian worldview, it is important that we understand this story correctly.

As with any story, within the story of Scripture lies a plot. At its most basic level, a plot involves something going wrong (narrative tension) and then being fixed (narrative resolution). With respect to Scripture, we can easily see how the biblical narrative of sin and redemption fits into this twofold movement. First, God creates the world with a purpose and a plan, but a problem arises that prevents God's purpose and plan from being realized (narrative tension). The problem is dealt with so that God's purpose and plan come to fulfillment (narrative resolution). This plot scheme, referred to as creation-fall-redemption, forms the basic structure of the overarching narrative of Scripture.[14]

---

12. While the whole of Scripture contains an overarching story, it is not a continuous narrative. Contained within the pages of the Bible is a collection of writings that were produced and assembled in stages over an extensive period of time. Even though we may recognize an overarching narrative that stretches throughout the Bible, we should still be careful to give due attention to the individuality of the various books that make up the canon.

13. Wright, New Testament and the People of God, 70.

14. Yet as J. Richard Middleton points out, while Christians may readily give lip service to this basic framework, it does not always function as a guide for reading Scripture. This happens because sometimes one can miss the forest for the trees! A person can get lost in the details of Scripture and lose sight of the overarching narrative within which those details are situated. Or a person can focus so much on the narrative resolution (redemption or salvation)—which

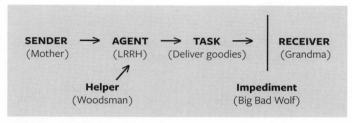

Figure 1.1 Plot analysis of Little Red Riding Hood
J. Richard Middleton, *A New Heaven and a New Earth: Reclaiming Biblical Eschatology* (Grand Rapids: Baker Academic, 2014), 59.

To better comprehend the dynamics of the biblical plot, we can use additional narratival categories: sender, agent, task, and receiver. To understand more clearly how these categories function, it is helpful to apply them to a simpler story before turning to the biblical story. The tale of Little Red Riding Hood serves as an excellent example for narrative analysis. The story begins with the girl, Little Red Riding Hood, being asked by her mother to bring a basket of goodies to her grandmother, who is sick. The narratival categories laid out in the beginning of the story can be identified as *sender* (the mother), *agent* (Little Red Riding Hood), *task* (deliver goodies), and *receiver* (the grandmother). These four elements make up the initial narrative sequence, but they do not yet form a plot because the narrative tension has not been introduced. Thus, the Big Bad Wolf enters the story and prevents Little Red Riding Hood from completing her task. The Big Bad Wolf acts as an *impediment* and provides the story with narrative tension. Finally, a woodsman comes to the aid of Little Red Riding Hood and serves as a *helper*, or a second agent, whose task is to aid in removing the impediment. The woodsman kills the wolf and assists Little Red Riding Hood in fulfilling her task (see fig. 1.1).[15]

We can apply these same categories of plot analysis to Scripture. In the opening of Genesis, the biblical version of sender, agent, task, and receiver is unveiled. The first few chapters of Genesis are not merely a prologue

admittedly occupies a majority of the biblical text—that the overall structure of the biblical plot is missed. This is especially true as it relates to the redemptive movements of Scripture being grounded in creation. Without having a proper understanding of the initial state (creation) and the nature of the problem (fall), one risks misreading the nature of the repair (redemption). See Middleton, *A New Heaven and a New Earth: Reclaiming Biblical Eschatology* (Grand Rapids: Baker Academic, 2014), 38.

15. Both N. T. Wright and J. Richard Middleton examine the biblical narrative through the motif of narrative analysis and use the story of Little Red Riding Hood to illustrate. See Wright, *New Testament and the People of God*, 69–73; and Middleton, *A New Heaven and a New Earth*, 57–59.

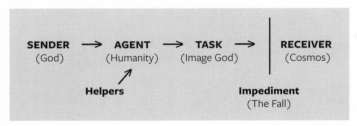

Figure 1.2 Plot analysis of the biblical narrative

that gives way to the real story; they reveal a crucial development that sets in motion the shape of the remainder of the story—Genesis through Revelation! In the narrative sequence of Genesis 1–2, God (sender) creates the human race (agent), giving humanity its earthly vocation to function as images of God (task) for the rest of creation (receiver). In Genesis 3, an *impediment* to humanity's task is introduced. Sin enters the narrative and tragically compromises the human task of imaging God. However, as in the tale of Little Red Riding Hood, the introduction of the impediment within the biblical narrative is not the end of the story. Rather, it is a summons for *helpers* to be introduced who assist the agents in their task—this portion of the plot constitutes much of the remainder of the biblical text (see fig. 1.2).[16] Given the importance of the first three chapters of Genesis to the biblical narrative, we will attend to some of the details of the story below to understand them further.

Genesis 1–2

Genesis 1–2 establishes the creation of the world and our place as humans within it. It offers a cosmology. Like any cosmology, its purpose is to provide a source of identity and orientation to the world; its function is to tell us who we are.[17] A key text for understanding and recognizing the plot development is Genesis 1:26–28:

16. Middleton, *A New Heaven and a New Earth*, 59–73.
17. The biblical creation story is not the only cosmology. Other ancient Near Eastern texts include their own accounts of creation as well. Many scholars have noted the similarities between various elements of the Genesis creation narratives and these other cosmologies—especially the Enuma Elish—but ultimately conclude that the Genesis narratives challenge and upend features found elsewhere in order to create its own alternative worldview. This occurs most notably in its monotheistic assertion and the role it grants to humanity within the cosmos. Rather than positing a divinely established hierarchical and dimorphic world where the majority of persons are created for the purpose of being cheap slave labor for the gods, the biblical creation story

Then God said, "Let us make humans in our image, according to our likeness, and let them have dominion over the fish of the sea and over the birds of the air and over the cattle and over all the wild animals of the earth and over every creeping thing that creeps upon the earth."

> So God created humans in his image,
> in the image of God he created them;
> male and female he created them.

God blessed them, and God said to them, "Be fruitful and multiply and fill the earth and subdue it and have dominion over the fish of the sea and over the birds of the air and over every living thing that moves upon the earth."

Here, among the creation of the cosmos, God creates humanity after God's own image and likeness. This is referred to as the *imago Dei* (image of God). There has been much historical debate as to what precisely it means that humans are made in the image of God. However, contemporary biblical scholars overwhelmingly agree that there are clues in the text itself and the surrounding cultures of the time that help us understand the meaning of this central human attribute. They conclude that ultimately the text points to a functional understanding of the image.[18] That is, being made in the image of God is related to the functions humans are entrusted to carry out as part of God's creation. Humans are given an earthly vocation to serve as God's representatives and agents in this world, sharing in God's rule and administration of earth's resources and creatures. Genesis 1:26–28 portrays the task as ruling animals and subduing the earth. Genesis 2:15 describes it as working and protecting

---

maintains that *all* humans are made in the *imago Dei* and are created for a governing purpose. See J. Richard Middleton, *The Liberating Image: The Imago Dei in Genesis 1* (Grand Rapids: Brazos, 2005).

18. There are three dominant approaches to understanding the image of God. The *substantial* or structural interpretation points to a capacity or capacities constitutive of being human that reflect God in some way. The most common human trait identified with this approach is humanity's capacity for rational thought. The *relational* interpretation—popular among theologians—highlights humans' relational nature to God, other humans, and creation, and it maintains that this relationality images God, who is also a relational being. The *functional* interpretation—widely held among biblical scholars—proposes that humans image God in their vocational function to serve as God's representatives and agents in the world, sharing in God's authority and power to rule over the earth's resources and creatures. Given the ancient Near Eastern context and the wider usage of "image of God" language outside the biblical texts, the functional interpretation seems the most faithful to the original sense of the phrase. See Marc Cortez, *Theological Anthropology: A Guide for the Perplexed* (New York: T&T Clark, 2010), 14–40; and Middleton, *Liberating Image*.

the garden. And Psalm 8:5–8, though not at the beginning of the Bible, reveals that God made humans to rule over the works of God's hands and that all things have been put under their feet. J. Richard Middleton summarizes these biblical passages: "In all these creation texts, the movement is what we might call 'missional'—from God via humans outward to the earth. The fundamental human task is conceived in rather mundane terms as the responsible exercise of power on God's behalf over our earthly environment."[19]

How we as humans are to wield that power and live out our earthly vocation as the *imago Dei* is a crucial plot point.[20] The Genesis narrative offers two complementary dimensions to humanity's task. First, there is a *developmental* dimension to the notion of rule, exemplified initially in God's creation of the world and then given by humans. Humanity's rule is modeled on God's rule. Genesis 1:1–2:3 depicts God's creation of the world as an act of *forming* and *filling*. On days one through three, the focus is largely on God *forming* the realms of the created order: day, night, sky, sea, and land. On days four through six, the focus is largely on God *filling* these regions with its occupants: luminaries, birds, fish, animals, and humans. In both acts, there is a progression from heaven (days one and four) to waters (days two and five) to earth (days three and six). This beautiful literary correspondence depicts a Creator God who carefully plans and constructs the world for the benefit of all creatures. Moreover, throughout the creation process, God does not hoard divine creative power but is generous with it and shares it with creatures—both human and nonhuman—so that they make their own contributions to the harmony and beauty of the world.[21]

19. Middleton, *A New Heaven and a New Earth*, 39.

20. Not all scholars welcome the notion of "rule" as central to a theological anthropology, given humanity's historical abuse of power. However, Middleton notes that the issue is not whether humans have power but *how* they organize and use such power. Consequently, the narrative of Gen. 1 functions as a polemic over and against ancient Near Eastern notions of humanity and kingship and was not intended to be oppressive but liberating and empowering. The biblical worldview presented at the beginning of Genesis served as an alternative vision to the ancient Near Eastern worldview. See J. Richard Middleton, "The Liberating Image? Interpreting the *Imago Dei* in Context," *Christian Scholar's Review* 24, no. 1 (September 1994): 13–25; and Middleton, *Liberating Image*, 185–297.

21. Some scholars even propose that the introductory statement in Gen. 1:2 that describes the earth as "formless" and "empty" corresponds to and anticipates the acts of forming and filling that occur in the subsequent verses: God bringing form and structure to that which was *formless* (days one through three) and God filling with living creatures that which was *empty* (days four through six). See Middleton, *Liberating Image*, 74–77, 287–96; and Middleton, *A New Heaven and a New Earth*, 50–52.

God's twofold creative activity of forming and filling is mirrored in the twofold task given to humanity to "fill the earth and subdue it," though the task is now reversed (Gen. 1:28). Humanity must first fill the earth before they can form it. The Creator has started the task of forming and filling, and now humans—as God's earthly representatives and agents—are called to continue God's creative activity. God fashions a highly dynamic, not static, world. The future lies open to countless possibilities, and humanity is granted a central task in developing these possibilities. Thus, to "rule" should not be understood as a license to exploit and abuse but to secure the well-being of others and assist in bringing the promise of each living thing to its full fruition. The earth is "very good" (1:31) when God completes the creative process, but it is not perfect in the sense that humans cannot continue to further its goodness. God's rest on the seventh day (2:1–3) represents the delegation from God as Artisan-Creator to humanity as images of this Artisan-Creator to develop the world around them.[22] Humanity lives as the image of God as it utilizes its power in a developmental and transformative way, which becomes the task of forming culture and developing civilization. Hence, as Genesis 1–11 unfolds, there is repeated interest in human cultural achievements and innovations.[23]

Second, there is a *priestly* dimension to the notion of rule. God creates the world in Genesis 1–2, and this world is presented throughout the rest of the Old Testament as a cosmic temple, equivalent to God's kingdom. Humanity has been placed as priests of creation in this temple, actively representing and mediating God's presence on earth as the image of God. Middleton elaborates on this priestly dimension:

> By our obedient exercise of power, humanity as *imago Dei* functions like a prism, refracting the pure light of God into a rainbow of cultural activities that scintillate with the creator's glory throughout the earth. By our

22. Many Old Testament scholars claim that the seventh day of creation institutes the Sabbath, but Middleton persuasively argues that there is no justification within the rhetoric of the text itself for this reading, even though this is how the text came to be read. See Middleton, *Liberating Image*, 88–90, 212, 289–96.

23. Gen. 2 portrays Adam and Eve as called to the task of agricultural cultivation of land and the domestication of animals, two tasks that constitute the minimal historical requirements for organized human society and culture. The garden is not just a natural phenomenon but a cultural project as well. Thus, Gen. 2 denotes agriculture as the first communal, cultural project of humanity. See Middleton, *A New Heaven and a New Earth*, 41–46; Walter Brueggemann, *Genesis: A Bible Commentary for Teaching and Preaching* (Atlanta: John Knox, 1982), 32; and Terence E. Fretheim, *God and World in the Old Testament: A Relational Theology of Creation* (Nashville: Abingdon, 2005), 48–53.

faithful representation of God, who is enthroned in the heavens, we extend the presence of the divine king of creation even to the earth, to prepare the earth for God's full—eschatological—presence, the day when God will fill all things. Then (when God fully indwells the earthly realm) the cosmic temple of creation will have been brought to its intended destiny.[24]

GENESIS 3

Despite this promising beginning, Genesis 3 immediately introduces an impediment to humanity's task. Sin enters the narrative and tragically compromises the human vocation to image God. Adam and Eve willfully rebel against God by eating fruit from the tree of the knowledge of good and evil, transgressing God's single prohibition. Consequently, every relationship is disrupted and distorted: between humans and God as Adam and Eve hide from God (3:8); between and among humans as Adam attempts to blame Eve (3:12); between an animal and humans as the serpent entices the woman (3:17); and even within the individual self as Adam and Eve are ashamed at their nakedness (3:7, 10).[25]

Moreover, the task of filling and forming given to humanity by God now becomes more difficult: pain is increased in childbearing (filling) and pain is increased in cultivating the land (forming).[26] Humanity is still called to live out its earthly vocation as the *imago Dei* (Gen. 5:1–2; 9:6), but their ability to do so is hampered. As Genesis 4–11 demonstrates, humans increasingly misuse their power against each other to create a world of violence, brutality, and abuse. God's original intention for the fullness of life is compromised as sin invades and corrupts the original flourishing of creation. And as Cain epitomizes, humanity begins to avoid its responsibility for its neighbor: "Am I my brother's keeper?"[27]

---

24. Middleton, *A New Heaven and a New Earth*, 49. For a fuller explanation of the cosmic sanctuary motif in the ancient Near East and biblical texts, see Middleton, *Liberating Image*, 81–88; and Middleton, *A New Heaven and a New Earth*, 46–49.

25. I am indebted to the work of Terence Fretheim for highlighting the relational model of creation present in Gen. 1–3, without reducing it to a particular understanding of the *imago Dei* in Gen. 1:26–28. Fretheim, *God and World in the Old Testament*, 13–22, 269–73. See also Bruce C. Birch, *Let Justice Roll Down: The Old Testament, Ethics, and Christian Life* (Louisville: Westminster John Knox, 1991), 82–83; and Bruce C. Birch and Larry L. Rasmussen, *The Predicament of the Prosperous* (Philadelphia: Westminster, 1978), 118–25.

26. The same Hebrew word for "pain" is used in both instances: *itsavon* (3:16–17).

27. Rabbi Jonathan Sacks offers an insightful Jewish reading of Gen. 1–11 that perceives the fundamental and repeated problem to be one of denying responsibility. See Jonathan Sacks, *To Heal a Fractured World: The Ethics of Responsibility* (New York: Schocken, 2005), 133–47.

As in the tale of Little Red Riding Hood, the impediment in the biblical narrative is not the end of the story. Rather, it is a summons for *helpers* to assist the agents in their task. Thus, much of the remainder of the biblical text relays the story of how God does not abandon humanity to its sinfulness after the fall but is continually at work to restore all of creation. Genesis 1–11 is immediately followed by God's call to Abraham and the promise that his lineage will become a great people—the nation of Israel—and that through them the rest of the world will be blessed. God rescues Abraham's descendants from Egypt so that they may fulfill this destiny, and God provides leaders and the law for them. Unfortunately, Israel's unfaithfulness prevents them from fully realizing its task. Thus, the New Testament opens with the gift of God's own Son, followed by the outpouring of God's Spirit, the ultimate *helpers* to restore humanity to its purpose and task, which we explore in further detail in the following chapters.[28]

But the one element that distinguishes the biblical narrative from that of Little Red Riding Hood is that the biblical story is not finished with the closing of the New Testament. The writing of Scripture has ended, but the narrative is ongoing because the task is not yet complete. Christians who locate themselves in this story are still awaiting Christ's second coming and the consummation of the kingdom of God. The New Testament hints at the ending (Rom. 8, 1 Cor. 15, parts of Revelation), but the intervening steps are not entirely clear. Thus, Christians today are still living in the final chapter, participating in this grand story.[29]

To summarize thus far, Christianity's story is about

a creator and his creation, about humans made in this creator's image and given tasks to perform, about the rebellion of humans and the dissonance of

28. The pneumatological dimension of redemption and new creation should not be overlooked. Both Wright and Middleton emphasize the significance of Christ with respect to the plot structure of the biblical narrative, but they do not grant the same primacy to the Spirit. See Wright, *New Testament and the People of God*, 139–43; and Middleton, *A New Heaven and a New Earth*, 57–73.

29. Wright, *New Testament and the People of God*, 141–43. Wright divides the biblical story into five acts: (1) Creation, (2) Fall, (3) Israel, (4) Jesus, and (5) the New Testament. While the fifth act was begun by the early church, it is not finished. As such, the church is living "under the 'authority' of the extant story, being required to offer an improvisatory performance of the final act as it leads up to and anticipates the intended conclusion. The church is designed . . . as a stage in the completion of the creator's work of art" (142). Moreover, Wright maintains that the gift of the Spirit guarantees the ultimate result but that this gift does not validate in advance all that the various characters may do or say; the actors are fallible (143).

creation at every level, and particularly about the creator's acting, through Israel and climactically through Jesus [and the Spirit], to rescue his creation from its ensuing plight. The story continues with the creator acting by his own spirit within the world to bring it towards the restoration which is his intended goal for it.[30]

This story is the first element of the Christian worldview and leads to the second: answers to the fundamental questions of life.

Answers

Having understood the overarching structure of the Christian story, we can see contained within it a set of answers to the four worldview questions delineated above.

Who are we? The biblical narrative maintains that we are made in the image of God. As such, humanity has a vocation to go forth and develop the earth as both cultural shapers and priests of creation. Contrary to other ancient Near Eastern usages of the image of God motif, the Christian story democratizes the image so that all humans, not just the pharaoh or king, bear the image and responsibility. Human beings, as the image of God, are called to use the power given to them in a creative and life-giving manner, such that the world around them is nurtured and empowered.[31]

Where are we? The biblical narrative situates humanity's existence in a good and beautiful world that was intentionally and purposefully created by God. This world serves as God's sanctuary, wherein God dwells and reigns.

What is wrong? The biblical narrative maintains that humanity has rebelled against its Creator, resulting in a cosmic dislocation in which the world is out of tune with its created intention. Humanity has fallen short of its calling, and the consequent destructive effects permeate the world. Whereas humanity was tasked to multiply and fill the earth (Gen. 1:28), contributing to the flourishing of God's world and extending God's divine presence, they instead fill the earth with violence (6:11, 13); humans corrupt that which God made and thereby grieve God. Humanity's violent misuse of power covers the earth with a cloud of physical and moral pollution that shuts the earth off from God's full presence.[32]

---

30. Wright, *New Testament and the People of God*, 132.
31. Middleton, *A New Heaven and a New Earth*, 43–45.
32. Middleton, *A New Heaven and a New Earth*, 52–55.

What is the solution? The biblical narrative claims that the Creator has not abandoned the world to its own demise, but instead God has acted, is acting, and will act within creation to deal with the widespread evil that is present because of human rebellion. Within Christianity we tend to talk about this solution as "salvation" or "redemption." Yet frequently these concepts are so narrowly defined that they are reduced to a spiritual or heavenly reality, completely untethered to earthly flourishing. A properly biblical version of salvation is holistic: it is also concerned with persons, the social order, and the natural world. Ultimately, through the gift of Jesus Christ and the outpouring of the Spirit, humanity's earthly vocation is renewed and empowered so that it can participate in the forgiveness, healing, and renewal that must take place in order for God to bring the world to the end for which it was made: to resonate fully with God's presence and glory.[33]

Praxis

Finally, the Christian story calls for action, by which the Christian worldview is lived out. Alasdair MacIntyre says that one cannot answer the question "What am I to do?" without first answering the question "Of which story am I a part?"[34] Once we understand the story to which Christianity subscribes and the answers it provides, what we are called to do in this world becomes clearer. The Christian story requires a particular way of being in the world. N. T. Wright suggests that this is better conceived of as a "being-*for*-the-world," since the Christian narrative designates humans as part of God's designed means of looking after this world and mediating God's presence to it. True, those who subscribe to the Christian worldview sometimes struggle to correlate their claims and their practice, but this is not a flaw of the Christian worldview itself but of human nature regardless of worldview. What we say and what we do are sometimes two distinct realities. "But in principle the Christian worldview supplies its adherents with a sense of direction, namely, the vocation to work in whatever way may be appropriate for the glory of the creator and the healing of his world."[35]

33. Wright, *New Testament and the People of God*, 133.
34. Alasdair MacIntyre, *After Virtue: A Study in Moral Theory*, 3rd ed. (Notre Dame, IN: University of Notre Dame, 2007), 216.
35. N. T. Wright, *New Testament and the People of God*, 133–34. Wright even suggests that one's failure to exemplify a life consistent with one's worldview is probably due in part to subscribing to another worldview at the same time (e.g., individualism, consumerism, nationalism). For

Conclusion: Putting the Pieces Together

Now that we understand worldviews, especially the Christian worldview, we can return to the initial question at the beginning of the chapter: What is the difference between benevolent service that non-Christians engage in and service that Christians engage in? Everyone can participate in acts of benevolence, but there is something unique about Christians who serve others because of the Christian worldview that shapes their orientation to service and its implementation. The Christian worldview situates our service to others as an integral part of our creation and calling as humans. Humanity was created in the image of God, and the earthly vocation that accompanies that identity—which God intended for humanity—leads to service in the world. From the very beginning, humanity was called to care for the life of this world. The fall does not eradicate this calling; it only necessitates that our calling become one of *redemptive* service, because our service now participates in the restoration of God's creational intent for the world—its redemption and salvation. "Whereas human power or agency was originally to be used for cultural development of our earthly environment, in a post-fall world, it is (also) to be used redemptively, for addressing the problem of human evil and brokenness."[36] After the fall, the creational mandate for humans becomes one of intercession on behalf of the world—human and nonhuman alike—until heaven and earth are transformed to fulfill God's purposes for justice and shalom.[37] This is the redemptive service (the praxis) to which we are called.

We are not left on our own to figure out this mission in a world gone awry. Made in the image of God, we find direction by means of God's own continual engagement in the cultivation and stewardship of the world through God's involvement with the Israelites, the incarnation of Jesus Christ, and the outpouring of the Spirit at Pentecost. The Christian story shows us how God engages in redemptive service. By looking at what God does, we can see what we are supposed to do as God's image bearers. The *imago Dei* (image of God) becomes the *imitatio Dei* (imitation of God). Our identity and mission, initiated at creation, comes from God's continual activity in the world and is carried out in our role as the people

---

more on hidden worldviews that can shape one's life and conflict with the Christian worldview, see Wilkens and Sanford, *Hidden Worldviews*, 27–182.

36. J. Richard Middleton, "A New Heaven and a New Earth: The Case for a Holistic Reading of the Biblical Story of Redemption," *Journal for Christian Theological Research* 11 (2006): 83.

37. Middleton, *Liberating Image*, 89–90; and Middleton, "A New Heaven and a New Earth," 74–77.

of God, body of Christ, and community of the Spirit. This trinitarian expression will be explored further in the remaining four chapters in part 1.

As much as one might be tempted to skip part 1 and move straight to part 2, discerning what we are to do in this world cannot be separated from the larger story from which our service emerges. Remember, worldview has to do with sight, and how we see the world affects how we interact with it. Looking further into the Christian story is not just about quickly gathering information for the purpose of moving into praxis. Rather, looking further into the Christian story to discover how the Christian worldview develops is itself a practice of formation. We are not just inquiring into how the story takes shape but also letting that story shape us. In so doing, our vision is changed and we begin to see the world as God sees it.

In the following chapters we thus look at the overarching narrative of Scripture, focusing on certain texts for illustration. It is beyond the scope of this work to engage with every passage that intersects with the concerns of the book. Rather, we aim to trace certain theological trajectories found within the Christian story that ultimately inform our praxis. Our goal is to orient our own actions and behaviors in light of what that story reveals. As Rabbi Jonathan Sacks says, the Bible is God's call to human responsibility.[38] And so we turn now to the next chapter to understand better what this human responsibility is and why it matters.

DISCUSSION QUESTIONS

1. Before reading this chapter, what would you have identified (if anything) as the difference between Christian service and non-Christian service?

2. What non-Christian worldviews can you identify? How do the stories, answers, and praxes of these worldviews differ from a Christian worldview?

3. What do you think about the proposal that to be made in the image of God means to be granted an earthly vocation to care for the life of this world? How can this idea be abused? How can we guard against such abuse?

4. Have you ever considered the service that you offer to others to be redemptive? What implications are there for understanding our service as such?

38. Sacks, *To Heal a Fractured World*, 28.

FOR FURTHER READING

Middleton, J. Richard. *The Liberating Image: The Imago Dei in Genesis 1*. Grand Rapids: Brazos, 2005.

————. *A New Heaven and a New Earth: Reclaiming Biblical Eschatology*. Grand Rapids: Baker Academic, 2014.

Sire, James W. *The Universe Next Door: A Basic Worldview Catalog*. 6th ed. Downers Grove, IL: InterVarsity, 2020.

Walsh, Brian J., and J. Richard Middleton. *The Transforming Vision: Shaping a Christian World View*. Downers Grove, IL: InterVarsity, 1984.

Wilkens, Steve, and Mark L. Sanford. *Hidden Worldviews: Eight Cultural Stories That Shape Our Lives*. Downers Grove, IL: InterVarsity, 2009.

2

Liberation and Law

The Formation of the People of God

The Christian worldview is formed by the narratives of Scripture. This story has the power to shape how we see the world and act within it. Thus, it is necessary to examine what the biblical story has to say concerning service to others. Unfortunately, too often our attempts to apply biblical texts to contemporary acts of benevolence disintegrate into a war of scriptural proof texts. Take, for example, the US House Agriculture Committee's debate in 2013 over a farm bill that included substantial cuts to the Supplemental Nutrition Assistance Program—a program for low-income individuals and families that help them purchase food. Bible verses were used by both supporters and opponents to validate their arguments. One representative opposed the cuts, citing Matthew 25 in support of feeding the hungry. He cited this passage because Jesus mentions not only feeding the hungry but also that such actions are equivalent to our treatment of Jesus himself. Another representative defended the cuts, citing Matthew 26:11, in which Jesus says we will always have the poor with us, and 2 Thessalonians 3:10, which says that anyone unwilling to work should not eat. He concluded that obligations to take care of the poor should be the responsibility of the church, not the government.[1]

1. Ron Nixon, "House Agriculture Committee Approves Farm Bill," The Caucus (blog), *New York Times*, May 16, 2013, https://thecaucus.blogs.nytimes.com/2013/05/16/house-agriculture -committee-approves-farm-bill; and Rick Ungar, "GOP Congressman Stephen Fincher on a

Setting politics aside for the moment—though we return to such important issues in part 2—there are several problems with using Scripture this way. To begin with, there are important exegetical (the critical explanation of a text) and hermeneutical (the interpretation of a text) questions that must be answered. What are the immediate passages before and after? What is the sociohistorical context? How should we allow ethics from ancient texts to inform contemporary ethics? To answer these questions, more work is required beyond merely quoting Scripture. In addition to these exegetical and hermeneutical issues lies the narrative: what is the larger story within which these texts emerge and how does that story shape our reading of these texts? While issues of praxis or ethics (What do I do?) are important and tend to be a prime motivator for turning to the biblical texts, praxis is fundamentally connected to the story. In the example above, both congressmen presented the Scripture verses apart from the overarching story within which those texts belong and from which they must be understood. This approach will inevitably distort the biblical narrative. While it is undoubtedly simpler and quicker to quote a verse that we think supports our view, as Christians we must take the time to understand the complexity of the texts themselves and how the texts fit within the larger narrative of Scripture. Only then can we orient our actions and behaviors in light of what that story reveals.

In this chapter we focus on the story that the Old Testament relays and the praxis that it demands from the Israelites as the people of God. The task to be the image of God becomes particularized as the narrative develops (see fig. 2.1). The Israelites are called to be the people of God. To the extent that they are faithful to this identity they will also be faithful to the mission to be a people engaged in redemptive service. God did not just arbitrarily desire such action for the Israelites; the command is grounded in God's own being and actions toward them. A fundamental theme in the Old Testament is that as God is, so should God's people be; as God acts, so should God's people act. Our redemptive action imitates God's redemptive action.

Mission from God—Starve the Poor while Personally Pocketing Millions in Farm Subsidies," *Forbes*, May 22, 2013, https://www.forbes.com/sites/rickungar/2013/05/22/gop-congressman -stephen-fincher-on-a-mission-from-god-starve-the-poor-while-personally-pocketing-millions -in-farm-subsidies. Rodney A. Werline notes how these two scriptural proof texts fail to recognize the complex settings in which these verses are embedded. See Werline, "Work, Poverty, and Welfare," in *The Bible in Political Debate: What Does It Really Say?*, ed. Frances Flannery and Rodney A. Werline (New York: Bloomsbury T&T Clark, 2016), 75–86.

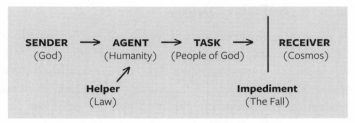

Figure 2.1 Plot analysis of the biblical narrative: Old Testament

Given that we cannot survey every relevant text in the Old Testament, we focus in this chapter primarily on the exodus and the Torah, Israel's laws. The former is important because it demonstrates the biblical idea that redemption embodies earthly flourishing in all aspects (not just the spiritual), and it reveals God's character and conduct toward those whose well-being is in jeopardy. The biblical laws are important because through their directives they reveal what it means to live as the people of God for the flourishing of others, especially the vulnerable, poor, and oppressed. In examining these aspects of the Israelites' story, it becomes clear what it means to be the people of God and how we are to engage the world as God's people.

The Exodus: Advent of the People of God

God created the world and intended goodness and well-being for it. While the fall introduces a disorder that allows for sin, evil, and death to corrupt God's good creation, God has not abandoned the world. On the contrary, God is at work restoring creation to the earthly flourishing initially intended. Scripture reveals that God intervenes in history to set things right—to redeem the world. In the Old Testament the central saving act is the exodus. From this event Israel emerges as the people of God, and their experience and memory of the exodus shapes much of the Old Testament. The exodus serves as a definitive event for understanding key aspects of redemptive service.[2] For our purposes, we will focus on what the exodus reveals about salvation, God, and humanity.

2. The canonical location of the book of Exodus implies that the "story of Israel as a moral community in relation to God is intended to play a crucial role in the shaping of subsequent generations of moral community in continuity with the biblical communities themselves." Bruce C. Birch, "Divine Character and the Formation of Moral Community in the Book of Exodus," in *The Bible in Ethics: The Second Sheffield Colloquium*, ed. John W. Rogerson, Margaret Davies, and M. Daniel Carroll R. (Sheffield, UK: Sheffield Academic, 1995), 119.

Salvation: Redemption as Holistic

Before turning to the exodus itself, we first consider what biblical redemption encompasses. Many Christians associate the word "salvation" with one's spiritual relationship with God that is established through the forgiveness of sins (justification). While this understanding is not wrong, to perceive salvation as *only* encompassing a single aspect of one's existence diminishes the biblical notion of redemption. According to J. Richard Middleton, Scripture presents salvation as "God's *deliverance* of those in a situation of need from that which impedes their well-being" and as "*restoration* to wholeness."[3] This twofold movement—deliverance and restoration—is not limited to the spiritual realm but includes all facets of one's existence: in relation to God, to fellow human beings, to the natural world, and to oneself.[4] Until the fall, all of these dimensions were present and flourishing. If redemption restores that which was lost, how could it not include all of these aspects? A holistic understanding of redemption as presented in the Bible is exemplified in the exodus.

The beginning of the book of Exodus paints a dismal picture. After the promises to Abraham of a seemingly bright future (Gen. 12:1–3), Abraham's descendants find themselves enslaved in Egypt. The book of Exodus opens with the Israelites initially fulfilling the creational mandate found in Genesis 1:28: to be fruitful, multiply, and fill the earth (Exod. 1:7). In fact, they are so successful in fulfilling the mandate that they become a threat to Pharaoh. His response to the growing number of Israelites is to enslave and oppress them (1:10–11). When this fails and the Israelites continue to multiply, the Egyptians intensify their oppression (1:13–14) and Pharaoh commands that every Hebrew boy who is born is to be killed (1:15–16, 22). Even though this measure does not work and the Israelites continue to increase in number (1:20), at every turn Pharaoh is set on working against God's desire for Israel's well-being and flourishing; redemption is needed.[5]

As the story continues, deliverance and restoration come to the Israelites by means of Yahweh. The Israelites are brought out from under Pharaoh's oppression and set free from the bondage of Egypt (*deliverance*

---

3. J. Richard Middleton, *A New Heaven and a New Earth: Reclaiming Biblical Eschatology* (Grand Rapids: Baker Academic, 2014), 79. In the Old Testament the word "shalom" is sometimes used to represent this comprehensive idea of well-being and flourishing.

4. Terence E. Fretheim excellently surveys the complex reality that the Bible demonstrates salvation to encompass. See Fretheim, "Salvation in the Bible vs. Salvation in the Church," *Word & World* 13, no. 4 (Fall 1993): 363–72.

5. Middleton, *A New Heaven and a New Earth*, 80.

from an impediment). The Israelites are also led to a new land—the promised land—where they can live in safety and God can dwell among them (*restoration* to the fullness of life). And what language is used to convey this earthly deliverance and restoration? The biblical text says that God "saves," "delivers," and "redeems" the Israelites from their bondage (Exod. 3:8; 6:6; 14:30; 15:13), which results in Yahweh becoming Israel's "salvation" (15:2). The exodus is thoroughly salvific, and yet it deals equally with the material realm as the spiritual. God's comprehensive deliverance and restoration is concerned with all aspects of the Israelites' lives. This holistic salvation is not limited to the exodus but is representative of salvation throughout the Old Testament (and the Bible generally).[6]

God: Divine Character and Conduct

It is easy to see God's divine action at work in the exodus story. But we will overlook a crucial aspect of the narrative if we do not also heed the presentation of God's character. The exodus is not an isolated, random deed from a powerful God about whom nothing else is known. It is intimately connected with God's character. And *who* God is makes all the difference in understanding *what* God does in the exodus. We cannot understand God's conduct apart from God's character.

Despite the Israelites' growing numbers, their situation under the tyranny of Pharaoh is unbearable. At first they won't even listen to Moses because their spirits are so broken by the prolonged exposure to cruel slavery (Exod. 6:9). After years of numbing oppression and hard labor, the Israelites groan and cry out (2:23). The verb "cry out" (*zaaq*) indicates misery but also complaint; the Israelites raise their voices to declare that things are not right, acceptable, or sustainable. This cry is not explicitly addressed to God; it is not a prayer but a human vocalization of agony and protest. Nonetheless, the narrator notes several times that the Israelites' cry is the reason God intervenes (2:23–25; 3:7–10; 6:5–8).[7] Exodus 3:7–8 says,

> Then the LORD said, "I have observed the misery of my people who are in Egypt; I have heard their cry on account of their taskmasters. Indeed, I know their sufferings, and I have come down to deliver them from the Egyptians

---

6. Middleton, *A New Heaven and a New Earth*, 79–83, 86–87; and Bruce C. Birch, *Let Justice Roll Down: The Old Testament, Ethics, and Christian Life* (Louisville: Westminster John Knox, 1991), 128–29.
7. Birch, *Let Justice Roll Down*, 115–16.

and to bring them up out of that land to a good and spacious land, to a land flowing with milk and honey, to the country of the Canaanites, the Hittites, the Amorites, the Perizzites, the Hivites, and the Jebusites."

In verse 7 Yahweh *sees* (or *observes*) the suffering of the Israelites, *hears* their cries of pain, and *knows* about their oppression. The first two actions—seeing and hearing—depict God's character as being inclined to care about and respond to human suffering. The last action—knowing—suggests something even further. The Hebrew word for "knowing" (*yada*) involves more than just cognition; there is also relationship and participation with the object that one knows. Yahweh is not just aware of Israel's oppression but cares about it and chooses to enter into it, participating in their suffering. Bruce Birch refers to this divine character trait as the vulnerability of God, wherein God freely chooses to respond to human need. This divine vulnerability leads to God's resolve to transform the Israelites' predicament.[8]

In verse 8 God is revealed as one who is partial to the dispossessed and opposed to evil. God is not neutral regarding oppression but acts on behalf of those in need. Yahweh *comes down*, *delivers*, and *brings up* the Israelites. The divine action is made present in the story through the various plagues wrought upon Egypt (Exod. 7–11) and as Yahweh fights on behalf of the Israelites to overthrow Pharaoh's army (14:14). Birch notes that the exodus "is but the beginning of a long list of canonical witnesses to God's special care for the poor, the hungry, the oppressed, the exploited, the suffering."[9]

Humanity: Agents in Partnership

While it is ultimately Yahweh who brings redemption in the exodus, God often uses human agents to assist in the process. Throughout the exodus narrative, God's wonder-working power is demonstrated through Moses' actions: his call by God to be a liberating agent (Exod. 3–4), his face-to-face confrontations with Pharaoh (5–12), his abuse and rejection by the Israelites (5:21; 14:10–12), and his mediation of God's power in Pharaoh's defeat (14:13–31). In 3:8 it is Yahweh who is going to bring out the Israelites, but in 3:10 Moses is the one sent by Yahweh to bring out the Israelites. Similarly, in 14:13 Moses tells the Israelites to stand by and

8. Birch, *Let Justice Roll Down*, 115–16, 119; and Birch, "Divine Character," 124–26.
9. Birch, *Let Justice Roll Down*, 121.

watch the deliverance that God will work, but then in 14:16 Yahweh has Moses stretch out his hand with his staff to divide the waters.[10]

Though Moses is the primary human agent through whom God works, there are other human agents essential to the story as well. The exodus begins with two midwives, Shiphrah and Puah, who fear God more than they fear Pharaoh and act to let the condemned baby boys live (Exod. 1:15–21). Moses' mother, Jochebed, is courageous and cunning as she hides Moses for three months to keep him alive (2:1–2). Moses' sister, Miriam, watches over Moses' basket and offers her mother as a nurse-maid (2:4–8). Pharaoh's daughter welcomes Moses into her family and sustains him as he grows up (2:5–10). Aaron assists Moses in his various tasks once he returns to Egypt (5:27–12:51), and both Aaron and Miriam play a role in leading the Israelites out of Egypt into their wilderness journey (Mic. 6:4).

Moreover, God's use of human agents not only is present in Israel's deliverance from Pharaoh but also continues in Israel's restoration to wholeness. After the Israelites depart Egypt and travel toward the promised land, they receive the biblical laws. These constitute God's instructions for holy living, providing for and ensuring communal flourishing. Many injunctions and exhortations of the law pertain especially to the treatment of the needy and marginalized, which we will examine closer below. "The experience of the exodus grounds Israel's insight that human society cannot function properly—salvation is incomplete—unless the most vulnerable members are protected, provided for, and nourished."[11] And this salvation cannot be made complete by God alone but must be embodied in the actions of the community toward one another.

In the exodus, God's power does not operate in isolation from human agency. The story of the exodus demonstrates that God partners with humanity to bring about God's desired redemption and flourishing of creation. At every turn we see an interplay of divine and human partnership, and at times even a correspondence of divine and human action. Just as God permitted created agents to participate in the act of creation (through filling and forming), God also permits created agents to participate in bringing about redemption.[12] Redemption is ultimately grounded

10. The exodus narrative replicates the pattern found at creation of the creation participating in divine action. Birch, *Let Justice Roll Down*, 126–28; and Middleton, *A New Heaven and a New Earth*, 84–85.

11. Middleton, *A New Heaven and a New Earth*, 88.

12. Middleton notes how nonhuman creation participates in the exodus too. See Middleton, *A New Heaven and a New Earth*, 84–85.

in God, but we have a part to play in realizing this redemption in our everyday lives and bringing healing and restoration to this broken world.

The Covenant: Life of the People of God

The exodus is the common experience out of which the faith community is born. It also initiates the Israelite covenant, of which the law codes are a fundamental piece. Within the covenant framework the laws establish expectations for the Israelites as the people of God; they detail what life is to look like as God's people. The law codes are not arbitrary rules for the Israelites to follow but covenant obligations. Fulfilling these obligations leads to blessing—a positive implication of the covenant relationship— while ignoring these obligations results in judgment—a negative implication of the covenant relationship.

Scholars identify four major law codes—or collections of legal materials—within the Pentateuch that are related to the Israelite covenant: the Decalogue (Exod. 20:2–17), the Book of the Covenant (Exod. 20:22–23:33), the Holiness Code (Lev. 17–26), and the Deuteronomic Laws (Deut. 12–26).[13] These law codes address a range of topics, both civil and cultic (religious).[14] Moreover, a substantial number of the biblical laws have humanitarian concerns, including generosity, justice, and equality among the Israelites, with special attention for the poor, widows, orphans, and sojourners. These particular groups are at the bottom of Israelite society. Because of their social location, they are vulnerable, and the laws seek to provide for them and protect them from abuses:

13. Law collections are typical within the ancient Near East and are not unique to the biblical texts. In fact, the biblical law codes are preceded by legal traditions in other civilizations, such as the Sumerians, Babylonians, Hittites, and Assyrians. See David L. Baker, *Tight Fists or Open Hands? Wealth and Poverty in Old Testament Law* (Grand Rapids: Eerdmans, 2009), 1–6. For a comparison between the humanitarian laws within the biblical law codes and other ancient Near Eastern law codes, see Baker, *Tight Fists or Open Hands?*; Roy E. Gane, *Old Testament Law for Christians: Original Context and Enduring Application* (Grand Rapids: Baker Academic, 2017), 126–33; J. David Pleins, *The Social Visions of the Hebrew Bible: A Theological Introduction* (Louisville: Westminster John Knox, 2001), 42–44; Enrique Nardoni, *Rise Up, O Judge: A Study of Justice in the Biblical World*, trans. Sean Charles Martin (Peabody, MA: Hendrickson, 2004), 1–41; and William Robert Domeris, *Touching the Heart of God: The Social Construction of Poverty among Biblical Peasants* (New York: T&T Clark, 2007), 151–68.

14. For an in-depth, introductory analysis of the law component of the biblical texts, see Pamela Barmash, ed., *The Oxford Handbook of Biblical Law* (Oxford: Oxford University Press, 2019).

1. The *poor* denote persons who are in particular need of help from the more prosperous members of the covenant community.[15]
2. The *widows* and *orphans* lack a patriarch in their family structure. In ancient Near Eastern society, a lack of a husband or father means that there is no protector or source of sustenance.
3. The *sojourners* are free persons who have left their native country or region and now reside among the Israelites. They have certain rights but are not regarded as full citizens of the community.[16]

In the biblical laws the poor, widows, orphans, and sojourners are sometimes explicitly listed as the benefactors of certain laws; other times their inclusion is implied, since they constitute some of the most at-risk persons in the Israelite community.[17]

While it would be naive to expect these ancient law codes—which were given in a vastly different historical, geographical, and cultural setting—to provide a detailed, step-by-step ethical map for the twenty-first century, they do present a certain disposition on behalf of the people of God toward those who are vulnerable, poor, and oppressed. These texts offer a general direction that can still guide us today, even as our faith is lived out in a different time and place. As we examine these law codes, what we will find is that the three themes noted above with respect to the exodus are also echoed in the law codes. First, salvation (or redemption) is holistic. God is not just concerned with the spiritual life of the Israelites but with all dimensions of life, which is why the law codes contain both cultic *and* civil laws. Second, God's character is shown in God's actions. The posture God commands of the Israelites toward their neighbors is connected to what God has done for them, especially the exodus. Third, humans are agents in partnership with God. Bringing about the flourishing of this earthly life requires the Israelites to be the means by which God's plan of redemption is realized.

15. For a rigorous study of poverty and the poor in the Old Testament, see Domeris, *Touching the Heart of God*; and Christoph Levin, "The Poor in the Old Testament: Some Observations," *Religion and Theology* 8, no. 3–4 (2001): 253–73.

16. A "sojourner" is distinct from a "foreigner." The latter also comes from another country but does not have any relationship with the covenant community. See Baker, *Tight Fists or Open Hands?*, 180.

17. Donald E. Gowan, "Wealth and Poverty in the Old Testament: The Case of the Widow, the Orphan, and the Sojourner," *Interpretation* 41, no. 4 (1987): 341–53; and Jeremiah Unterman, *Justice for All: How the Jewish Bible Revolutionized Ethics* (Lincoln: University of Nebraska Press, 2017), 41–84.

Humanitarian Laws

LAWSUITS

One significant disparity between those at the top of society and those at the bottom, even in ancient cultures, is in their respective access to legal restitution for crimes and injustice. Lawsuits in ancient Israel were often decided by elders who sat at the town gate to discuss the affairs of the local community.[18] Difficult cases could be taken before judges or the king, though the king was still subject to the law of God and did not possess absolute legal authority.[19] A just legal system is essential to any healthy community. If it becomes corrupt, it will inevitably be those at the bottom of society who will be exploited because they do not have the power or means to protect themselves or participate in the dysfunctional system. Thus, the Old Testament law codes are designed to benefit weak members of society, addressing three specific matters related to just lawsuits. The first is that of witnesses. Witnesses established truth in legal cases, and consequently, a false testimony could cause serious harm (Exod. 20:16; 23:1–2; Deut. 5:20). For this reason, multiple witnesses are required, and appropriate punishment is meted out to a false witness (Deut. 17:6; 19:15–21). The second area of concern is that of impartiality. The law codes prohibit bias toward both the rich and the poor (Exod. 23:3, 6–7; Lev. 19:15; Deut. 16:18–19). Prohibiting favoritism toward the poor might surprise us, but the point is that God is on the side of justice, which forbids partiality to anyone, wealthy or poor. The last area of concern is that of bribes. Bribes—whether gifts or payments—are unacceptable in Israelite society because they are likely to influence a judge in favor of a litigant who is able and willing to pay (Exod. 23:8; Deut. 16:19–20; 27:25). The poor do not have the resources to purchase justice and so are particularly vulnerable in a system that requires or is influenced by such acts.[20]

SHARED HARVESTS

Justice without generosity can be callous. What good is access to a fair judicial system when one is starving? The law codes command the Israelites to be generous in sharing their harvests in a variety of ways.

18. Examples of this can be seen in Gen. 23:10, 18; Deut. 21:19–20; 22:15–21; 25:7–9; Ruth 4:1–12; 1 Kings 21:8–14; Job 29:7; Prov. 31:23; Amos 5:10, 12, 15; Zech. 8:16.

19. Examples of the presence and activity of judges can be seen in Deut. 16:18; 17:8–13; 19:17–18; 25:1–2; 2 Chron. 19:5–11. Examples of the judicial function of kings can be seen in 1 Sam. 8:5; 2 Sam. 8:15; 14:4–11; 15:2–6; 1 Kings 3:9, 16–28; 7:7; 2 Kings 8:3–6; Ps. 72:1–2; Prov. 16:10; 29:14; Jer. 21:11–12; 22:15–16.

20. Baker, *Tight Fists or Open Hands?*, 199–222.

For example, every three years the tithe—which consisted primarily of agricultural produce—was not to be taken to the sanctuary but stored in the towns for the purpose of providing for those in need (Deut. 14:28–29; 26:12–13). This triennial tithe leveraged a religious practice for social purposes; what was normally used to serve God was given to serve the needy. There are also laws prescribing that every seventh year (the sabbatical year) the land be allowed to rest by lying fallow and the poor allowed to eat from the produce that grows of its own accord during that year (Exod. 23:10–11; Lev. 25:1–7). Provision for the needy was supplied in the other remaining years through laws concerning gleaning and "scrumping" (eating food from someone's fields without permission), laws designed to ensure that those in need had sustenance every year, not just intermittently. Landowners were to leave a portion of their crops in the fields for those in need to come and gather (Lev. 19:9–10; 23:22; Deut. 24:19–22).[21] And landowners were also to allow passing neighbors to satisfy their hunger by partaking of the harvest, though the passerby is limited in what they can eat so as not to take advantage of the hospitality (Deut. 23:24–25).[22]

GENEROUS LOANS

Needy people are at risk of exploitation. The biblical law codes seek to prevent such injustices from arising in Israel. When a person was in need, loans were to be provided without interest (Exod. 22:25; Lev. 25:35–38; Deut. 23:19–20).[23] Given that the interest charged in the ancient Near East could be as high as one-third or one-half of the loan, these laws provided significant protection for the poor. A person's need is not an opportunity for profit. Every seven years all debts of fellow Israelites were to be canceled (Deut. 15:1–3). This provision offered a way out for needy persons who had tried to pay off their debt but were unable to do so. Moreover, creditors were to be no less generous toward the end of the seven-year period—when they may not be paid back—than at the beginning (Deut. 15:7–11).

21. Ruth is a prominent biblical example of a needy person gleaning in the field because of the provision of the law (Ruth 2). Ruth belonged to all three vulnerable groups mentioned in Deut. 24:19–22: sojourner, orphan (because she had left her parents), and widow. See Baker, *Tight Fists or Open Hands?*, 238–39.

22. Baker, *Tight Fists or Open Hands?*, 223–51.

23. Though the law in Exodus specifies only money, and the law in Leviticus specifies only money and food, Baker argues that none of the laws exclude other items. Deuteronomy's addition of "anything" to the list of what should be lent interest free should be understood as making explicit what is already implicit in the earlier formulations. See Baker, *Tight Fists or Open Hands?*, 262–63.

Within a system of borrowing and lending, security ensures that loans are promptly repaid. Within Israel, requiring security—or a pledge—was permitted as long as it was balanced with compassion and the borrower was not deprived of the basic essentials for survival. A creditor could request the cloak of a person for a pledge, but it had to be returned by the evening so that the individual could use it as a blanket to keep themselves warm while sleeping (Exod. 22:26–27; Deut. 24:12–13). A creditor could not, however, take a widow's cloak as a pledge (Deut. 24:17) or anyone's set of millstones, since without them there would be no way to grind flour or bake bread (Deut. 24:6). And the creditor was prohibited from entering the debtor's house to retrieve the pledge (Deut. 24:10–11). This injunction preserves the debtor's dignity, since the debtor is allowed to choose the object for a pledge and bring it out.[24]

Fair Trade

The law also addresses fair trade between persons. There are laws that require that poor hired laborers be paid their wages on the day they were earned (Lev. 19:13; Deut. 24:14–15). More than others, these people depended on prompt payment. In commerce, there were also laws to enforce that the measurements used to conduct business were accurate (Lev. 19:35–36; Deut. 25:13–15). Sellers were not to manipulate weights and measures in order to obtain ill-gotten profits from unsuspecting buyers.[25]

Parity

Certain laws were meant to produce greater equality between those at the top and bottom of society. With respect to sacrifices, poor persons were allowed to fulfill the cultic requirements with less expensive offerings (Lev. 12:8; 14:21–22). Israel also regularly observed the Sabbath and religious holidays (Exod. 20:10; 23:12; Deut. 5:14; 12:12, 18; 16:11, 14; 26:11). These days were religious in nature, but they also had a social function by providing regular times of rest and recreation for everyone—not just the ones who were free and could afford to work and rest when they desired. Without laws to regulate rest and recreation for all, many poor persons would likely have continued to work nonstop while the wealthy enjoyed their breaks. There was also the Jubilee Year that occurred after seven cycles of seven years in the fiftieth year (Lev. 25). During this year freedom

24. Baker, *Tight Fists or Open Hands?*, 252–85.
25. Baker, *Tight Fists or Open Hands?*, 286–304.

was proclaimed for all the inhabitants of the land. Any land that had been sold in the preceding years was to be returned to its original owner. Bonded laborers—who had been forced to sell themselves because of poverty—were to be freed so that they could return to their own family and land.[26]

Motivation: Imitation of God

It is important not only to see *what* was required of the Israelites as the people of God but also to understand *why* these mandates were given. The motivation for these laws is just as important as the laws themselves. Throughout the Old Testament a principle at work is that of imitating God. Many people today are familiar with this idea, though it is more widely associated with the New Testament than the Old Testament (thanks to the popular slogan WWJD: What Would Jesus Do?). The idea behind the WWJD phrase is that, as Christians, we are to imitate Jesus as a moral model. How Jesus would act in a given situation is how we should act. But the idea of imitating God is not just a New Testament concept; it emerges first in the Old Testament (WWYD: What Would Yahweh Do?). God is not just a source of divine commandments (law codes), but God's character and actions serve as the source and basis of Israel's morality too.[27] As Joe Pettit rightly notes, "Ethical life is not merely a matter of following commandments, but of imitating God."[28] This idea is widely recognized and commonly referred to as *imitatio Dei* (imitation of God).[29]

26. Baker, *Tight Fists or Open Hands?*, 76–97, 159–74, 287–96. Regardless of whether the Jubilee Year was regularly observed—if at all—the laws still embody values that resonate with the overall ethos of the humanitarian laws of the Old Testament. Moreover, the prophet Isaiah uses images from the Jubilee to challenge his hearers to make radical changes to their lifestyle (Isa. 58) and to anticipate the messianic age (Isa. 61).

27. In the same way that the creation concept of *imago Dei* in Genesis took an ancient Near Eastern concept and democratized it (applied it to all, not just kings and pharaohs), so too does the concept of *imitatio Dei*. Ancient near Eastern cultures held that political leaders were representative of the gods and thus were to maintain justice, including advocating for the poor and vulnerable. In Israel, this responsibility was not limited to the leaders of Israel but given to all the people. Joe Pettit, "The Spoil of the Poor Is in Your Houses: Profits and Prophets in a Disrupted Society," *Journal of the Society of Christian Ethics* 27, no. 1 (2007): 36–39; and Leslie J. Hoppe, *There Shall Be No Poor among You: Poverty in the Bible* (Nashville: Abingdon, 2004), 25.

28. Pettit, "Spoil of the Poor Is in Your Houses," 39.

29. Both Jewish and Christian scholars have acknowledged the presence of the *imitatio Dei* theme in the Old Testament, even outside the law codes. See E. J. Tinsley, *The Imitation of God in Christ* (Philadelphia: Westminster, 1960), 27–64; Martin Buber, *Mamre: Essays in Religion*, trans. Greta Hort (Westport, CT: Greenwood, 1970), 32–43; David S. Shapiro, "The Doctrine of the Image of God and *Imitatio Dei*," in *Contemporary Jewish Ethics*, ed. Menachem Marc Kellner (New York: Sanhedrin, 1978), 127–51; Bruce C. Birch, "Moral Agency, Community, and

If humans are created to image God, it follows that humans are also intended to reflect the character of God. Being created in the image of God is the grounds for imitating God.[30] The pattern that began in Genesis is codified in the life of Israel, especially in their humanitarian obligations to others. Being the people of God gives us a particular mission: as God is, so should God's people be; as God acts, so should God's people act.

There are several explicit examples of *imitatio Dei* among the humanitarian laws. In Exodus 20:8–11, Israel's weekly rhythm of work and rest imitates God's own action in creation by working for six days and resting on the seventh:

> Remember the Sabbath day and keep it holy. Six days you shall labor and do all your work. But the seventh day is a Sabbath to the LORD your God; you shall not do any work—you, your son or your daughter, your male or female slave, your livestock, or the alien resident in your towns. For in six days the LORD made heaven and earth, the sea, and all that is in them, but rested the seventh day; therefore the LORD blessed the Sabbath day and consecrated it.

Rest for all—including slaves and sojourners—is to be provided on a weekly basis in imitation of God.

Leviticus 19:2 offers a clear command for the Israelites to imitate God:

> Speak to all the congregation of the Israelites and say to them: You shall be holy, for I the LORD your God am holy.[31]

While it might be tempting to understand this mandate merely as a spiritual directive or a reference to cultic and ceremonial duties in the temple, it is clear from the verses that follow that the Israelites are summoned to a holiness that is thoroughly material and practical. It is a holiness of conduct that encompasses specific social obligations, several of which

the Character of God in the Hebrew Bible," *Semeia* 66 (1994): 29–33; Eryl W. Davies, "Walking in God's Ways: The Concepts of *Imitatio Dei* in the Old Testament," in *In Search of True Wisdom: Essays in Old Testament Interpretation in Honour of Ronald E. Clements*, ed. Edward Ball (Sheffield, UK: Sheffield Academic, 1999), 99–115; John Barton, "Imitation of God in the Old Testament," in *The God of Israel*, ed. Robert P. Gordon (Cambridge: Cambridge University Press, 2007), 35–46; and Karen Elizabeth Durant, "Imitation of God as a Principle of Ethics Today: A Study of Selected Psalms" (PhD diss., University of Birmingham, England, 2010).

30. Some of the passages employing the concept of *imitatio Dei* in connection with the Sabbath are linked to creation narratives (e.g., Exod. 20:8–11).

31. Cf. Lev. 11:44; 20:7, 26; 21:8.

concern the humanitarian laws noted above: generosity for the poor and sojourner during harvest time (Lev. 19:9–10; cf. 23:22), faithfulness in paying hired help (19:13), integrity in the judicial process (19:15), love and care for the sojourners living among them (19:33–34), and honesty in commercial transaction (19:35–36). God's holiness acts as both a model and a motivating force in the development and maintenance of holy character among the Israelites, which is to be expressed in their daily activities. This connection is continually emphasized, as the refrain "I am the LORD" or "I am the LORD your God" is repeated no less than fifteen times throughout Leviticus 19.

In Deuteronomy 10:17–18 the Israelites are presented with this description of God:

> For the LORD your God is God of gods and Lord of lords, the great God, mighty and awesome, who is not partial and takes no bribe, who executes justice for the orphan and the widow, and who loves the strangers, providing them food and clothing.[32]

All of these attributes and actions of Yahweh are echoed in the humanitarian laws concerning lawsuits and shared harvests. The commands to pursue justice in the legal system and demonstrate generosity to those in need are grounded in God's own character and behavior. In Deuteronomy 15:12–15 God's activity in the exodus provides a blueprint for the Israelites' behavior:

> If a member of your community, whether a Hebrew man or a Hebrew woman, is sold to you and works for you six years, in the seventh year you shall set that person free. And when you send a male slave out from you a free person, you shall not send him out empty-handed. Provide for him liberally out of your flock, your threshing floor, and your winepress, thus giving to him some of the bounty with which the LORD your God has blessed you. Remember that you were a slave in the land of Egypt, and the LORD your God redeemed you; for this reason I lay this command upon you today.

In the exodus the Israelites were the recipients of God's liberating work and blessing, and now Israel is called to imitate these same actions of release and blessing toward those who have become slaves.

32. Cf. 2 Chron. 19:7.

The principle of *imitatio Dei* is also implicit in the humanitarian laws that invoke Israel's experience in Egypt as a motivating refrain. For example, Deuteronomy 24:17–22 says,

> You shall not deprive a resident alien or an orphan of justice; you shall not take a widow's garment in pledge. Remember that you were a slave in Egypt and the LORD your God redeemed you from there; therefore I command you to do this.
>
> When you reap your harvest in your field and forget a sheaf in the field, you shall not go back to get it; it shall be left for the alien, the orphan, and the widow, so that the LORD your God may bless you in all your undertakings. When you beat your olive trees, do not strip what is left; it shall be for the alien, the orphan, and the widow.
>
> When you gather the grapes of your vineyard, do not glean what is left; it shall be for the alien, the orphan, and the widow. Remember that you were a slave in the land of Egypt; therefore I am commanding you to do this.

This appeal occurs multiple times throughout the humanitarian laws: Exodus 22:21; 23:9; Leviticus 25; Deuteronomy 5:12–14; 10:19; 16:11–12. Israel's experience of Egypt should have a significant bearing on the values and concerns they demonstrate in their communal life. The laws remind the Israelites of their experience in Egypt and of the exodus. In remembering, the Israelites are to follow and imitate the example of Yahweh—the one who heard their cry, had compassion, and liberated them—not the example of the Egyptians, who severely oppressed them. Unfortunately, as we will see in the next chapter, the Israelites do just the opposite of what God desires of them.

Conclusion

As the story unfolds, the Israelites are called to image God by being the people of God. They had been rescued from Egypt for this purpose, and they had been given biblical laws for living as the people of God. In both instances, redemption encompasses all aspects of life (both spiritual and material), is fundamentally grounded in God's being, and requires active human participation in the mission of God. Both narratives highlight the vulnerable, poor, and oppressed. Initially, Israel itself is the subject to these conditions from which God brings them out. God then charges the Israelites to attend to those in their own midst who find themselves vulnerable, poor, and oppressed by protecting and providing for such people. Redemptive service is thus not optional or marginal to the Israelites' identity and mission as the people of God; it is required and central. Their failure in this aspect of the covenant with God results in their undoing.

DISCUSSION QUESTIONS

1. The Israelites' exodus began with their crying out. Who is crying out today in pain? Whose disruptive voice do you need to hear in order to partner with God to bring deliverance and restoration?

2. Have you ever thought about God being moved by our suffering? How does this affect your understanding of God?

3. In addition to the poor, the Old Testament specifies widows, orphans, and sojourners as especially vulnerable people. In our society, in addition to the poor, what groups of vulnerable people should be listed?

4. Even though the humanitarian laws were formulated for a much different time and place than our own, do you see any parallels between the problems the laws were addressing and the problems we have today? If so, do the laws provide any insight into how we might go about addressing contemporary problems?

5. What significance does redemptive service have, knowing that by engaging in it, we are not just participating in the mission of God but also imitating God?

FOR FURTHER READING

Baker, David L. *Tight Fists or Open Hands? Wealth and Poverty in Old Testament Law*. Grand Rapids: Eerdmans, 2009.

———. "Why Care for the Poor? Theological Foundations of Old Testament Laws on Wealth and Poverty." *Proceeding of the Irish Biblical Association* 29 (2006): 1–23.

Birch, Bruce C. *Let Justice Roll Down: The Old Testament, Ethics, and Christian Life*. Louisville: Westminster John Knox, 1991.

Domeris, William Robert. *Touching the Heart of God: The Social Construction of Poverty among Biblical Peasants*. New York: T&T Clark, 2007.

Fretheim, Terence E. "Salvation in the Bible vs. Salvation in the Church." *Word & World* 13, no. 4 (Fall 1993): 363–72.

Hoppe, Leslie J. *There Shall Be No Poor among You: Poverty in the Bible*. Nashville: Abingdon, 2004.

Malchow, Bruce V. *Social Justice in the Hebrew Bible*. Collegeville, MN: Liturgical Press, 1996.

Nardoni, Enrique. *Rise Up, O Judge: A Study of Justice in the Biblical World*. Translated by Sean Charles Martin. Peabody, MA: Hendrickson, 2004.

Wright, Christopher J. H. *Old Testament Ethics for the People of God*. Downers Grove, IL: InterVarsity, 2004.

3

A Distorted Mess

A Broken Covenant and a Broken People

Israel's life as God's covenant people is, unfortunately, not a perfect success. As the Old Testament narrative moves beyond the Torah, the Israelites struggle to be the people of God, especially in their neglect of the vulnerable, poor, and oppressed. The prophets enter the story to reveal these shortcomings and call Israel to account for its failures.[1] While many times the prophets are identified as the social justice heroes of Scripture, the prophets actually have little new to say about this issue. Much of the abuses the prophets denounce are violations of the biblical laws we examined in the previous chapter. Their message is not a deviation from the prior Old Testament faith tradition but a continuation of it. The prophets' radicality consists more in their rhetorical strategy than in their ideas. Their forceful and intense way of speaking about the covenantal expectations make their concerns stand out. As Terence Fretheim puts it, "They got 'in your face' with respect to long-standing communal commitments."[2] While it is not wrong to view the

---

1. There are prophets during the early periods of the kingship in Israel (e.g., Samuel, Nathan, Elijah, and Elisha) who are highlighted in the historical books. Some of these prophets become involved in matters of social justice on occasion. See the story of King Ahab and Elijah in 1 Kings 21, as well as that of King David and Nathan in 2 Sam. 12:1–15. However, the prophetic literature in the Old Testament represents a shift from stories about the prophets (their activity) to collections of their preached oracles (their message).

2. Terence E. Fretheim, "The Prophets and Social Justice: A *Conservative* Agenda," *Word & World* 28, no. 2 (Spring 2008): 160. Moreover, the concerns that the prophets raise would need to have been reasonably well known by their audiences or their message would have been incomprehensible.

prophets as champions of social justice, they are only so because of what they have inherited and what they are calling Israel to be faithful to again.[3]

As we survey the prophetic texts, we see an echo of the three themes identified in the previous chapter with respect to the exodus and the Torah, but this time directed at Israel's deficits: the Israelites have failed to understand the connection between how one lives (materiality) and how one worships (spirituality); failed to express faithfully the same redemption that is part of their own history and testimony; and failed to be agents of redemption for the oppressed around them.[4] The message of the prophets reveals just how central Israel's care for the vulnerable, poor, and oppressed is to fulfilling the call to be the people of God.

Below, we focus on the prophets' message, paying particular attention to Israel's failure with respect to their humanitarian responsibility. Then we turn briefly to the promise of the future offered by some of the prophets. This hopeful outlook anticipates the events of the New Testament and is necessary to note before looking at that portion of the story. Thus far we have refrained from quoting Scripture at length, but we make an exception in this chapter because one cannot grasp the severity of the prophets' message without reading their precise words. Since their rhetorical style makes their message so poignant, it is necessary to convey the prophetic message as it is recorded.

The Problem: Failure to Be the People of God

Covenant Disobedience

The prophets do not convey their own thoughts to Israel; they speak as representatives of God. Thus, their oracles are presumed to be the very

---

3. Joe Pettit makes a helpful distinction between prophets and ethicists: "Prophets point to injustice and, in doing so, demand a response. Ethicists take their time trying to figure out what that response should be, and they are right to take their time, as the proper response may be highly complex and quite tentative" (Joe Pettit, "The Spoil of the Poor Is in Your Houses: Profits and Prophets in a Disrupted Society," *Journal of the Society of Christian Ethics* 27, no. 1 [2007]: 35–36). His point is that while the prophet establishes the responsibility for change, it is the ethicist who prescribes how that change should be carried out. Consequently, in viewing the biblical prophets' messages, one should expect not blueprints to solve problems but instead passion and fervor that demand repentance. However, to move forward, both are required.

4. The context for some prophetic books is Judah (in the south), while for others it is Israel (in the north). However, to avoid switching back and forth between references to Judah and Israel, I use only Israel as the designated audience, with the understanding that this designation encompasses both kingdoms. Though I am treating the prophetic literature holistically, due attention should be given to the particular context within which each prophet preached.

words of God and give insight into God's pathos.[5] The overarching issue in the prophets' message is that Israel is not reflecting its covenant commitments in its behavior toward one another, and thus their relationship with Yahweh is now broken. Their movement away from each other is a movement away from God.

Isaiah 5:1–7

In Isaiah 5:1–7 we find a Song of the Vineyard that presents this situation in parable form. The first four verses state the following:

> [1]I will sing for my beloved
>   my love song concerning his vineyard:
> My beloved had a vineyard
>   on a very fertile hill.
> [2]He dug it and cleared it of stones
>   and planted it with choice vines;
> he built a watchtower in the midst of it
>   and hewed out a wine vat in it;
> he expected it to yield grapes,
>   but it yielded rotten grapes.
>
> [3]And now, inhabitants of Jerusalem
>   and people of Judah,
> judge between me
>   and my vineyard.
> [4]What more was there to do for my vineyard
>   that I have not done in it?
> When I expected it to yield grapes,
>   why did it yield rotten grapes?

The beginning of the song depicts Yahweh as the vinedresser who has systematically cared for the vineyard by digging, clearing, planting, and building. As the vinedresser, Yahweh has done everything necessary to reap an excellent harvest, including planting choice vines. While this particular parable does not explicitly mention the exodus as part of the preparation process, God's faithfulness to Israel by means of the exodus is assuredly in the background (cf. Jer. 2:2; Hosea 11:1–4; Amos 3:1–2; Mic. 6:3–4). Yet, despite Yahweh's nurturing actions toward Israel, the vineyard fails

---

5. Abraham Joshua Heschel, *The Prophets: Two Volumes in One* (Peabody, MA: Hendrickson, 2007), 25–26.

to yield grapes corresponding to the select stock it was sown with and instead produces "rotten grapes." The vineyard does not reflect the special thought and care with which it was planted. Imagine the disappointment of the vinedresser.

The song then relays the consequences for Israel's unfaithfulness and unfruitfulness:

> [5]And now I will tell you
>   what I will do to my vineyard.
> I will remove its hedge,
>   and it shall be devoured;
> I will break down its wall,
>   and it shall be trampled down.
> [6]I will make it a wasteland;
>   it shall not be pruned or hoed,
>   and it shall be overgrown with briers and thorns;
> I will also command the clouds
>   that they rain no rain upon it.

The elements of protection are removed, the care that had been demonstrated is abandoned, and the one essential element that fosters its growth—rain—is stopped. Without protection, care, and rain, the vineyard has little hope of survival.

The song concludes by making explicit to whom and to what the parable alludes:

> [7]For the vineyard of the LORD of hosts
>   is the house of Israel,
> and the people of Judah
>   are his cherished garden;
> he expected justice
>   but saw bloodshed;
> righteousness
>   but heard a cry!

This song recounts the history of Israel and Judah. The exceptional harvest that Yahweh once expected in return for all the effort was one of justice (*mishpat*) and righteousness (*tsedaqa*).[6] While each of these words has its

---

6. Hemchand Gossai, *Social Critique by Israel's Eighth-Century Prophets: Justice and Righteousness in Context* (Eugene, OR: Wipf & Stock, 1993), 251–54. Biblical scholars who are

own range of meanings, when they appear together they generally refer to God's just ordering of the world and just rule as reflected in social and political relationships. However, the harvest God finds is just the opposite: there is no justice and there is no righteousness. The English translation fails to capture the play on words, which is based on the Hebrew words sounding like each other. Yahweh expects "justice" (*mishpat*) but finds "bloodshed" (*mispah*); expects "righteousness" (*tsedaqa*) but instead hears a "cry" (*seaqa*)—not unlike the cry from the enslaved Israelites in Egypt that God heard (cf. Exod. 3:7, 9). In an ironic turn, the Israelites have now become the oppressors, and their abuses are causing others to cry out. Thus, there will be judgment, though this should not come as a surprise (cf. Exod. 22:21–24).[7]

Micah 3:1–3

The prophet Micah's condemnation is violently descriptive of how justice is being polluted among God's people. In Micah 3:1–3 he says,

> [1]And I said:
> Listen, you heads of Jacob
>   and rulers of the house of Israel!
> Should you not know justice?—
>   [2]you who hate the good and love the evil,
> who tear the skin off my people
>   and the flesh off their bones,
> [3]who eat the flesh of my people,
>   flay their skin off them,
> break their bones in pieces,
>   and chop them up like meat in a kettle,
>   like flesh in a caldron.

While these words should not be understood literally, the images of extreme suffering and pain are quite vivid. The rulers and leaders of Israel who have been entrusted with the responsibility to care for the powerless

---

concerned with justice in the Old Testament frequently note that a repeating refrain is that of "justice and right(eousness)" (*mishpat* and *tsedaqa*). The two terms are linked more than fifty times in the Old Testament, indicating that it is a common idiom, though it is almost entirely absent in the Torah but prevalent in the prophets (especially Isaiah) and the Psalms. For a comprehensive treatment of the phrase, see Moshe Weinfeld, *Social Justice in Ancient Israel and in the Ancient Near East* (Minneapolis: Fortress, 1995); Gossai, *Israel's Eighth-Century Prophets*; and Walter J. Houston, *Justice for the Poor? Social Justice in the Old Testament in Concept and Practice* (Eugene, OR: Cascade Books, 2020), 150–80.

7. Gossai, *Israel's Eighth-Century Prophets*, 251–54.

have now become instruments of abuse. "Self-interest has replaced covenantal responsibilities, and personal concerns have taken the place of
societal demands."[8]

Amos 5:7 and 6:12

The prophet Amos notes how justice and righteousness—things that
are life-giving and life-preserving—have been corrupted. In Amos 5:7 he
declares,

> [7]Ah, you who turn justice to wormwood
> and bring righteousness to the ground!

And in 6:12 he says,

> [12]But you have turned justice into poison
> and the fruit of righteousness into wormwood.

God has instructed Israel how to live; they know what is "right." Living
according to those standards produces "justice," which is the fruit or
effect of righteousness. But the Israelites have turned aside from those
instructions, allowing injustice to spread. The result of perverting justice
and righteousness is likened to wormwood—a shrub that produces a bit-
ter liquid—and poison: the effects are deadly.[9] The imagery of Amos 5:7
is one of throwing or casting down righteousness. "Thus, when [righ-
teousness] is thrown to the ground, there is the image of Israel disrobing
itself of that which has kept and sustained it in a special relationship with
Yahweh. The casting away of [righteousness] becomes the point at which
Israel has rejected the binding element with Yahweh. The relationship is
not annulled, but it is broken."[10]

Worship of God but Neglect of Neighbor

The prophets lament that the Israelites attend to the cultic laws but
neglect the humanitarian laws.[11] The Israelites are still attending to the

---

8. Gossai, *Israel's Eighth-Century Prophets*, 300–302.
9. Donald E. Gowan, "The Book of Amos," in *The New Interpreter's Bible Commentary*,
ed. Leander E. Keck et al. (Nashville: Abingdon, 2015), 5:571.
10. Gossai, *Israel's Eighth-Century Prophets*, 213.
11. There is debate among scholars whether the prophets' critique of the cultic is a call for
an abolition of the cultic or for an interrelationship between the cultic and social justices. See

religious aspects of their lives, but they are violating the social aspects. Their cultic practices and ceremonies are disconnected from their social responsibilities. But God desires to be worshiped holistically and not merely by what takes place within the temple. One cannot truly worship God without an active commitment to the welfare of others. This critique is repeated by several prophets. For them, the truest form of worship is imitation of God in social relations; there is no separation of the inner spiritual life and the outer communal and political life.[12]

Isaiah 1:10–17 and 58:1–12

There are two extensive passages in the book of Isaiah that address this issue. Isaiah 1:10–17 says,

> [10]Hear the word of the LORD,
>   you rulers of Sodom!
> Listen to the teaching of our God,
>   you people of Gomorrah!
> [11]What to me is the multitude of your sacrifices?
>   says the LORD;
> I have had enough of burnt offerings of rams
>   and the fat of fed beasts;
> I do not delight in the blood of bulls
>   or of lambs or of goats.
>
> [12]When you come to appear before me,
>   who asked this from your hand?
>   Trample my courts no more!
> [13]Bringing offerings is futile;
>   incense is an abomination to me.
> New moon and Sabbath and calling of convocation—
>   I cannot endure solemn assemblies with iniquity.
> [14]Your new moons and your appointed festivals
>   my soul hates;

Gossai, *Israel's Eighth-Century Prophets*, 265–71. Gene M. Tucker suggests that these texts are not a complete rejection of cultic activity, observing that Israel's songs of worship constantly emphasize the link between piety and social concerns (Ps. 15:1–2; 24), and even Isaiah himself was in the temple when he had his vision in Isa. 6 (cf. Isa. 1:10–17). See Tucker, "The Book of Isaiah 1–39," in *The New Interpreter's Bible Commentary*, ed. Leander E. Keck et al. (Nashville: Abingdon, 2015), 4:57–58. The point is not what is wrong with the worship but what is wrong with the worshipers. The idea is not to replace ritual with social action but to insist that what goes on in worship correspond with what goes on in society.

12. Pettit, "Spoil of the Poor Is in Your Houses," 39.

they have become a burden to me;
 I am weary of bearing them.
[15]When you stretch out your hands,
 I will hide my eyes from you;
even though you make many prayers,
 I will not listen;
 your hands are full of blood.
[16]Wash yourselves; make yourselves clean;
 remove your evil deeds
 from before my eyes;
cease to do evil;
 [17]learn to do good;
seek justice;
 rescue the oppressed;
defend the orphan;
 plead for the widow.

The religious leaders are engaging in proper cultic practices, but this is not enough for a proper relationship with Yahweh. Their behavior is not only ineffectual but distasteful. The Israelites' hands are full of blood—a metaphor for acts of violence—and they must be cleaned. The cleansing consists of a twofold movement of *ceasing* to do evil and *pursuing* the good, specified as seeking justice, rescuing the oppressed, defending the orphan, and pleading for the widow.[13] The cleansing of bloody hands is not just a ritual cleansing but a transformation of one's life. It is not just a change in attitude that is required but a proactive care for the powerless members of society who were supposed to be provided for and protected according to the biblical laws.[14]

Isaiah 58 also details God's expectation that Israel will fulfill its social obligations and even likens it to worship by describing it in cultic terms ("fast"). Isaiah 58:1–5 says,

[1]Shout out; do not hold back!
 Lift up your voice like a trumpet!
Announce to my people their rebellion,
 to the house of Jacob their sins.
[2]Yet day after day they seek me
 and delight to know my ways,

13. Gossai, *Israel's Eighth-Century Prophets*, 255–57.
14. Tucker, "Book of Isaiah 1–39," 191.

as if they were a nation that practiced righteousness
    and did not forsake the ordinance of their God;
they ask of me righteous judgments;
    they want God on their side.
[3]"Why do we fast, but you do not see?
    Why humble ourselves, but you do not notice?"
Look, you serve your own interest on your fast day
    and oppress all your workers.
[4]You fast only to quarrel and to fight
    and to strike with a wicked fist.
Such fasting as you do today
    will not make your voice heard on high.
[5]Is such the fast that I choose,
    a day to humble oneself?
Is it to bow down the head like a bulrush
    and to lie in sackcloth and ashes?
Will you call this a fast,
    a day acceptable to the LORD?

The Israelites seek Yahweh, but the ways in which they delight to know God are not the ways of covenant law. Instead, the ways they practice are those of the ritual cult. The fast described is that of religious mourning, which is also a ritual of repentance. Hence, the prophet portrays the Israelites' confusion as to why their spiritual acts of worship are not recognized and rewarded by God. They wonder if they are doing the ritual correctly. But what seems pious on the outside is equated by God as rebellion and sin because they are worshiping in ways that seem correct while ignoring the injustice around them.[15]

What kind of fast *is* God looking for? What would please God and cause God to hear and answer Israel's cries? Isaiah 58:6–12 provides an answer:

[6]Is not this the fast that I choose:
    to loose the bonds of injustice,
    to undo the straps of the yoke,
to let the oppressed go free,
    and to break every yoke?
[7]Is it not to share your bread with the hungry
    and bring the homeless poor into your house;

---

15. John D. W. Watts, *Isaiah 34–66*, Word Biblical Commentary 25 (Waco: Word, 1987), 274–77.

when you see the naked, to cover them
> and not to hide yourself from your own kin?
[8]Then your light shall break forth like the dawn,
> and your healing shall spring up quickly;
your vindicator shall go before you;
> the glory of the LORD shall be your rear guard.
[9]Then you shall call, and the LORD will answer;
> you shall cry for help, and he will say, "Here I am."

If you remove the yoke from among you,
> the pointing of the finger, the speaking of evil,
[10]if you offer your food to the hungry
> and satisfy the needs of the afflicted,
then your light shall rise in the darkness
> and your gloom be like the noonday.
[11]The LORD will guide you continually
> and satisfy your needs in parched places
> and make your bones strong,
and you shall be like a watered garden,
> like a spring of water
> whose waters never fail.
[12]Your ancient ruins shall be rebuilt;
> you shall raise up the foundations of many generations;
you shall be called the repairer of the breach,
> the restorer of streets to live in.

Verses 6–7 catalog the specific, tangible needs on which the people should be focused. These are not abstract problems but concrete circumstances facing the Israelites. As verse 9 makes clear, God is capable of hearing their cry and responding, but only when proper righteousness, not hypocrisy, is manifested. Proper righteousness is manifested in practical actions by recognizing surrounding injustices, working to stop those who are enacting the wrong, and reaching out to aid the victims. If the Israelites want God to turn toward them, they must turn toward their neighbor. There is no spiritual or cultic substitute for such righteousness.[16]

AMOS 5:21–24

Like Isaiah, the prophet Amos condemns reliance on cultic practices while injustice is tolerated. Amos 5:21–24 says,

16. Tucker, "Book of Isaiah 1–39," 520–22.

²¹I hate, I despise your festivals,
  and I take no delight in your solemn assemblies.
²²Even though you offer me your burnt offerings and grain
    offerings,
  I will not accept them,
and the offerings of well-being of your fatted animals
  I will not look upon.
²³Take away from me the noise of your songs;
  I will not listen to the melody of your harps.
²⁴But let justice roll down like water
  and righteousness like an ever-flowing stream.

Amos attacks all of the elements of Israel's worship: feasts, assemblies, sacrifices, offerings, and songs. The beginning of verse 24 indicates a sharp contrast between that which is thought to be effective (the cultic practices of vv. 21–23) and that which is important and essential (the justice and righteousness of v. 24). In essence, one cannot worship God without an active commitment to the welfare of others. To do so is hypocritical and useless.[17]

Micah 6:1–8

In Micah 6:1–8 the prophet warns that Israel's priorities are mistaken. This passage can be viewed as a court scene, wherein Yahweh is the prosecutor and Israel the defendant. Verses 1–2 indicate that something has gone awry in the relationship between Yahweh and Israel:

¹Hear what the LORD says:
  Rise, plead your case before the mountains,
  and let the hills hear your voice.
²Hear, you mountains, the case of the LORD,
  and you enduring foundations of the earth,
for the LORD has a case against his people,
  and he will contend with Israel.

Verses 3–5 present Yahweh's account of all the good works that Yahweh has done for Israel:

³"O my people, what have I done to you?
  In what have I wearied you? Answer me!

17. Gossai, *Israel's Eighth-Century Prophets*, 260–61.

> [4]For I brought you up from the land of Egypt
>   and redeemed you from the house of slavery,
> and I sent before you Moses,
>   Aaron, and Miriam.
> [5]O my people, remember now what King Balak of Moab devised,
>   what Balaam son of Beor answered him,
> and what happened from Shittim to Gilgal,
>   that you may know the saving acts of the LORD."

Verses 6–7 present Israel's response and attempt to restore the broken relationship:

> [6]"With what shall I come before the LORD
>   and bow myself before God on high?
> Shall I come before him with burnt offerings,
>   with calves a year old?
> [7]Will the LORD be pleased with thousands of rams,
>   with ten thousands of rivers of oil?
> Shall I give my firstborn for my transgression,
>   the fruit of my body for the sin of my soul?"

This list of cultic possibilities attempts to appease Yahweh by means of total dedication (burnt offerings), the most desirable kind of sacrificial animal (calves a year old), lavish sacrifices (thousands of rams and ten thousands of rivers of oil), and one's most valuable possession (a firstborn child).[18] The questions in these verses push the point to the extreme: Is anything adequate to move God to accept me, particularly when I have defied God and now want to repent and restore the relationship? Israel's response assumes that the sacrificial system will remedy all woes and restore their broken relationship with Yahweh. But verse 8 makes clear that Yahweh's requirement is not more or better sacrifices:[19]

> [8]He has told you, O mortal, what is good;
>   and what does the LORD require of you
> but to do justice, and to love kindness,
>   and to walk humbly with your God?

The Israelites have been preoccupied with what they can do to please God through religious ritual and ceremony (vv. 6–7). But Yahweh shifts

---

18. Ralph L. Smith, *Micah–Malachi*, Word Biblical Commentary 32 (Waco: Word, 1984), 51.
19. Gossai, *Israel's Eighth-Century Prophets*, 261–63.

the emphasis away from the realm of the temple to the people's everyday lives. In doing so, there is nothing really new here (v. 8). The people know the great stories of deliverance and have the teachings of Moses. The three things God expects echoes what we find in the Torah (cf. Deut. 10:12–13). First, the people must *do* justice (*mishpat*), not merely wish for it or talk about it. In the book of Micah this means to work for fairness and equality for all, especially the weak and powerless who are exploited by others. Second, the people must love kindness. The Hebrew word for "kindness" (*hesed*) is a complex term that has to do with love, loyalty, and faithfulness. It describes an essential element in relationships, including that between God and humanity. Thus, Israel's relationship of covenant faithfulness to Yahweh should emerge from their love of God, not merely from duty or fear of punishment. And third, the people must walk humbly with their God. To "walk" means to live in a certain way, but the Hebrew word for "humbly" (*sana*) is more difficult to translate because it is not the typical word for "humility." It is probably better understood as "carefully." The people of God are to live carefully, according to what God wants. Walking with God ensures that they are imitating God's steps, making Yahweh their constant companion and conforming their will and actions to God's. As we have already seen, one cannot imitate God without looking after the vulnerable, poor, and oppressed (cf. Jer. 22:15–16).[20]

JEREMIAH 7:1–11

Finally, the prophet Jeremiah also highlights the dissonance between Israel's worship and its ethics. Jeremiah 7:1–11 says,

> [1]The word that came to Jeremiah from the LORD: [2]Stand in the gate of the LORD's house, and proclaim there this word, and say, Hear the word of the LORD, all you people of Judah, you who enter these gates to worship the LORD. [3]Thus says the LORD of hosts, the God of Israel: Amend your ways and your doings, and let me dwell with you in this place. [4]Do not trust in these deceptive words: "This is the temple of the LORD, the temple of the LORD, the temple of the LORD."
>
> [5]For if you truly amend your ways and your doings, if you truly act justly one with another, [6]if you do not oppress the alien, the orphan, and the widow or shed innocent blood in this place, and if you do not go after

---

20. Daniel J. Simundson, "The Book of Micah," in *The New Interpreter's Bible Commentary*, ed. Leander E. Keck et al. (Nashville: Abingdon, 2015), 5:725–27; and Kenneth L. Barker and Waylon Bailey, *Micah, Nahum, Habakkuk, Zephaniah*, New American Commentary 20 (Nashville: Broadman & Holman, 1999), 113–15.

other gods to your own hurt, [7]then I will dwell with you in this place, in the land that I gave to your ancestors forever and ever.

[8]Here you are, trusting in deceptive words to no avail. [9]Will you steal, murder, commit adultery, swear falsely, make offerings to Baal, and go after other gods that you have not known [10]and then come and stand before me in this house, which is called by my name, and say, "We are safe!"—only to go on doing all these abominations? [11]Has this house, which is called by my name, become a den of robbers in your sight? I, too, am watching, says the LORD.

In verse 2, the Israelites are entering the temple to worship the Lord, and what follows is a description of what legitimates worship and what nullifies it. Some people are providing a false sense of security with their religious sloganeering (v. 4). But these lying words (v. 8) gloss over a societal structure that is rotten to the core. Verse 9 specifically references prohibitions from the Decalogue, including worship of other gods and four of the sins against neighbor. These are fundamental covenantal stipulations, and yet the Israelites enter into worship in the temple thinking they're safe and in the right, only to go right back out to commit the same crimes and sins. The people have no shame, and the temple is no longer a place of worship under these circumstances, despite the peoples' pretense of worship. The temple can become the dwelling place of God again only if there is a radical reformation of Israel's moral life. It must engage in fair and just dealings, protect and care for the innocent and weak members of society, and demonstrate unqualified devotion and loyalty to God. What transpires outside the temple either legitimizes or undermines what happens in the temple.[21]

Specific Injustices

Beyond general critiques of the Israelites' neglect of their social commitments, the prophets also detail specific ways in which the Israelites have not upheld the humanitarian laws. The justice system is compromised because bribes are accepted (Isa. 1:23; 5:23; Ezek. 22:12; Amos 5:12; Mic. 3:11), innocent persons are slandered by false witnesses (Isa. 32:7), oppressive laws are created (Isa. 10:1–2), and justice is denied (Isa. 10:2; Jer. 5:28). Those in need are exploited and abused as garments are taken in

21. Patrick D. Miller, "The Book of Jeremiah," in *The New Interpreter's Bible Commentary*, ed. Leander E. Keck et al. (Nashville: Abingdon, 2015), 4:634–37, 641.

pledge (Amos 2:8), interest is charged on loans (Ezek. 22:12), houses and fields are seized (Isa. 3:14; Mic. 2:2), and people are subject to extortion (Ezek. 22:7, 12). Merchants are intentionally cheating their customers by falsifying weights and measurements in the sale of goods (Amos 8:5–6). The king is demanding laborers but refusing to give them their wages (Jer. 22:13). And Hebrew slaves that were released according to biblical laws are being forced back into subjection (Jer. 34:15–17). Remember the constant refrain in the biblical laws to protect the poor, widows, orphans, and sojourners? Now listen to the prophets' condemnation of how these persons are being treated: their faces are grinded on, they are trampled, pushed out of the way, oppressed, extorted, crushed, afflicted, brought to ruin, left undefended, deprived of their rights, turned aside from justice, and robbed. The people of Yahweh have blasphemed Yahweh's name through their behavior. Consequently, they are no longer recognizable as the people of God.

This oppression has enabled certain persons to live lifestyles of gross lavishness, especially in comparison to the poor among them. The prophets note that the affluent own fine jewelry and luxurious ornaments (Isa. 3:13–26). They own multiple houses that are built out of fine materials and are extravagantly decorated, as well as multiple fields that are magnificent and plentiful (Isa. 5:8–9; Jer. 22:13–17; Amos 3:15; 5:11). They are fat with the wealth they have gained and the food and drink they have consumed (Amos 4:1; 6:4–6; Jer. 5:26–28). Yet each description of affluence is followed by a corresponding indictment and judgment. The issue is not wealth itself but the overindulgence and extravagance displayed in light of the state of the poor and oppressed, as well as the means by which the wealth was gained. Obtaining wealth with a disregard for the condition of the poor or on the backs of the poor is a direct insult and offense to Israel's relationship with Yahweh and the expectations of the covenant.

Future Hope: A New People of God

Despite Israel's unfaithfulness and broken covenant with Yahweh, God does not abandon Israel. After judgment there is hope for the future, and the prophets provide a glimpse into what lies ahead. Yet God's future with Israel will not be a simple renewal of their past. The prophetic hope for what is to come includes new visions of God's reign and new understandings of the role of God's people.[22] This is seen clearly in Jeremiah 31:31–34:

> [31]The days are surely coming, says the LORD, when I will make a new covenant with the house of Israel and the house of Judah. [32]It will not be like the covenant that I made with their ancestors when I took them by the hand to bring them out of the land of Egypt—a covenant that they broke, though I was their husband, says the LORD. [33]But this is the covenant that I will make with the house of Israel after those days, says the LORD: I will put my law within them, and I will write it on their hearts, and I will be their God, and they shall be my people. [34]No longer shall they teach one another or say to each other, "Know the LORD," for they shall all know me, from the least of them to the greatest, says the LORD, for I will forgive their iniquity and remember their sin no more.

The prophet Ezekiel speaks of the newness of this covenant in terms of a new heart and a new spirit. In Ezekiel 11:19–20 (cf. 18:31; 36:26) Yahweh says,

> [19]I will give them one heart and put a new spirit within them; I will remove the heart of stone from their flesh and give them a heart of flesh, [20]so that they may follow my statutes and keep my ordinances and obey them. Then they shall be my people, and I will be their God.

The prophet Isaiah also references the new things that God will do. In Isaiah 43:19 (cf. 42:9; 48:6) Yahweh says,

> [19]I am about to do a new thing;
>   now it springs forth; do you not perceive it?
> I will make a way in the wilderness
>   and rivers in the desert.

The prophetic message is clear: despite Israel's unfaithfulness, God still desires to be in relationship with them. The relationship between God and Israel will not end because of their disobedience, but a new chapter in the story will be written and constitute a new covenant.

While certain things will change in this age to come, what will remain is God's continued concern with how the people of God embody and live

---

22. Bruce C. Birch, *Let Justice Roll Down: The Old Testament, Ethics, and Christian Life* (Louisville: Westminster John Knox, 1991), 271.

out God's justice and righteousness. These covenantal obligations will not disappear, for they are grounded in the very nature of God. God fills Zion with "justice and righteousness" (Isa. 33:5), loves justice (Isa. 61:8), and acts with "steadfast love, justice, and righteousness in the earth, for in these things I delight, says the LORD" (Jer. 9:24). The age to come, despite its newness, will continue to reflect these characteristics. In describing the future, Isaiah 29:19–21 says,

> [19]The meek [poor] shall obtain fresh joy in the LORD,
>   and the neediest people shall exult in the Holy One of Israel.
> [20]For the tyrant shall be no more,
>   and the scoffer shall cease to be;
>   all those alert to do evil shall be cut off—
> [21]those who cause a person to lose a lawsuit,
>   who set a trap for the arbiter in the gate
>   and undermine justice for the one in the right.

And Isaiah 32:16–17 notes,

> [16]Then justice will dwell in the wilderness
>   and righteousness abide in the fruitful field.
> [17]The effect of righteousness will be peace,
>   and the result of righteousness, quietness and trust forever.

A few prophetic passages connect the future age with the ideal king—later identified as the Messiah—who will fulfill his role as the ultimate protector of the poor. Of him Isaiah 9:6–7 says,

> [6]For a child has been born for us,
>   a son given to us;
> authority rests upon his shoulders,
>   and he is named
> Wonderful Counselor, Mighty God,
>   Everlasting Father, Prince of Peace.
> [7]Great will be his authority,
>   and there shall be endless peace
> for the throne of David and his kingdom.
>   He will establish and uphold it
> with justice and with righteousness
>   from this time onward and forevermore.
> The zeal of the LORD of hosts will do this.

And in Isaiah 11:1–5 the prophet proclaims,

> [1]A shoot shall come out from the stump of Jesse,
>   and a branch shall grow out of his roots.
> [2]The spirit of the LORD shall rest on him,
>   the spirit of wisdom and understanding,
>   the spirit of counsel and might,
>   the spirit of knowledge and the fear of the LORD.
> [3]His delight shall be in the fear of the LORD.
>
> He shall not judge by what his eyes see
>   or decide by what his ears hear,
> [4]but with righteousness he shall judge for the poor
>   and decide with equity for the oppressed of the earth;
> he shall strike the earth with the rod of his mouth,
>   and with the breath of his lips he shall kill the wicked.
> [5]Righteousness shall be the belt around his waist
>   and faithfulness the belt around his loins.

Finally, Isaiah 42:1–4 says,

> [1]Here is my servant, whom I uphold,
>   my chosen, in whom my soul delights;
> I have put my spirit upon him;
>   he will bring forth justice to the nations.
> [2]He will not cry out or lift up his voice
>   or make it heard in the street;
> [3]a bruised reed he will not break,
>   and a dimly burning wick he will not quench;
>   he will faithfully bring forth justice.
> [4]He will not grow faint or be crushed
>   until he has established justice in the earth,
>   and the coastlands wait for his teaching.

The prophet Jeremiah also echoes Isaiah's hopes for a future king:

[5]The days are surely coming, says the LORD, when I will raise up for David a righteous Branch, and he shall reign as king and deal wisely and shall execute justice and righteousness in the land. [6]In his days Judah will be saved, and Israel will live in safety. And this is the name by which he will be called: "The LORD is our righteousness." (Jer. 23:5–6; cf. 33:14–16)

Thus, the anticipation of a new age for the people of God emerges in the prophets, through whom we catch glimpses of what this future will entail. As we turn to the New Testament these prophetic words are fulfilled in the person of Jesus Christ and the gift of the Spirit in the outpouring of Pentecost. Here the people of God receive new identities as the body of Christ and the community of the Spirit, and these identities will continue to point to the mission of care for the vulnerable, poor, and oppressed. Justice and righteousness are still to be lived out in this new age, modeled by the Messiah and enabled by the Spirit. The mandate for redemptive service does not end but is transformed christologically and pneumatologically as God remains committed to the life and flourishing of this world.

Identity and Mission as the People of God

Too often Christians move past the Old Testament, especially the Torah, as though this part of the story were no longer applicable to our lives. While the incarnation of Jesus Christ inaugurates a new creation and the age of the kingdom of God, even Jesus himself said he did not come to abolish the law and prophets but to fulfill them (Matt. 5:17). Thus, we should expect continuity between the main ideas we have observed thus far and what transpires in the New Testament. So, what lessons can we glean from the story of the Israelites as the people of God?

First, redemptive service means being concerned with both the spiritual and material well-being of those around us. The salvation that God desires for the world today is still comprehensive, and we must attend to bringing holistic healing and restoration. If we try to split the spiritual from the material or ignore one to the detriment of the other, we will fail.

Second, redemptive service means that, as the people of God, we are to image God's justice and righteousness in our justice and righteousness. God's deliverance of the afflicted still requires human hands. God can and will act, and he desires that we partner with him and mediate healing and restoration to the world around us.

Third, redemptive service is grounded in the very being of God. The Old Testament reveals a God who is invested in the well-being of creation and has chosen a people through whom restoration will be mediated to the whole world. God's own actions and initiatives *to* and *for* the Israelites were supposed to be imitated *in* and *through* them toward others. As the people of God (identity), they were to reflect their God (mission). To the extent that we engage in redemptive service, we are not just enacting good social practices but mediating God's own desires and actions for others' well-being. We are imitating God and thus fulfilling our creational call to image God.

Finally, redemptive service is an essential characteristic of the people of God and is to be embodied in their day-to-day actions toward one another. As David Baker observes, "Hard hearts and tight fists have no place in the covenant community."[23] Though we do not live by the legal requirements of the Torah today, God still requires God's people to live in service to one another, especially the vulnerable, poor, and oppressed. Although the precise details of Israel's humanitarian laws are no longer applicable, the principles remain: we are responsible for the well-being of our neighbors. To fail to live out our communal calling and responsibility to one another is to fail to be the people of God. As the prophets show, this failure brings judgment upon us that no amount of religious piety or activity can offset. The prophets' indictments disclose how integral righteous social engagement is to living as God's people. The Israelites neglected their mission and bore the consequences of it. Today, redemptive service is still required and central to our identity and mission.

DISCUSSION QUESTIONS

1. Before reading this chapter, what did you know about the causes of Israel's exile, and how would you have described the message the prophets delivered to Israel? Does reading this chapter change your perspective? If so, how?

2. The prophets warn against worshiping God in the temple while neglecting one's neighbors outside the temple. How might we translate that message into a caution to the twenty-first-century church today?

3. The prophets call out specific injustices among the Israelites that lead to the oppression of those most vulnerable in their midst. If the prophets lived today and were addressing the American church, what specific injustices might they call out as a violation of our identity as the people of God?

23. David L. Baker, *Tight Fists or Open Hands? Wealth and Poverty in Old Testament Law* (Grand Rapids: Eerdmans, 2009), 283.

4. In the introduction to part 1, we explored how the parable of the good Samaritan connects seeing and doing. How does the Old Testament's story of the Israelites as the people of God inform the way we see others? How does it inform the way we act toward others?

FOR FURTHER READING

Fretheim, Terence E. "The Prophets and Social Justice: A *Conservative* Agenda." *Word & World* 28, no. 2 (Spring 2008): 159–68.

Gossai, Hemchand. *Social Critique by Israel's Eighth-Century Prophets: Justice and Righteousness in Context*. Eugene, OR: Wipf & Stock, 1993.

Heschel, Abraham Joshua. *The Prophets: Two Volumes in One*. Peabody, MA: Hendrickson, 2007.

Houston, Walter J. *Contending for Justice: Ideologies and Theologies of Social Justice in the Old Testament*. New York: T&T Clark, 2006.

———. *Justice for the Poor? Social Justice in the Old Testament in Concept and Practice*. Eugene, OR: Cascade Books, 2020.

4

Reign and Renewal

The Ministry and Mission of Jesus Christ

The biblical narrative, thankfully, does not stop after the prophets. If it did, the story would be rather depressing, as well as incomplete! Yet while we would not want to make the mistake of assuming the biblical account ends with the closing of the Old Testament, we must also not make the mistake of assuming that it begins afresh in the New Testament—as if the narrative of Jesus were its own self-contained story. The plotline of the Gospels is directly connected with the story developed in the Old Testament. Israel's narrative is the backstory to Jesus, making the four Gospels the climax to the story of Israel. Failing to recognize this leads to the temptation to individualize the Gospels and read them as a story for personal, spiritual devotion. However, the story of the Gospels is more properly *Israel's* story and only becomes part of *our* story as we situate ourselves within God's covenant people. The Gospels are, thus, the story of how Israel's God enacts his reign through Jesus Christ, and consequently how Jesus rescues the whole created order—not just individual souls—from the disorder that had been plaguing it since the garden.[1]

In the previous chapters we observed how the creational mandate for humanity to function as the image of God (Gen. 1) is taken up in the Old

---

1. Max Turner, *Power from on High: The Spirit in Israel's Restoration and Witness in Luke-Acts* (Sheffield, UK: Sheffield Academic, 1996), 434–35.

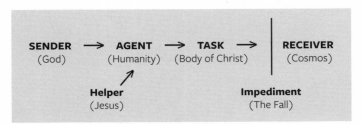

Figure 4.1 Plot analysis of the biblical narrative: New Testament

Testament by Israel through their identity and mission as the people of God. As we turn to the New Testament, this identity and mission does not disappear. Quite the contrary! As the plot develops further, the people of God also become known as the body of Christ (Rom. 12:4–5; 1 Cor. 12:12–31; Eph. 4:15–16; Col. 1:18, 24), and a new layer is added to our identity and mission due to the person and work of Jesus Christ (see fig. 4.1).[2] Whereas in the Old Testament the people of God received the Torah—biblical laws that prescribed and guided their redemptive service to others—there is no comparable set of law codes in the New Testament. Rather, Jesus Christ himself demonstrates the redemptive service to which we are called.

Jesus is another "helper" sent to humans to assist in their task of fulfilling their earthly vocation, but the nature of this helper is vastly different from that of the Torah. The law was *external* to both God and the Israelites, though it reflected God's character and actions in its directives, detailing for the Israelites how to live as the people of God. Jesus Christ, however, is not external to God or humanity. The witness of the incarnation affirms that Jesus is both God *and* human. As fully God, Jesus' actions and words not only reflect God's actions and words but *are* God's very actions and words here on earth. As fully human, Jesus shows, with actions and words, how humanity is to live, and in his own embodiment Jesus fulfills God's desire and goal for humanity as a human; Jesus is *the* image of God par excellence. While we can think of Jesus as a helper in the narrative sense, we should recognize the vast difference between him and the law.

Since the New Testament provides a christological lens through which to understand our identity and mission, it is necessary to take a closer look at

2. Terence Fretheim says, "The church, in continuity with Israel, is to take up the mission to which the people of God have long been called. It is to be noted that many of the central mission texts in the New Testament are specifically grounded in the Old Testament (Luke 24:45–47; Acts 13:47; 15:14–18; Rom. 15:8–12; Gal. 3:8–9)" (Fretheim, *Exodus* [Louisville: Westminster John Knox, 1991], 214). This continuity is also clearly seen when comparing Exod. 19:5–6 and 1 Pet. 2:4–10.

the story and what new plotlines are provided that inform our worldview. In this chapter we focus on the story of Jesus Christ as presented in the Gospels, highlighting his coming as the advent of the kingdom of God and the new creation. These might seem like two separate concepts, but they are actually two ways of talking about the same reality. "Kingdom of God" emphasizes the coming *reign* of God, whereas "new creation" emphasizes the coming *renewal* of what God initiated at the beginning. These two realities are connected in the person of Jesus Christ, who is both the messianic king inaugurating as well as manifesting the kingdom and the beginning of the new creation itself. Jesus' kingdom project is the rescue and renewal of God's creation project.[3]

"Behold the King": The Coming of the Kingdom of God

If all we needed to know about Jesus was his incarnation, death, and resurrection, then there is a considerable amount of the Gospels that we should just cut out! While that sounds like a silly proposal, many times that is exactly how the narrative of Jesus is treated. Of course, there is sustained focus on the beginning of Jesus' life as God coming in the flesh (incarnation). And yes, there is sustained focus on the end of Jesus' life, dying on the cross for our sins (death) and being raised to life again (resurrection). But what about the middle portion? What about his life between the moments of birth and death? To discount the life of Jesus is to discount the majority of the content of the Gospels, since the writers all seem to value the time between Jesus' birth and death. Particularly, this middle content focuses on Jesus' kingdom-inaugurating work. To neglect this is to misunderstand Jesus altogether![4]

At the beginning of his ministry, Jesus proclaims that the kingdom of God is near (Mark 1:14–15). After his resurrection, Jesus continues to talk

---

3. G. K. Beale, "The New Testament and New Creation," in *Biblical Theology: Retrospect and Prospect*, ed. Scott J. Hafemann (Downers Grove, IL: InterVarsity, 2002), 164; and N. T. Wright, *Simply Jesus: A New Vision of Who He Was, What He Did, and Why He Matters* (New York: HarperOne, 2011), 213. In the Gospel of John when Jesus is being sentenced to crucifixion, Pilate unwittingly identifies Jesus with two significant titles that aptly summarize Jesus' life and mission: "Behold the man" and "Behold the king" (author's translation) (John 19:5, 14). We will use these two designations to explore the themes of new creation and the kingdom of God below.

4. N. T. Wright notes this lacuna in the church today and highlights how the creeds reinforce this truncated notion of the significance of Jesus. See Wright, *How God Became King: The Forgotten Story of the Gospels* (New York: HarperOne, 2012), 3–24.

about the kingdom with his disciples before he ascends to heaven (Acts 1:1–3). Between these bookends of Jesus' life are a plethora of parables, sayings, and enacted dramas related to the kingdom. Moreover, when Jesus sends out the twelve and then the seventy-two, he tells them to preach the message of the kingdom of God (Luke 9:1–2; 10:8–11). The prevalence of material related to the kingdom in the Gospels—especially the Synoptic Gospels—leads Nicholas Perrin to remark that the "kingdom of God was not simply at the heart of Jesus' agenda; it *was* his agenda."[5]

While the kingdom of God is front and center in Jesus' life and ministry, the precise meaning of "kingdom" (*basileia*) is somewhat complex. Although contemporary English associations with the word "kingdom" may conjure up ideas of a particular place or people, this understanding misses the dynamic sense of the Greek word *basileia* as "kingship" or "rule." The phrase "kingdom of God" does not refer to a thing called the "kingdom"; rather, it is a proclamation about the God who is king. When Jesus proclaims that the kingdom of God is near, it means that God is taking over as king. To be part of this kingdom is to come under God's rule.[6]

The "kingdom of God" is not a new concept that Jesus proclaims; it is rooted in the Old Testament Scriptures. While the phrase "kingdom of God" does not occur in most translations, God's kingship is a prevalent theme throughout the Old Testament—and later Jewish literature—as both a present and future reality. On the one hand, many of the psalms celebrate the rule of the God who is a great king reigning over all the earth (Pss. 10:16–18; 47:1–9; 93:1; 95:3–7; 96:10–13; 97:1; 145:1, 10–13). On the other hand, a number of prophetic passages recognize the extent of human rebellion against God's rule such that there will be a day when God's kingship will be more effectively established (Isa. 33:20–22; 45:21–24; 52:7–10; Zech. 14:9). Thus, when Jesus announces the coming of the kingdom, his hearers understand his proclamation, as it resonates with their Jewish beliefs concerning God's reign.[7]

---

5. Nicholas Perrin, *The Kingdom of God: A Biblical Theology* (Grand Rapids: Zondervan, 2019), 25. The Gospel of Matthew uses the Jewish equivalent "kingdom of heaven" instead of "kingdom of God," though there is no discernible difference in meaning. "Kingdom of God" or its equivalent is found within the Synoptic Gospels over seventy times, not including the parallels. See R. T. France, "Kingdom of God," in *Dictionary for Theological Interpretation of the Bible*, ed. Kevin J. Vanhoozer (Grand Rapids: Baker Academic, 2005), 420.

6. France, "Kingdom of God," 420.

7. France, "Kingdom of God," 421. Wright notes that the idea of Yahweh's kingship is also present even where explicit "king" or "kingdom" language is absent in the Old Testament. He offers the example of God as "shepherd" as an equivalent image for "king." Wright, *Simply Jesus*, 47–49.

Having established *what* the kingdom is, there still remains the question of *when* the kingdom is. When Jesus proclaimed the kingdom of God, did he intend to communicate a present or future reality? Although historically scholars have been divided on how to answer this question, there is a growing consensus that the answer is not either/or but rather both/and. The kingdom is not *either* a present *or* a future reality; the kingdom is *both* a present *and* a future reality. How can this be? Jesus brought the immediate presence of the kingdom of God, but its climactic appearance won't transpire until Christ's second coming. Some refer to this as the "already/not yet" tension: the kingdom of God has *already* broken into human history through Jesus and his followers but is *not yet* complete.[8] Let's now take a closer look at the characteristics of this kingdom, beginning with John the Baptist and then examining Jesus himself.

John the Baptist: Preparing the Way

The Old Testament closes with the prophets, and the New Testament opens with another one: John the Baptist (Matt. 11:9; Luke 1:76; 7:26). John prepares the way for Jesus, and his voice and message stand in continuity with the prophetic voices of the past. Yet John's ministry also marks the emergence of the kingdom of God (Matt. 11:12–13; Luke 16:16; Acts 1:21–22; 10:36–37). As a transitional figure, John's preparatory work includes calling out a newly reconstituted Israel and declaring the community expectations within this kingdom of God. In so doing, John introduces the themes of Jesus' ministry to the crowds and begins the process of revealing God's salvation.[9]

At the beginning of John's ministry, we find him in the wilderness baptizing. His commissioning as a prophet borrows from that of the Old Testament prophets. Just as the word of God came to the prophets of old to propel them into their prophetic ministry, so does the word of God come to John to launch his ministry (cf. 1 Kings 18:1; Jer. 1:2; Ezek. 1:3; Hosea 1:1; Joel 1:1; Jon. 1:1; Luke 3:2). In the Gospels of Matthew and Mark, John's clothing demonstrates that he is a prophet by recalling the attire of the prophet Elijah (cf. 2 Kings 1:8; Matt. 3:4; Mark 1:6).[10]

8. Perrin, *Kingdom of God*, 28–34.

9. Perrin, *Kingdom of God*, 75, 82–85; and Richard B. Vinson, *Luke*, Smyth & Helwys Bible Commentary (Macon, GA: Smyth & Helwys, 2008), 88.

10. Mikeal C. Parsons, *Luke*, Paideia: Commentaries on the New Testament (Grand Rapids: Baker Academic, 2015), 64–65; and M. Eugene Boring, "Matthew," in *The New Interpreter's Bible Commentary*, ed. Leander E. Keck et al. (Nashville: Abingdon, 2015), 7:90.

John's public ministry is introduced by a quotation from Isaiah that, in its original context, describes a voice preparing the way for Yahweh's return to Zion but now identifies John as the voice calling out and preparing the way for the Lord—Jesus—who will return to Zion and bring God's salvation (Matt. 3:3; Mark 1:2–3; Luke 3:4–6; John 1:23).[11] The central message of John's preaching is a baptism of repentance and forgiveness. Ritual washings were common among the Jews (like at Qumran and the temple), though John's baptism is not a repeated ritual but a once-for-all baptism with eschatological implications. Repentance and forgiveness are central to the gospel taught by Jesus to the apostles, to be spread to all the nations (Luke 24:47; Acts 3:19; 5:31; 26:18–20), which is also associated with baptism in Acts (Acts 2:38).[12]

Like the prophets of old, John had a message of repentance and forgiveness that included attention to a person's behavior toward their neighbor. Thus, we arrive at the significance of John's message for our purposes: it was about not just repentance and forgiveness but also producing fruit in one's life in keeping with repentance. In essence, John was calling for ethical renewal among the Israelites—not unlike his predecessors, the prophets. It is not just a baptism of repentance and forgiveness of sins that counts (religious ritual) but also a life that bears fruit worthy of repentance (covenant obligations).

While all four Gospels attest to John's ministry of baptism (Matt. 3:1–6; Mark 1:2–6; Luke 3:1–6; John 1:19–28), only the Gospel of Luke provides an extended record of his message to the people coming to be baptized:

> John said to the crowds coming out to be baptized by him, "You brood of vipers! Who warned you to flee from the coming wrath? Therefore, bear fruits worthy of repentance, and do not begin to say to yourselves, 'We have Abraham as our ancestor,' for I tell you, God is able from these stones to raise up children to Abraham. Even now the ax is lying at the root of the trees; therefore every tree that does not bear good fruit will be cut down and thrown into the fire."
>
> And the crowds asked him, "What, then, should we do?" In reply he said to them, "Whoever has two coats must share with anyone who has none,

---

11. Throughout the Gospel of Luke and the book of Acts, whenever the story introduces the public ministry of a key character, it uses a prominent quote of Old Testament Scripture. This literary technique helps to signal that each new stage of the narrative is continuing to fulfill the divine commissioning, and this is certainly the case with the introduction of John the Baptist (cf. Luke 4:18–19; Acts 2:17–21; 13:47). Robert C. Tannehill, *Luke*, Abingdon New Testament Commentaries (Nashville: Abingdon, 1996), 80.

12. Boring, "Matthew," 90–91.

and whoever has food must do likewise." Even tax collectors came to be baptized, and they asked him, "Teacher, what should we do?" He said to them, "Collect no more than the amount prescribed for you." Soldiers also asked him, "And we, what should we do?" He said to them, "Do not extort money from anyone by threats or false accusation, and be satisfied with your wages." (Luke 3:7–14; cf. Matt. 3:7–10)

Not mincing any words, John calls the crowds coming to him a brood of vipers! He describes the approaching people as evildoers who expect baptism to save them from God's impending judgment. Such a label may also be implicating the people's connection to Satan—*the* viper—rather than to Abraham, the prized forefather of the Israelites. Accordingly, the negative characterization indicates that the crowds coming to John are living outside the covenant, a theme of the text that immediately follows John's scathing address in Luke 3:8.[13]

We see in this passage that John's name-calling is triggered by their lack of fruit attesting to a repentant life. Pedigree alone cannot protect a person (lineal descent from Abraham); rather, it is living in such a way that one's actions attest to the professed change. John's message was that neither the rights of birth nor the ritual of baptism could substitute for repentance and ethical reform. These things are worthless by themselves unless the people bear fruit in keeping with repentance; a change in direction must be validated by a change in behavior.

John the Baptist is also depicted in connection with the prophets in his warning of the coming eschatological judgment and in his use of fruit-bearing language. John's message here has strong correlations with Isaiah's message (Isa. 5:1–7). Like Isaiah, John not only compares covenantal obedience with fruit-bearing but also focuses the terms of covenant obedience on issues of social justice. In particular, the fruit John has in mind is utterly practical and focused on one's neighbor. Three times various factions of the crowd ask him what they need to do to bear fruits worthy of repentance. First, John instructs anyone who has an extra tunic or food to share with those who have none.[14] This complements Jesus' later words concerning love and sharing (Luke 6:30–36). Second, John instructs tax

---

13. Parsons, *Luke*, 66; and R. Alan Culpepper, "Luke," in *The New Interpreter's Bible Commentary*, ed. Leander E. Keck et al. (Nashville: Abingdon, 2015), 8:65–66.

14. Some translations render the Greek word in Luke 3:11 as "coats" (*chitōnas*), but this is misleading. The reference is not to an extra outer garment but to a basic garment that is worn next to the skin. See Tannehill, *Luke*, 81.

collectors to refrain from collecting more than they are owed. At the time, the right to collect taxes (tolls and customs duties owed to the Romans) was auctioned off to the highest bidder, with the winner paying in advance. When the highest bidder—the chief tax collector—set out to collect the taxes, he aimed to recoup not only the original amount paid but also any other expenses he might incur from hiring other collectors under him as well as any profits he desired. Thus, the people who owed money were liable to be exploited financially in order to make money for these collectors. The third response by John—directed to soldiers—is to tell the soldiers not to extort money, similar to his instructions to the tax collectors. The soldiers were likely being sent to enforce the demands of the tax collectors. In his response to the tax collectors, John also places emphasis on inward contentment, as acts of social justice are related to inward attitudes.[15]

All three of John's commands call for an end to a lifestyle based on greed and accumulation of material possessions, especially with needy neighbors in view. The crowds are challenged to demonstrate their concern for the well-being of others by sharing whatever they do not need for their own survival. The tax collectors and soldiers are to refrain from exploiting their positions for personal gain at the expense of others. These fruits of repentance begin to constitute a redeemed community that reflects the reign of God. Commenting on John the Baptist's message, Nicholas Perrin says, "Because right worship (vertical) presupposes well-ordered human relationships (horizontal), the faithful of Yahweh must concern themselves not only with getting right with God but also with getting right with one another, with special attention to the disenfranchised in their midst (Isa. 56:4–7; Jer. 7:4–8; Ezek. 22:6–7)."[16]

The salvation or redemption John proclaims is holistic and pertains to all dimensions of life, not just the spiritual—similar to what we observe in the Old Testament. God's concern with the material aspects of this world remains a key part of the Christian story. If John the Baptist functions to prepare the way for Jesus and marks the emergence of the kingdom of God, we should certainly anticipate that Jesus' message and ministry will stand in continuity with John the Baptist's and that Jesus' furtherance of the kingdom will exhibit the same characteristics.

15. Culpepper, "Luke," 66–67; Parsons, *Luke*, 66–68; Perrin, *Kingdom of God*, 83–85; Tannehill, *Luke*, 81–82; and Vinson, *Luke*, 90–92.
16. Perrin, *Kingdom of God*, 84–85.

Jesus Christ: Showing Us the Way

John the Baptist's ministry leads to and marks the beginning of Jesus' own ministry. All four Gospels record Jesus' baptism by John and the subsequent descent of the Spirit upon him. Each Gospel then develops its narrative about Jesus' life and ministry. However, only in the Gospel of Luke do we find an inaugural sermon by Jesus that details the good news of the kingdom of God that Jesus will then go about proclaiming and performing (Luke 4:43).[17]

After his baptism and forty days of testing in the wilderness, Jesus returns to his hometown of Nazareth and enters into public ministry. Here we learn about the character of Jesus' mission from Jesus himself. The placement of this scene at the beginning of Jesus' ministry in the Gospel of Luke suggests that the rest of the Lukan story—Acts as well as Luke—should be read in light of it. It is the public announcement of Jesus' messianic vocation.[18] Luke 4:16–21 says,

> When he came to Nazareth, where he had been brought up, he went to the synagogue on the Sabbath day, as was his custom. He stood up to read, and the scroll of the prophet Isaiah was given to him. He unrolled the scroll and found the place where it was written:
>
>> "The Spirit of the Lord is upon me,
>>> because he has anointed me
>>>> to bring good news to the poor.
>>> He has sent me to proclaim release to the captives
>>>> and recovery of sight to the blind,
>>>>> to set free those who are oppressed,
>>> to proclaim the year of the Lord's favor."
>
> And he rolled up the scroll, gave it back to the attendant, and sat down. The

---

17. Bruce C. Birch, *Let Justice Roll Down: The Old Testament, Ethics, and Christian Life* (Louisville: Westminster John Knox, 1991), 121–22. Matthew 13:53–58 and Mark 6:1–6 also record Jesus' preaching at Nazareth, but both omit the details of the public discourse and situate the scene later in Jesus' ministry. The Gospel of Luke is unique in both the placement of this event and the details of the content.

18. Some refer to this pericope as the Nazareth manifesto. Parsons, *Luke*, 80–81; Tannehill, *Luke*, 91. Luke intentionally rearranges the Markan narrative sequence, indicating a programmatic function of Luke 4:18–19 for Jesus' ministry. Whereas Mark places Jesus' appearance in his hometown synagogue much later in the narrative, after Jesus has already been ministering for a while (Mark 6:1–6), Luke moves the appearance to the very beginning of his narrative about Jesus to help frame Jesus' ministry that follows. See Richard B. Hays, *The Moral Vision of the New Testament: A Contemporary Introduction to New Testament Ethics* (New York: HarperOne, 1996), 115.

eyes of all in the synagogue were fixed on him. Then he began to say to them, "Today this scripture has been fulfilled in your hearing."[19]

God's particular concern for the vulnerable, poor, and oppressed that we observed in the Old Testament becomes incarnate in Jesus, who announces that this will be the focus of his own ministry.[20] The text from Isaiah that Jesus reads aloud in the synagogue announces that God's own agent will put an end to injustice and oppression, and Jesus claims he is that agent. By virtue of the Spirit resting on Jesus—which has already descended earlier in the narrative at his baptism (Luke 3:22)—Jesus declares himself to be the anticipated Messiah who has received this commission from God.

The recipients of Jesus' ministry in Luke 4 are the poor, captive, blind, and oppressed. While it may be fitting to understand these conditions spiritually—which is not altogether inappropriate in the Gospel of Luke—they are also grounded in concrete reality. Jesus' anointing is not just for spiritual matters but social ones too.[21]

To announce good news to the poor means that Jesus is sent to those who are economically disadvantaged and to those who are spiritually impoverished. During Jesus' time it is estimated that 90 percent of the population were peasant farmers and village craftspeople who produced most of the wealth, but much of it was siphoned off to the top 10 percent by taxes, tithes, and charges for sacrifices and temple service.[22] Jesus echoes his mother's song when he reads this part of the Isaiah text: in Mary's Magnificat she praises the Lord for lifting up the lowly and sending the rich away empty (Luke 1:52–53). Jesus also echoes his cousin's commands to the crowd to share with those who have not (3:10–11). Later Jesus announces God's blessing on the poor (6:20); refers to the fulfillment of the charge to bring good news to the poor in his response to John (7:22); includes the poor on the guest list of the kingdom banquet (14:13, 21); highlights

19. The cited text in Luke 4:18–19 is a paraphrase of Isa. 61:1–2 and 58:6, with certain Lukan modifications. These modifications reflect a well-known rhetorical exercise known as "paraphrase," wherein the writer takes liberties to alter the form of expression from the original text while still retaining the original idea. See Parsons, *Luke*, 48.

20. Later in the Gospel of Luke, Jesus' kingdom proclamation is put in relationship to the law and the prophets (Luke 16:16).

21. Parsons, *Luke*, 81. Later in the narrative John the Baptist will inquire as to whether Jesus is actually the Messiah. Jesus' response to him is to list all the *physical* acts he has performed (Luke 7:18–23), which correlate with the *physical* conditions of people described in Luke 4.

22. David P. Gushee and Glen H. Stassen, *Kingdom Ethics: Following Jesus in Contemporary Context*, 2nd ed. (Grand Rapids: Eerdmans, 2016), 138–39.

them in his parable as true children of Abraham (16:19–31); designates them as beneficiaries of the charity of the rich (18:22); and admires their generosity in contrast to the gifts of the rich (21:3–4).[23]

To proclaim release to the captives means that Jesus is sent to those who are enslaved physically and to those who are enslaved to sin. The "captives" here probably include at least three groups of people. Given the preceding reference to the poor, there are those imprisoned for monetary debt (Luke 7:40–42); those with physical ailments regarded as a result of Satan's bondage (Luke 13:16) or the devil's oppression (Acts 10:38); and those who need to be released from their sin, also depicted as a form of bondage (Acts 8:22–23).[24]

To bring recovery of sight to the blind means that Jesus is sent to those who are physically and spiritually without sight. Jesus' healing ministry certainly includes those who are blind (Luke 7:21; 18:35–43). But sight and light are also used metaphorically for perceiving revelation and sharing in salvation (Luke 1:78–79; 2:30–32; Acts 13:47; 26:18, 23). And to set free the oppressed means that Jesus is sent to those who are subject to unwelcome forces of restraint and unwanted demons (cf. Luke 8:29).[25]

The reference to the proclamation of the year of the Lord's favor is an allusion to the Jubilee Year legislation from Leviticus 25. Every fifty years family property was to revert to its original owners and indentured servants were to be released.[26] Jesus' ministry signals that the time of deliverance for the vulnerable, poor, and oppressed has come, and in that respect, his work fulfills the ideal social concern of the Jubilee Year. Jesus declares this imminent "year of the Lord's favor" to be the inbreaking of the kingdom of God (Luke 4:43), and it is already being fulfilled (4:20–21).[27]

Jesus' concern for the poor, captive, blind, and oppressed is not a new idea. His reading of Isaiah demonstrates a continuation of the Old Testament storyline, as does connecting himself with the promises of the Jubilee Year. Richard Hays summarizes the significance of Luke 4:

---

23. Culpepper, "Luke," 84; Parsons, *Luke*, 81; Tannehill, *Luke*, 91–92; and Vinson, *Luke*, 120.

24. Culpepper, "Luke," 84; Parsons, *Luke*, 81; and Tannehill, *Luke*, 92.

25. Culpepper, "Luke," 84–85; Parsons, *Luke*, 81; and Tannehill, *Luke*, 92.

26. The emphasis on release in Luke 4:18 recalls the Jubilee Year in 4:19, as the Jubilee Year is also referred to as the "year of release" (Lev. 25:10 LXX). See Tannehill, *Luke*, 93.

27. Culpepper, "Luke," 84–85; and Parsons, *Luke*, 81–82. N. T. Wright maintains that the genealogy of Jesus in the Gospel of Matthew presents Jesus as Israel's Jubilee in person (Matt. 1:2–16). See Wright, *How God Became King*, 67–74. Jesus' proclamation is immediately followed by casting out demons and healing: two signs of the inbreaking of the kingdom of God. See Perrin, *Kingdom of God*, 152–68.

Jesus' messianic activity is the work of *liberation*, and the direct link of the gospel to the message of the prophets is to be found in the prophetic call for *justice.* . . . The particular Isaiah texts that are conflated in Luke's account are significant: Isaiah 61 promises the deliverance and restoration of Israel, and Isaiah 58 is a powerful statement of God's demand for service to the poor. . . . By evoking these texts at the beginning of his ministry, Luke's Jesus declares himself as the Messiah who by the power of the Spirit will create a restored Israel in which justice and compassion for the poor will prevail. All of Jesus' miracles and healings throughout Luke's Gospel are therefore to be read as signs of God's coming Kingdom, in which the oppressed will be set free.[28]

At first this is welcome news to those Israelites listening to his proclamation. However, the tide turns when Jesus explains that these benefits will not be limited to the Israelites alone. Jesus tells those gathered around him that his ministry will be marked by radical inclusiveness (of the Gentiles). Commenting on this, Mikeal Parsons says of the Israelites, "They have understood themselves to be the primary beneficiaries of Jesus's message. They can all relate to being poor, captive, blind, or oppressed. They are ready for deliverance, but they are not prepared to share it."[29]

Hereafter in the narrative, Jesus' ministry and mission will include the poor, captive, blind, and oppressed, as well as every other kind of first-century outcast: sinners, demoniacs, prodigals, prostitutes, the unclean, the lame, tax collectors, women, Samaritans, and even Gentiles. And Jesus' concern for the downtrodden and outcasts is revealed not only in his ministry but also in his teachings. His healings, deliverances, and celebrations are all to be understood as particular manifestations of God's rule now appearing: this is what it looks like when God is in charge (Luke 10:9; 11:20; 14:15–24).[30] Jesus' mission was to begin to mend this broken world, and to do so, he had to mend broken people. In short, the inbreaking of the kingdom brought restoration to those broken by life's circumstances.[31]

---

28. Hays, *Moral Vision of the New Testament*, 166. Jesus is presented as a prophet like Moses, a liberator of his people. Even his death and resurrection are referred to in the Gospel of Luke as his "exodus" (Luke 9:31). See Hays, *Moral Vision of the New Testament*, 117–18.

29. Parsons, *Luke*, 83.

30. Gordon D. Fee, "The Kingdom of God and the Church's Global Mission," in *Called and Empowered: Global Mission in Pentecostal Perspective*, ed. Murray W. Dempster, Byron D. Klaus, and Douglas Petersen (Peabody, MA: Hendrickson, 1991), 12–13, 17; and Tannehill, *Luke*, 98. In the psalms that praise Yahweh as king, a repeated theme is that when Yahweh reigns the result will be proper justice and the removal of all corruption and oppression. See Wright, *Simply Jesus*, 43–53.

31. Birch, *Let Justice Roll Down*, 121–22.

"Behold the Man": The Coming of the New Creation[32]

In addition to the advent of the kingdom of God, Jesus' coming is the advent of the new creation as well. The Bible begins by detailing God's handiwork in creating the world. Unfortunately, the original creation becomes corrupted, though it is not abandoned. The Old Testament recounts God's continued work to redeem and restore fallen creation. But when we turn to the pages of the New Testament, it is clear that this work of restoration has not yet been fully realized. Jesus thus comes along as the foundation stone of the new creation.[33]

Whereas Paul explicitly references the idea of new creation in 2 Corinthians 5:17 and Galatians 6:15—along with indirect indicators elsewhere (Rom. 8:18–22)—this theme is already present in an implicit, though significant, way in the Gospel of John. In this Gospel, the coming of Jesus is simultaneously the coming of creation's renewal. Life has its origins, as well as its consummation, in God. This theme of creation's renewal appears at the beginning and the end of the Gospel, in which John evokes multiple allusions to Genesis 1–2 to connect the story of Jesus to the story of the creation of the world. In and through Jesus there is another beginning, and thus God is creating once again. Moreover, Jesus is the pinnacle of this new creation, and as *the* image of God (John 1:14, 18; 14:9–11) he renews the creation of humanity.[34]

---

32. The word for "man" in John 19:5 is *anthrōpos*, which usually means "human" in the general sense and not male in the specific sense. However, because John is ultimately comparing the first Adam and second Adam, the use of "man" here helps this parallel stand out more clearly.

33. Above we noted that healings and exorcisms were signs of the inbreaking of the kingdom. But they are also signs of the beginning of the new creation. Healings were the beginning reversal of the curse of the old, fallen world; miracles were an inbreaking of the new creation to come. Moreover, Jesus' ministry of casting out demons demonstrated the beginning of his decisive defeat of Satan—the one who had brought creation into captivity. See Beale, "New Testament and New Creation," 162, 165, 173. For an in-depth study of creation motifs throughout the New Testament, see Paul Sevier Minear, *Christians and the New Creation: Genesis Motifs in the New Testament* (Louisville: Westminster John Knox, 1994).

34. There are other themes throughout the Gospel that echo the creation themes of Genesis. For example, the prominent motif of life utilized throughout the Gospel points toward creation's eschatological renewal. The word "life" is repeated forty-seven times. The language of new birth in John 3:3–8, in essence, expresses the gift of new life. Three of Jesus' "I am" statements explicitly note the connection between Jesus and life: "I am the bread of life" (6:35, 48, 51), "I am the resurrection and the life" (11:25), and "I am the way, the truth, and the life" (14:6). The placement of the theme of life at the end of the Gospel in its climactic purpose statement (20:30–31) strongly supports viewing this theme as central for the Gospel of John. See Jeannine K. Brown, "Creation's Renewal in the Gospel of John," *Catholic Biblical Quarterly* 72, no. 2 (2010): 277–78; Carlos Raúl Sosa Siliezar, *Creation Imagery in the Gospel of John* (New York: Bloomsbury T&T Clark, 2015); and Clinton W. Klink III,

John's prologue (John 1:1–18) immediately takes the reader back to the first chapter of Genesis, repeating the opening words from Genesis 1: "In the beginning." This clear connection evokes the story of creation as the starting place for John's Gospel about Jesus. The dominant themes of life and light that are found in Genesis 1 also figure strongly in John's prologue, and John's use of "word" (*logos*) calls to mind God's creative activity in Genesis of calling forth creation by means of speech. For John to describe all things as coming into existence through Jesus—the Word—is no coincidence. It signals that creation is the overarching context within which John will tell his story of Jesus and that creation will provide a means by which to understand Jesus' life and mission. "By evoking this context, John signals that the Jesus story will illuminate the ongoing story of God's creation and provide its culmination."[35]

Throughout the Gospel of John the story of Jesus echoes the story of creation in other ways, but it is in the passion and resurrection that we once again find strong allusions to Genesis 1–2. At this juncture of the narrative, John places the events that transpire within the imagery of Eden. The Gospel of John is the only Gospel to set all the climactic moments of the end of Jesus' life in a garden. The author begins the passion story in a garden (John 18:1, 26) and describes the location of both the crucifixion and tomb as gardens (19:41). After the resurrection, Mary assumes Jesus to be the gardener, which in one sense is wrong—it is Jesus—but in another sense is right: Jesus has returned as the divine gardener in the garden of his creation (John 20:15; cf. Gen. 3:8–10). These subtle impressions invite comparison with the first garden, Eden.[36]

Moreover, the Gospel of John compares the first Adam and second Adam. This theme permeates the passion and resurrection accounts in John, coming to the fore in Pilate's proclamation of Jesus: "Behold the man!" (John 19:5). The narrative uses an unwitting Pilate to speak a theological truth to emphasize Jesus' enfleshment. In the Septuagint—the Greek translation of Old Testament Scripture—we find a similar phrase in Genesis 3:22 in God beholding Adam, announcing the curses and banishment

---

John, Zondervan Exegetical Commentary on the New Testament (Grand Rapids: Zondervan, 2016), 160–62.

35. Brown, "Creation's Renewal in the Gospel of John," 277. Mary L. Coloe notes how the Johannine prologue mirrors the structure of Gen. 1. See Coloe, "Theological Reflections on Creation in the Gospel of John," *Pacifica* 24 (February 2011): 2–4.

36. Brown, "Creation's Renewal in the Gospel of John," 279–81; and Klink III, *John*, 845. Coloe provides further details that confirm this connection between the passion narrative and creation. See Coloe, "Creation in the Gospel of John," 4–6, 8.

from the garden. In Genesis the title declares his alienation from God and his existence in a state of death. But in the Gospel of John a reversal of death has begun with the coming of Jesus—a new Adam—who brings life (John 1:4; 14:6) and enters into the broken conditions of the world and humanity in order to recreate them. To behold the man in the Gospel of John is to identify Jesus as the new Adam.[37]

Furthermore, when the resurrected Jesus appears to the disciples, he comes bringing peace and the gift of the Spirit. Three times Jesus offers peace to them (John 20:19, 21, 26). Though this typical Jewish salutation can function as a mere greeting, Jesus' use certainly entails a deeper meaning that is connected to the Old Testament's idea of *shalom*—the wholeness or flourishing of the world. Christ thus proclaims that the eschatological peace of God is now present through him, and thus the brokenness of creation is being mended through him.[38] And so, Jesus offers the breath of life to the disciples and says, "Receive the Holy Spirit" (John 20:22). Here we have another clear allusion to the creation narratives, as John uses the same rare verb used by the Septuagint in Genesis 2:7 to communicate the breath of life into Adam (cf. Ezek. 37:9). John wants the reader to understand this act of Jesus as one of creation, inaugurating a new humanity by breathing the Spirit into his followers. This breath of life (Spirit) is a fundamental reality of the new creation (more on this in the following chapter).[39]

Jesus as the Image of God, Humanity as the Image of Jesus

If the story of the New Testament is one of the coming kingdom of God and new creation, how does that inform our praxis? How do these new contours of the narrative inform our vocation to be the image of God and engage in redemptive service? To answer these questions, we must first look at some other New Testament texts before returning to the story of Jesus. Beyond the Gospel accounts, the New Testament notion of the

37. Craig S. Keener, *The Gospel of John: A Commentary*, vol. 2 (Peabody, MA: Hendrickson, 2003), 1123; Klink, *John*, 777–79; and Brown, "Creation's Renewal in the Gospel of John," 281–82. For other places in which the New Testament develops an Adam Christology, see James D. G. Dunn, *Christology in the Making: A New Testament Inquiry into the Origins of the Doctrine of the Incarnation*, 2nd ed. (Grand Rapids: Eerdmans, 1989), 98–128.

38. Coloe, "Creation in the Gospel of John," 8–10.

39. Brown, "Creation's Renewal in the Gospel of John," 282–83; Marc Cortez, *Resourcing Theological Anthropology: A Constructive Account of Humanity in the Light of Christ* (Grand Rapids: Zondervan, 2017), 47–48; and Klink, *John*, 861–65.

image of God focuses on one particular human, Jesus Christ, setting forth a christocentric understanding that draws from the Old Testament idea but also transforms it.[40]

Hebrews 2:6–9 takes the universal anthropology found in Psalm 8 (which is itself a commentary on Gen. 1:28–30) and interprets it christologically. Whereas the psalmist declares that God has crowned humanity with "glory and honor" and put everything "under their feet," the author of Hebrews declares that Jesus is the one crowned with glory and honor and everything is now subject to him. Jesus is presented as having dominion over creation—God's intention for humanity from the beginning—and as being the ruler of the cosmos. Earlier in Hebrews 1:3 Jesus is said to be the radiance of God's glory and the exact representation (image) of God's being. And in 2 Corinthians 4:4–6 and Colossians 1:15–20 Jesus is explicitly identified as the image of God.[41]

If, according to the New Testament, Jesus is the image of God, what does that mean for the rest of humanity? Are we to abandon this identity and vocation? The short answer is no. The New Testament does not intend to discard the rest of humanity in favor of Jesus as the sole image. But it does posit that Jesus Christ is the fulfillment of what God had intended from the beginning and, accordingly, is *the* image of God. Correspondingly, Jesus is the image or standard by which we are to orient ourselves and into which we are transformed.[42]

John Kilner offers a helpful conceptual distinction between Jesus as the image of God and humans as the image of God. Kilner notes that while the identity of the image of God applies to both parties, there is a clear difference. For both Jesus and humanity, being identified as God's image entails a special *connection* to God and a *reflection* of God, but they do so in different ways. Jesus shares a complete and exact identity with God such that the two are essentially one—anyone who has seen Jesus has seen the Father (John 14:9)—and thus Christ constitutes a complete picture of what God intends for people in God's image. Humans, however, are not yet fully

40. See E. J. Tinsley, *The Imitation of God in Christ* (Philadelphia: Westminster, 1960), 67–180.

41. See Stanley J. Grenz, "Jesus as the *Imago Dei*: Image-of-God Christology and the Non-Linear Linearity of Theology," *Journal of the Evangelical Theological Society* 47, no. 4 (December 2004): 618–20; and Craig L. Blomberg, "'True Righteousness and Holiness': The Image of God in the New Testament," in *The Image of God in an Image Driven Age: Explorations in Theological Anthropology*, ed. Beth Felker Jones and Jeffrey W. Barbeau (Downers Grove, IL: IVP Academic, 2016), 74–85.

42. Grenz, "Jesus as the *Imago Dei*," 621–24.

the image of God because they are not yet fully transformed. Colossians 1:15 states that Christ is the image of God, but in 3:10 notes that humans at large are still in the process of putting on their new self and still need renewal according to God's image in Christ. Ephesians 4:20–24 echoes this idea, describing the process of putting off one's old self in exchange for the new self that is created to be like God. In 2 Corinthians 4:4 Christ is declared to be the image of God, but in 3:18 people are described as being transformed into the divine image. The image of God in Christ is the standard by which we need to conform, but we are not yet fully there. We are recreated in the image of the Image, but the transformation to the divine image is gradual and progressive, reaching its climax at the eschatological resurrection (Rom. 8:29–30). In light of this, Kilner suggests describing humanity as a "likeness-image" that is *similar* to but not an exact representation of the original, whereas Jesus is an "imprint-image" that is *identical* to—an exact representation of—the original.[43]

If Jesus is God's image—the imprint-image—then conforming to Jesus is equivalent to conforming to God's image. With this christological transformation of the Old Testament's notion of the image of God, we have a corresponding christological transformation of the understanding of the human vocation, not abandoning the thrust of the plot toward redemptive service but propelling it forward in new—but not altogether different—ways.

Our calling to redemptive service is now to be oriented toward and participate in Jesus' own redemptive service. While his ultimate work of redemptive service was literally to go to the cross—a work that we should not understand to be part of our calling as likeness-images—the rest of his life provides direction for how we are to live out our own vocations as likeness-images.[44] We mentioned the notion of WWYD (What Would Yahweh Do?) in chapter 2, and now as the story develops in the New Testament it becomes WWJD (What Would Jesus Do?). The Old Testament

43. John F. Kilner, *Dignity and Destiny: Humanity in the Image of God* (Grand Rapids: Eerdmans, 2015), 59–60.

44. While Jesus is the image into which we are being transformed, he is also the last Adam and the true Israel. And therefore, his literal death is particular to this aspect of his mission. But he dies and rises again as both the new Israel and the new creation. "The church, as Christ's risen body, now carries on the commission of the true Adam and Israel to subdue the earth for God as his vicegerent." Beale, "New Testament and New Creation," 164. However, though we are not called to reenact Jesus' literal death, the New Testament does use the language of "taking up one's cross" to communicate the idea of self-sacrifice and self-denial in our pursuit of following Christ (Matt. 10:38; 16:24; Mark 8:34; 10:21; Luke 9:23; 14:27).

showed humanity's mission to imitate Yahweh's redemptive action, and now the New Testament shows humanity's mission to imitate Jesus Christ: as Jesus is, so should Jesus' people be; as Jesus acts, so should Jesus' people act.[45]

And what did Jesus do? He went about proclaiming and performing the kingdom of God and offering hope and change toward a new creation. He was doing this not just as a divine person but also as fully human. When reading the Gospels, we are not just observing a life and mission that belongs to God alone. It is also an invitation for humanity to participate in this calling. Being transformed into Jesus' image is not just a spiritual transformation but a holistic transformation, renewing humans and our call to service in this world. The kingdom of God clarifies our vocation—defining and delineating our work—and the gift of new creation empowers us toward it. We are to live out this transformed existence in the present.

Christ brings the good news of forgiveness of sins and personal salvation, but he also brings the good news of the kingdom of God and new creation. Jesus interprets his life and mission in terms of the messianic expectations of Isaiah: in Christ's person and work, the long-expected reign of God is decisively breaking in, and along with it comes a renewal of the whole earth. The Old Testament expectations of full-orbed shalom are being fulfilled in Jesus. He displays shalom by healing the blemishes that are incompatible with shalom. Jesus repeatedly concerns himself with the vulnerable, poor, and oppressed, along with all those cast out and living on the margins of society. Jesus' messianic activity is the work of liberation, of healing and making whole everything that was disordered. In the New Testament, to be the body of Christ is to continue Christ's work of ushering in the kingdom of God and bringing to fruition God's shalom. We are to be icons of Christ, imaging his justice in our justice.

Conclusion

Identity drives mission. Bearing the image of Christ as the body of Christ harmonizes our vocation with Christ's vocation to further the kingdom of God in this world until that kingdom comes on earth as it is in heaven (Matt. 6:10). Jesus' life was marked by a mission for others. He visited

45. For an extensive look at how Christology can inform ethics, see Richard A. Burridge, *Imitating Jesus: An Inclusive Approach to New Testament Ethics* (Grand Rapids: Eerdmans, 2007); and Gushee and Stassen, *Kingdom Ethics*.

small villages proclaiming that the kingdom of God was at hand, telling parables about this kingdom that God desires, and enacting that kingdom through his healings and deliverances. To the extent that people are faithful as the body of Christ (identity), they will be faithful as people engaged in redemptive service (mission). Redemptive service is not optional or marginal but required and central to Christians' identity and mission as the body of Christ.

We noted above that while Jesus begins the work of the kingdom of God and new creation, neither is fully realized during his ministry. God once again partners with humanity. It is all too easy to assume that "if Jesus really was king of the world, he would, as it were, do the whole thing by himself. But that was never his way—because it was never God's way. It wasn't how creation itself was supposed to work. And Jesus' kingdom project is nothing if not the rescue and renewal of God's creation project."[46]

And what does Jesus do along the way? He calls others to participate in this process and then leaves them a parting gift (the Spirit) to enable them to do it. Jesus was not a lone ranger. He proclaimed and performed the kingdom of God (Mark 1:15), but he also gathered a community of followers and commissioned them to do the same (Mark 1:17). Jesus' followers are entrusted to continue the task he started and further the kingdom of new creation here on earth. The same words Jesus spoke then, Jesus proclaims to us today: "Follow me."

DISCUSSION QUESTIONS

1. What surprised you in this chapter about the kingdom of God?
2. What are the consequences of understanding the categories from Luke 4 (poor, captive, blind, and oppressed) solely in spiritual terms? What are the consequences of understanding them solely in material terms?
3. How does the theme of creation employed by the Gospel of John with respect to Jesus' life and mission enrich your understanding of Jesus?
4. Sometimes the discontinuity between the Old Testament and the New Testament is emphasized without acknowledging the continuity. What

46. Wright, *Simply Jesus*, 213.

surprises you about the similar concern for the vulnerable, poor, and oppressed found in the Gospels that we also see in the Old Testament?

5. With respect to redemptive service, what is one thing you could do to grow in your likeness-image of Jesus?

6. Returning to the parable of the good Samaritan and the intersection of seeing and doing, how do the life and mission of Jesus inform the way we see others? How do they inform the way we act toward others?

FOR FURTHER READING

Brown, Jeannine K. "Creation's Renewal in the Gospel of John." *Catholic Biblical Quarterly* 72, no. 2 (2010): 275–90.

Coloe, Mary L. "Theological Reflections on Creation in the Gospel of John." *Pacifica* 24 (February 2011): 1–12.

Perrin, Nicholas. *The Kingdom of God: A Biblical Theology*. Grand Rapids: Zondervan, 2019.

Wright, N. T. *How God Became King: The Forgotten Story of the Gospels*. New York: HarperOne, 2012.

———. *Simply Jesus: A New Vision of Who He Was, What He Did, and Why He Matters*. New York: HarperOne, 2011.

5

A Fresh Wind

The Outpouring of the Spirit and Its Effects

The ending of the Gospels is framed as a new beginning. Jesus' resurrection is not the end of the story. Jesus' mission is passed along to us to live out in this world. Just as God created humans in the garden to be his image bearers and to reflect his sovereign rule in the world, God once again commits to that trust after Christ's ascension, intending to spread his reign throughout the world through human beings. Humans are the vital element in God's kingdom project. We were cocreators in creation, and now God is calling us to be cocreators in new creation.

What does the kingdom community of new creation look like? The rest of the New Testament gives us a glimpse, especially the Acts of the Apostles. As its name suggests, the book of Acts recounts what Jesus' followers did immediately after his ascension. This story was written intentionally as the second part of Jesus' story. Whereas the Gospel of Luke is concerned with all that Jesus did and taught (Acts 1:1), Acts is focused on what his followers did and taught as they followed Jesus' Way.[1]

Continuing beyond the Gospels, a new layer is added to our identity and mission. In the book of Acts, the outpouring of the Spirit at Pentecost

---

1. "The Way" is used in Acts to denote the movement initiated by Jesus (Acts 9:2; 19:9, 23; 22:4; 24:14, 22). See J. Bradley Chance, *Acts*, Smyth & Helwys Bible Commentary (Macon, GA: Smyth & Helwys, 2007), 146.

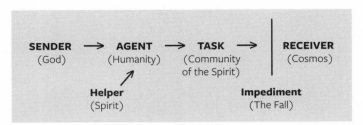

Figure 5.1 Plot analysis of the biblical narrative: New Testament

creates a community of the Spirit (see fig. 5.1). With this gift of the Spirit, the church can heed Jesus' call to follow him and continue the work of the kingdom of new creation that he began.[2] The book of Acts demonstrates the pneumatological underpinnings of this reality.

In this chapter we attend to the patterns of the Spirit in the Old Testament to see how they illuminate the work of the Spirit in the New Testament, especially in the life of Jesus and the early Christian community. Then we highlight how the presence of the Spirit among the early Christian community transformed their interactions with one another. Finally, we offer some reflective thoughts to conclude part 1 of this book.

Pentecost: The Advent of the Community of the Spirit

Old Testament Patterns of the Spirit

While it is not until the New Testament that we find a full personalization of the Spirit and the revealing of a trinitarian God, the Spirit of God in the life and history of Israel foreshadows the Spirit's presence and activity in the New Testament. We offer here a brief overview of two patterns of the Spirit found in the Old Testament that will help us comprehend more fully the work of the Spirit in the New Testament. First, the Spirit in the Old Testament authenticates and empowers those chosen by God to leadership. This happens with Joseph (Gen. 41:38–40); Moses and the seventy elders (Num. 11:16–17, 25); Joshua (Num. 27:18–23); multiple judges of Israel (Judg. 3:7–11; 6:33–34; 11:29; 13:24–25; 14:5–6, 19; 15:12–15); Saul (1 Sam. 10:6, 10–11; 11:6); and David (1 Sam. 16:13; 2 Sam. 23:2).

---

2. The work of the Spirit in the Old Testament is also related to creation and life. See Robert L. Hubbard Jr., "The Spirit and Creation," in *Presence, Power and Promise: The Role of the Spirit of God in the Old Testament*, ed. David G. Firth and Paul D. Wegner (Downers Grove, IL: InterVarsity, 2011), 71–91; and Christopher J. H. Wright, *Knowing the Holy Spirit through the Old Testament* (Downers Grove, IL: InterVarsity, 2006), 13–34.

The Spirit is present in these leaders' lives to validate and equip them. Moreover, in the prophetic anticipation of a future leader (recall the discussion from chap. 3 on the future, ideal king), the Spirit is given to that leader to authenticate and empower him for his reign (Isa. 42:1; 61:1). This king—whom the New Testament identifies as the Messiah—will receive the fullest endowment of the Spirit recorded in Scripture (Isa. 11:2) and will be a unique man of the Spirit.[3]

Second, the Spirit is transferred from person to person in association with the transfer of leadership. This occurs with Moses to the seventy elders (Num. 11:10–30); Moses to Joshua (Num. 27:18; Deut. 34:9); Elijah to Elisha (2 Kings 2:9, 15); and Saul to David (1 Sam. 10:10; 16:13–14). In all of these instances, the transfer of leadership from one person to the next entails a transfer of the Spirit for the purposes of authenticating and empowering the successor. In addition to this transferring, there is a prophetic anticipation for a future time when the Spirit will be poured out on the community at large. The Spirit who rests on the Messiah will be shared with the restored people of God (Isa. 44:3; Joel 2:28–29), and the future outpouring will create a community of the Spirit (Isa. 59:21; Ezek. 36:26–27; 37:5–6, 14).[4]

New Testament Demonstrations of the Spirit

The New Testament, especially the Gospel of Luke and the Acts of the Apostles, reflects both of these themes from the Old Testament. First, as prophesied, Jesus is the unique bearer of the Spirit, which authenticates his messiahship and empowers his ministry. The Gospel accounts attest that from the very beginning of Jesus' life, the Spirit's presence was upon him and working through him. Luke records that Jesus' conception is made possible by the presence and power of the Spirit: "The angel answered, 'The Holy Spirit will come on you, and the power of the Most High will overshadow you. So the holy one to be born will be called the Son of God'" (Luke 1:35). Reminiscent of the Spirit hovering over the waters in creation (Gen. 1:2), the Spirit now hovers over Mary to bring about a new creation through the conception of Jesus. Moreover, the description

3. David G. Firth, "The Spirit and Leadership: Testimony, Empowerment and Purpose," in Firth and Wegner, *Presence, Power and Promise*, 259–80; Wonsuk Ma, "Isaiah," in *A Biblical Theology of the Holy Spirit*, ed. Trevor J. Burke and Keith Warrington (Eugene, OR: Cascade Books, 2014), 34–45; and Wright, *Knowing the Holy Spirit through the Old Testament*, 35–62.

4. Firth, "Spirit and Leadership," 259–80; and Roger Stronstad, *The Charismatic Theology of St. Luke* (Peabody, MA: Hendrickson, 1984), 13–27.

of the Spirit as a power from on high alludes to the words of Isaiah, who
said that when the Spirit was poured out from on high, the renewal of
Israel would take place (Isa. 32:15).[5] John the Baptist speaks of Jesus as
one who will baptize with the Spirit (Luke 3:16). As Jesus is baptized by
John, the Spirit descends on Jesus, and he becomes the unique bearer of
the Spirit (Luke 3:22). Full of the Spirit, Jesus is led into the desert, where
he successfully resists temptations and emerges in the power of the Spirit
(Luke 4:1, 14). Finally, when preaching in the synagogue in Nazareth (Luke
4:16–21), Jesus offers his understanding of the Spirit's descent upon him
in his baptism: the Spirit's presence and power in his life is programmatic
for his entire ministry (Acts 10:38).[6] This pneumatic gifting makes it possible for Jesus to complete his messianic vocation and to proclaim and
perform the kingdom of God.

Second, the presence of the Spirit does not end with the story of Jesus
but continues with his followers, as Jesus is no longer just the Spirit bearer
but also the Spirit baptizer who authenticates and empowers the community of faith through his transfer of leadership. The Gospel of Luke
concludes with Jesus commanding his disciples to remain in Jerusalem
to await power from on high. The beginning of Acts continues where the
Gospel leaves off and reiterates Jesus' command to wait in Jerusalem, this
time specifying that the power is the gift of the Holy Spirit. The day of
Pentecost brings an outpouring of the Spirit onto the community of the
disciples that empowers the church to continue Jesus' work and transfers
the mantle of leadership from Christ to the early church to continue in
his place.

Commenting on this, Roger Stronstad says,

> The Pentecostal narrative is the story of the transfer of the charismatic Spirit
> from Jesus to the disciples. In other words, having become the exclusive bearer
> of the Holy Spirit at His baptism, Jesus becomes the giver of the Spirit at
> Pentecost. . . . By this transfer of the Spirit, the disciples become the heirs and
> successors to the earthly charismatic ministry of Jesus; that is, because Jesus
> has poured out the charismatic Spirit upon them the disciples will continue
> to do and teach those things which Jesus began to do and teach (Acts 1:1).[7]

5. Max Turner, *Power from on High: The Spirit in Israel's Restoration and Witness in Luke-
Acts* (Sheffield, UK: Sheffield Academic, 1996), 159.
6. Stronstad, *Charismatic Theology of St. Luke*, 45.
7. From Luke's perspective, there is an *essential* relationship between the descent of the
Spirit on Jesus and the outpouring of the Spirit on the community at Pentecost. Stronstad,
Charismatic Theology of St. Luke, 49.

Whereas in the Gospel of Luke Jesus is empowered by the Spirit to *inaugurate* the kingdom of new creation, in the Acts of the Apostles this kingdom of new creation *continues* to unfold in the early church by means of the outpouring of the Spirit on all flesh.[8] In the book of Acts, Luke's vision of the power of the Spirit in the church extends in a more comprehensive and egalitarian way to the whole people of God by means of Pentecost. As Peter explains, the gift of the Spirit is not just for one or two individuals but for the whole community, marking them as a community of the Spirit (Acts 2:17–18, 39). Implied in this gift of the Spirit for *all* is the empowering of *all* to continue Jesus' mission and ministry of the kingdom, with the Spirit first descending on Jesus to fulfill the prophetic vision and promise of justice proclaimed in the Old Testament (Luke 4:16–21; 16:16).[9] The community of the Spirit inherits Jesus' mission and ministry to proclaim and perform this same kingdom of God, extending God's renewal and reign in the world.[10] But humans cannot be Jesus' likeness-image without receiving the Spirit.

The Community of the Spirit: "Witnesses" to the Kingdom of New Creation

At the end of the Gospel of Luke and the beginning of the book of Acts, among Jesus' parting words to his disciples is that they will be his "witnesses"

8. Richard B. Hays, *The Moral Vision of the New Testament: A Contemporary Introduction to New Testament Ethics* (New York: HarperOne, 1996), 116. Murray W. Dempster refers to this as the "Pentecost/kingdom sequential connection" (Dempster, "Evangelism, Social Concern, and the Kingdom of God," in *Called and Empowered: Global Mission in Pentecostal Perspective*, ed. Murray W. Dempster, Byron D. Klaus, and Douglas Petersen [Peabody, MA: Hendrickson, 1991], 23). Charles H. Talbert convincingly argues for a significant correspondence between the content and sequence of events and persons found in Luke and Acts, which constitute a primary architectonic pattern that helps us properly understand the Lucan writings. He says, "As far as we know, only Luke-Acts in early Christianity reflects the conviction that both the story of Jesus and the story of the apostolic church are incomplete without the other as complement." Talbert, *Literary Patterns, Theological Themes and the Genre of Luke-Acts* (Missoula, MT: Scholars Press, 1974), 15.

9. The Spirit of prophecy that rests on Moses is shared with seventy elders, and Moses expresses the wish that the Spirit be given to all Israel (Num. 11:26–30), which Joel's promise fulfills. Turner, *Power from on High*, 288.

10. The idea of the kingdom of God has not been abandoned as the story develops beyond Jesus. In fact it is mentioned in the concluding statement of the book of Acts summarizing Paul's work in Rome, where it says he was there for two years preaching the kingdom of God and teaching about Jesus (Acts 28:30–31). Hays, *Moral Vision of the New Testament*, 121; and Dempster, "Evangelism, Social Concern, and the Kingdom of God," 24–39. Murray W. Dempster describes this link between the Old Testament moral tradition, Jesus' kingdom ethic, and the Pentecostal community of the Spirit as a hermeneutical line of continuity. See Dempster, "Pentecostal Social Concern and the Biblical Mandate of Social Justice," *Pneuma* 9, no. 2 (Fall 1987): 148.

(*martyres*) (Luke 24:48; Acts 1:8). While contemporary associations with "witness" or "witnessing" are usually limited to proclamation of the gospel, this is too narrow an understanding of what Jesus means. To bear authentic witness to the kingdom can only be done through both words and actions—not unlike Jesus' own proclamation and performance of the kingdom. A *spoken witness* and a *social witness* are necessary in order for God's reign in Jesus to be accurately and authentically made present. A community of the Spirit, therefore, has to witness through its own life as a community of visibly redeemed creation, expressing the kingdom ideals of God's love for all and desiring justice to rule throughout creation.[11]

A Community of Justice and Righteousness

We noted above that Luke's description of the coming of the Spirit in Luke-Acts is an allusion to Isaiah 32:15 (Luke 1:35; 24:49; Acts 1:8). But what follows in Isaiah 32:16 also has import for how we understand the outpouring of the Spirit in the New Testament, especially at Pentecost. Isaiah 32:15–16 says,

> until a spirit from on high is poured out on us,
>   and the wilderness becomes a fruitful field,
>   and the fruitful field is deemed a forest.
> Then justice will dwell in the wilderness
>   and righteousness abide in the fruitful field.

Verse 15 metaphorically describes Israel's return from exile: the wilderness will become a fruitful field. Verse 16 then describes this glorious future, specifying that justice and righteousness will be present. Isaiah proclaims that the outpouring of the Spirit will be the means by which justice and righteousness are made manifest. This is true in Isaiah, and it is the same in Luke-Acts. The presence of the Spirit, both in Jesus and in the early Christian community, generates renewal. We observed elements of this in the previous chapter when looking at Jesus (Luke 4), and now we examine how this takes shape in the Christian community in Acts. While the word "justice" is not explicitly used in Acts, the type of community prophesied in Isaiah is fulfilled in Acts.

---

11. Murray Dempster divides church ministry into three aspects: kerygmatic, koinoniac, and diakonic. For him this encompasses the proclamation of the word (kerygmatic), Christian fellowship (koinoniac), and outward service (diakonic). See Dempster, "Evangelism, Social Concern, and the Kingdom of God," 22–39.

In the first part of Acts, when the narrative is focused on the events in Jerusalem, there are two summary accounts of note. Acts 2:42–47, which immediately follows Pentecost, says,

> They devoted themselves to the apostles' teaching and fellowship, to the breaking of bread and the prayers. Awe came upon everyone because many wonders and signs were being done through the apostles. All who believed were together and had all things in common; they would sell their possessions and goods and distribute the proceeds to all, as any had need. Day by day, as they spent much time together in the temple, they broke bread at home and ate their food with glad and generous hearts, praising God and having the goodwill of all the people. And day by day the Lord added to their number those who were being saved.

Acts 4:32–35, which immediately follows after a second Pentecost, says,

> Now the whole group of those who believed were of one heart and soul, and no one claimed private ownership of any possessions, but everything they owned was held in common. With great power the apostles gave their testimony to the resurrection of the Lord Jesus, and great grace was upon them all. There was not a needy person among them, for as many as owned lands or houses sold them and brought the proceeds of what was sold. They laid it at the apostles' feet, and it was distributed to each as any had need.

Both passages directly connect the outpouring of the Spirit with the subsequent paradisal community.[12] Though none of these activities are explicitly attributed to the Spirit, the communal life depicted here corresponds with the kingdom hopes that are conveyed in the Gospel of Luke and also corresponds with the aims of Jesus' ministry for Israel's transformation. If it is not the outpouring of the Spirit that has affected these things, what else could account for it? The narrative leads the reader to assume that this communal life results from what immediately preceded it: the reception

---

12. William J. Larkin Jr. notes that the "structure Luke points to is not a coercive communism that dispenses with private property through once-for-all expropriation to a common fund. Luke . . . sees all churches as living out not only their responsibility for the poor (Acts 20:5) but also their interdependence through caring for one another. . . . Seen in this light, what Luke calls for is fully normative. With a mindset of unity we will view our economic resources as available to meet others' needs. We will voluntarily, periodically supply our local assembly's common fund for the poor." Larkin, *Acts* (Downers Grove, IL: InterVarsity, 1995), 83. See also Craig L. Blomberg, *Neither Poverty nor Riches: A Biblical Theology of Possessions* (Downers Grove, IL: InterVarsity, 1999), 160–67.

of the Spirit.[13] These two summary passages indicate the tangible effect and impact of the Spirit in the life of the believers—both as individuals and as a community. "In this community there are no poor left in need, nor hungry to mourn, nor rich who oppress, and they are freed from the fear of their enemies to serve God."[14]

The outpouring of the Spirit empowers them not only to spread the gospel but to live the gospel too. God's people are re-formed as a renewed community and social order. Scholars have noted the parallels between Jesus' ascent to heaven and the giving of the Spirit at Pentecost (Acts 1–2) and Moses' ascent to God on Mount Sinai and his reception of the law that he gives to the Israelites (Exod. 19). While the similarities are not necessarily equivalent, the law provided instruction on what the community should do (mission) because of who the community was (identity). In the book of Acts, the gifting of the Spirit is for the renewing of the community and its life, which becomes most visible after Pentecost. Thousands of new believers are added to the original nucleus, and the community in Jerusalem takes on a distinctive form of life (Acts 2:42–47; 4:32–35). Pentecost is not a giving of a law per se, but it is a giving of the Spirit to help live out the "law" of Jesus and the kingdom of new creation that God is bringing forth (mission).[15] The most obvious difference between Pentecost and the Mount Sinai event is that the community of the Spirit is not limited to Israel alone but intended for all who would repent and be baptized (identity).

Acts 4:34 further shows that the outpouring of the Spirit informs the life of the community, as the wording in Greek is identical to Deuteronomy 15:4 in the Septuagint, only modifying the verb from the future tense ("will . . . be no one in need") to the past tense ("was not a needy person among them"). This strongly suggests that Luke understood the early Christian community in Acts as a manifestation of the radical communal vision of Deuteronomy, in which the people's devotion to Yahweh is evidenced by their treatment of one another (Deut. 15:4–5, 7–8). In Deuteronomy, caring for the lowliest and neediest person of the community served as a barometer for the community's obedience to their covenant relationship

---

13. David W. Pao, *Acts and the Isaianic New Exodus* (Grand Rapids: Baker Academic, 2000), 131–35; and Turner, *Power from on High*, 412–15.

14. Turner, *Power from on High*, 413.

15. Matthias Wenk, *Community-Forming Power: The Socio-Ethical Role of the Spirit in Luke-Acts* (New York: T&T Clark, 2000), 246–51, 258; Turner, *Power from on High*, 285–89; and Hays, *Moral Vision of the New Testament*, 122–23.

with God; the same is true in Acts.[16] "In the church's common life of economic sharing, we see the fruition—or at least first fruits—of the mission that Jesus announced in Luke 4:16–21: to bring a restored Israel in which good news is proclaimed and enacted for the poor and oppressed."[17]

Recall from chapter 4 that John the Baptist prepared the way for Jesus and initiated the kingdom of God with his ministry of repentance and forgiveness through water baptism. For John, true repentance and forgiveness is evidenced by proper fruit, most notably fruit borne out in relationships with one's neighbors. Jesus, too, continued to spread the kingdom of God, exemplifying and echoing John's demand for proper fruit. At the end of the Gospel of Luke and the beginning of the book of Acts, the theme of repentance and forgiveness is still at the center of the story (because the kingdom of God is still at the center of the story!). Jesus tells his disciples to wait in Jerusalem until the Spirit comes upon them, telling them that repentance and forgiveness of sins is to be proclaimed in his name to all nations, beginning in Jerusalem, then Judea and Samaria, and finally to the ends of the earth (Luke 24:46–49; Acts 1:7–8).[18] If John the Baptist's message of repentance and forgiveness requires proper fruit, and if Jesus' mission of repentance and forgiveness bears proper fruit, it stands to reason that the early church's ministry of repentance and forgiveness was also accompanied by proper fruit. And predictably, the communal life that emerges from the outpouring of the Spirit is evidence of the proper fruit of repentance and forgiveness. Their communal life is a manifestation of the fruitful field of justice and righteousness from Isaiah 32.

Excursus: "The Poor You Will Always Have with You": Deuteronomy 15 in the Gospels

Acts is not the only book of the New Testament that references Deuteronomy 15. Earlier in the Gospels, Jesus' anointing at Bethany contains an allusion to Deuteronomy 15:11. The disciples chide Mary for wasting expensive perfume on Jesus' feet and suggest that it should have been

16. Peter T. Vogt, "Social Justice and the Vision of Deuteronomy," *Journal of the Evangelical Theological Society* 51, no. 1 (March 2008): 39, 41–42. Vogt notes the eschatological nature of the Deuteronomy passage as it envisions a society as it ought to be one day.

17. Hays, *Moral Vision of the New Testament*, 124.

18. The narrative of the book of Acts mimics this movement, focusing on events in Jerusalem (Acts 2:1–8:4), then turning toward Judea and Samaria (8:5–40), and finally demonstrating its spread to the ends of the earth (9:1–28:31).

sold to provide for the poor (Matt. 26:6–13; Mark 14:3–9; John 12:1–8). In response, Jesus says that they will always have the poor, but they will not always have him.

In discussions concerning benevolence, someone inevitably raises the issue of this statement from Jesus: "If Jesus said we will always have the poor with us, what is the point?" At best, this sentiment expresses someone's genuine puzzlement over the words of Jesus. At worst, this remark serves as a proof text to excuse Christians from redemptive service. So, how are we to understand this verse? What was Jesus trying to communicate?

Danger is never far when we cherry-pick a verse or two of Scripture and use it as evidence to prove our views. Pulling Jesus' statement out of its context—both in the Gospels and in the whole of Scripture—is a good example of how we can misconstrue Scripture when we are not attentive to the story within which it is situated.

In unpacking Jesus' words, we will limit our discussion to the Matthean passage, though the other Gospels support this interpretation as well. Matthew 26:11 includes some important exegetical points that help us properly understand Jesus' words. First, this verse clearly alludes to Deuteronomy 15:11, which is part of the Deuteronomic law codes. This part of the law code is concerned with the sabbatical year in which all debt would be canceled every seven years. God forbids strategically refusing to lend to a neighbor when the seven-year cycle is almost complete. Deuteronomy 15:10–11 says,

> Give liberally and be ungrudging when you do so, for on this account the LORD your God will bless you in all your work and in all that you undertake. Since there will never cease to be some in need on the earth, I therefore command you, "Open your hand to the poor and needy neighbor in your land."

The Deuteronomic observation that there will always be poor in the land is placed between God commanding the Israelites to give freely and happily (v. 10) as well as openhandedly (v. 11). In Deuteronomy, the persistence of poverty is hardly an excuse to give up! And if the original context for this comment is not a justification to ignore the needs of our neighbors, the allusion to this verse in the New Testament is not either.[19]

---

19. Michael J. Wilkins, *Matthew*, NIV Application Commentary (Grand Rapids: Zondervan, 2004), 829; and M. Eugene Boring, "Matthew," in *The New Interpreter's Bible Commentary*, ed. Leander E. Keck et al. (Nashville: Abingdon, 2015), 7:348.

Second, it is important to keep in mind the broader context of Matthew 26:11 within Matthew. Several times in the Gospel, Jesus emphasizes giving to the poor (Matt. 5:42; 6:2–4; 19:16–22; 25:31–46). All these passages demonstrate Jesus' concern and call to care for the poor, and in Matthew 25 Jesus even says that to give to the poor is to give to Jesus himself! Given this, it would seem quite conflicting to interpret Jesus' words about the poor in 26:11 as implying that we should therefore disregard the poor in our midst.

Third, Matthew 26:11 represents only a portion of the communal vision offered in Deuteronomy 15, which presents a tension between what Israel should be (15:4) and what it actually is (15:11). Matthew's use of Deuteronomy emphasizes the latter—life's disappointments (Deut. 15:11)—whereas the book of Acts emphasizes the former—the eschatological ideal society (Deut. 15:4). Both of these views must be held together—one acknowledging the present, broken reality and the other the hopeful, transformed future. The book of Acts' usage of Deuteronomy does not negate Matthew's, but it does strongly suggest that Matthew 26:11 does not imply that caring for the poor should be abandoned or is futile.[20]

How, then, should we understand Jesus' statement? The proximity of Matthew 25:31–46 to 26:6–13 indicates that these two passages can be read in juxtaposition. Both texts are ultimately about a person's acts toward Jesus. In Matthew 25, those who attend to the needs of the poor are praised and said to *figuratively* minister these acts to Jesus himself. In Matthew 26, the unnamed woman who anoints Jesus is praised as she *literally* ministers to him. The difference between the two passages is timing. In the absence of Jesus, one can minister to him by ministering to the poor. In the presence of Jesus, especially in the context of the approaching passion, anointing him with oil is the best way of ministering to him. Earlier in the Gospel, Jesus himself notes that behavior can change depending on the time and season (Matt. 9:14–15). Given the timing of the moment in Matthew 26, the unique circumstances of the hour warrant that the woman's homage to Jesus could have been performed only while he was still with them. However, in his absence—which is soon approaching—his disciples have an ongoing obligation to care for the needy in their midst, and in doing so, they too will be ministering to Jesus, though in a different way.[21]

20. Vogt, "Social Justice and the Vision of Deuteronomy," 41.
21. Wilkins, *Matthew*, 829; and Boring, "Matthew," 348.

This understanding corresponds not only with the entirety of the Gospel of Matthew but also with the entirety of Scripture. We are called to love God, just as the unnamed woman demonstrates her loving devotion to Jesus by anointing him—and we are called to love our neighbors, serving the vulnerable, poor, and oppressed in our midst. These two affections and actions are not mutually exclusive.

A Community of Love

Social renewal is an effect of the Spirit, because ultimately the Spirit who is poured out is a Spirit of love.[22] "Love" is not explicitly mentioned in reference to the Spirit in Acts. But elsewhere in the New Testament the Spirit is associated with love (Rom. 5:5; 1 John 4:7–21), and there is a long historical precedent for identifying the Spirit as love.[23] Thus, we can plausibly identify Pentecost as an outpouring of the gift of love, which helps make sense of the communal dynamics described in the narrative. The community presented in Acts 2:42–47 and 4:32–35 reveals a lived-out example of the fulfillment of the twofold Great Commandment: love for God and love for neighbor (Luke 10:27).[24] Commenting on this, Amos Yong says, "The love of God ignites love for God, expressed in the prayers and praises of the people directed to God, and generates neighborly love, seen in the generosity and solidarity of the people with each other, as well as with those who were added to the community on a daily basis. . . . Is this not also a manifestation of the love of God, even if not explicitly called such here?"[25]

22. To claim that Pentecost is a baptism of love is not to deny the theme of power that has traditionally been associated with the pneumatology of the book of Acts. The proposal in this chapter is not to replace that theme but to expand it to include the fullness of the effects of this outpouring. Even some early Pentecostal figures proposed a baptism of love alongside that of power. See Amos Yong, *Spirit of Love: A Trinitarian Theology of Grace* (Waco: Baylor University Press, 2012), 59–74.

23. While one does not want to violate the integrity of the Acts narrative and superimpose categories onto the text that are not present, when reading the biblical story canonically it is appropriate to understand Luke's outpouring of the Spirit as a baptism of divine love—not reduced solely to this but inclusive of it. For three historical models that connect the Spirit with love, see Yong, *Spirit of Love*, 3–19.

24. The Gospel of Luke is the only Gospel that follows the Great Commandment immediately with an illustration of it: the parable of the good Samaritan (cf. Matt. 22:34–39; Mark 12:28–34).

25. Yong, *Spirit of Love*, 98. Moreover, this connection between altruism and the Spirit is not unique to the early Christian community. Recent studies have demonstrated this same correlation among Pentecostal communities that emphasize the work of the Spirit in the believer's life. See Margaret M. Poloma and Ralph W. Hood Jr., *Blood and Fire: Godly Love in a Pentecostal*

Aaron Kuecker maintains that in Luke-Acts, the Spirit transforms individuals, causing them to turn away from pure self-interest to the other.[26]
While he does not label this outward movement from oneself to others
as "love," it easily could be understood as such. The gift of God's Spirit
in the book of Acts is referred to as a baptism (Acts 1:5; 11:16; cf. Luke
3:16) and an infilling (Acts 2:4; 4:8, 31; 7:55; 9:17; 13:9, 52). Both concepts
suggest being inundated by the Spirit—either completely submersed or
filled—which brings an overflow of God into human lives so that they are
no longer full of themselves but of God.[27] And if God is love (1 John 4:8,
16), then this fullness of the Spirit acts as a centrifugal force that disrupts
our tendency to focus on ourselves and instead propels us outward toward
others; this is love.

The Spirit's reorientation of individuals immediately follows Acts
4:32–35, juxtaposing Barnabas, who is described as one "filled" with the
Spirit (4:31; 11:24), with Ananias and Sapphira, who are described as
being "filled" with Satan (5:3). Filled with the Spirit, Barnabas turns away
from himself and outward toward others by selling his field and bringing
all the money to the apostles. Conversely, Ananias and Sapphira, who are
filled with Satan rather than the Spirit, turn inward toward themselves
and away from others by selling a field but keeping some of the money
and lying about it.[28] In Acts 6:1–7 when the widows are being overlooked
in the daily distribution of food—likely a result of the sudden influx and
growth of the community after Pentecost—and the apostles are looking to
address the oversight, one of their qualifications for service is that persons
be "full of the Spirit" (6:3).[29] Why specify that persons need to be full of

Emerging Church (New York: New York University Press, 2008); Matthew Lee and Margaret M.
Poloma, *A Sociological Study of the Great Commandment in Pentecostalism: The Practice
of Godly Love as Benevolent Service* (Lewiston, NY: Edwin Mellen, 2009); and Margaret M.
Poloma and John C. Green, *The Assemblies of God: Godly Love and the Revitalization of
American Pentecostalism* (New York: New York University Press, 2010).

26. Aaron Kuecker's main focus is on how this dynamic is at work with respect to ethnic
identities in the narrative. See Aaron Kuecker, *The Spirit and the "Other": Social Identity,
Ethnicity and Intergroup Reconciliation in Luke-Acts* (New York: Bloomsbury, 2011), 18–19.

27. Yong, *Spirit of Love*, 98–99.

28. Aaron Kuecker maintains that for Luke there is a contrast between the influence of the
Spirit and the influence of Satan, which impinges on one's relationship with others (e.g., Luke
22:3–4). He also notes that this juxtaposition between the two influences emerges in the temptation scene of Jesus as well. See Kuecker, *Spirit and the "Other,"* 78–80, 136–47.

29. "Being full of . . . wisdom" is an additional criterion, which is also connected to the work
of the Spirit in a person's life. See Tremper Longman III, "Spirit and Wisdom," in *Presence,
Power and Promise: The Role of the Spirit of God in the Old Testament*, ed. David G. Firth
and Paul D. Wegner (Downers Grove, IL: InterVarsity, 2011), 95–110.

the Spirit to serve the widows? Because a Spirit-filled life orients a person toward others, an effect that is nothing if not love (cf. 1 John 3:17–18). Both of these instances exhibit love for neighbor, even if not explicitly labeled as such in the narrative.

Furthermore, this outpouring of the Spirit of love renders former identities and social divisions meaningless, as all are welcome in the kingdom. In the book of Acts not only do we see the Spirit pushing people outward toward others but we also see those on the margins being brought toward the center. We observe this in the initial outpouring of the Spirit at Pentecost, the reference to Joel pointing to a revolutionized community (Acts 2), and also throughout Acts as groups previously excluded from being fully part of the people of God are now welcomed into the community: the Samaritans (8:4–25), the Ethiopian eunuch (8:26–39), and the Gentiles (10–11).[30] This Spirit of love is a liberating force that transcends the categories that human beings routinely use to justify marginalization and exploitation of others (cf. Gal. 3:26–29).[31]

Conclusion

Recall how the biblical story began in Genesis. Humanity was created in the image of God with an earthly vocation to serve and care for the life of the world around them. The fall complicated humanity's ability to fulfill this task, but the calling did not vanish. After the fall, our earthly vocation becomes one of redemptive service, as our efforts to serve and care for the life of the world participate in the restoration of God's creational intent. God entrusts this task to the Israelites, who were called to image God as the people of God. God provided the law to assist the Israelites toward this end, but they failed to live out this calling.

In the New Testament, the story of the kingdom of God and new creation is a story about God, who has come in the person of Jesus Christ to

30. Matthias Wenk, "The Fullness of the Spirit: Pentecostalism and the Spirit," *Evangel* 21, no. 2 (Summer 2003): 43; Wenk, *Community-Forming Power*, 236, 291–307. For other works related to these ideas, see Wenk, "Community-Forming Power: Reconciliation and the Spirit in Acts," *Journal of the European Pentecostal Theological Association* 19 (1999): 17–33; and Wenk, "The Holy Spirit as Transforming Power within a Society: Pneumatological Spirituality and Its Political/Social Relevance for Western Europe," *Journal of Pentecostal Theology* 11, no. 1 (2002): 130–42.

31. The 1906 Azusa Street Revival is an example of a move of the Spirit among a community that resulted in social barriers being overcome. See Gastón Espinosa, *William J. Seymour and the Origins of Global Pentecostalism: A Biography and Documentary History* (Durham, NC: Duke University Press, 2014).

enact redemptive service, the ultimate act of which was to go to the cross. But to focus on the cross alone neglects all the other moments of Jesus' life—birth through resurrection—that also constitute Jesus' redemptive service. Moreover, it is in Jesus' image that we are transformed and reoriented toward the vocation to care and serve the world once again.

Only with the reception of the Spirit at Pentecost can people truly become Jesus' likeness-image and thus be enabled and empowered to continue Jesus' kingdom work of redemptive service. Jesus entrusts his ministry to his followers. As the book of Acts demonstrates, the presence of the Spirit transforms individuals, turning them toward their neighbors and away from themselves. As conduits for the work of the Spirit and constituting a community of the Spirit, we are enabled to work toward the realization of the kingdom of God, bringing forth his reign of justice, love, and shalom. Thus, a Spirit-filled life is one that is lived in redemptive service to our neighbors. To the extent that persons are a community of the Spirit (identity), they will also be a people engaged in redemptive service (mission). While this brief overview does not exhaust the New Testament texts concerned with redemptive service, it establishes a clear trajectory that we are to follow in order to live out our calling as the image of God.[32] Redemptive service is, thus, not optional or marginal to Christians' identity and mission as the community of the Spirit; it is required and central.

The writing of Scripture has ended, but the overarching narrative continues because the task is not yet complete. As the people of God, the body of Christ, and the community of the Spirit, we are called to take up the mission of redemptive service in the world. Doing so is how we image God in and to the world.[33] Attention to redemptive service exhausts neither the whole of the gospel story nor the whole of our mission in life. But it is at the heart of the gospel story and, thus, should be at the heart of our story too. Hopefully, tracing this theme throughout the biblical story will help us develop a proper worldview that enables us to see those around us who are hurting and in need. Just like God heard the cries of the Israelites in Egypt, we need to attune our ears to hear the cries of those suffering today and be moved by those cries. Loving our neighbors begins with

32. The following are some other New Testament passages concerned with redemptive service: Rom. 15:25–28; 1 Cor. 16:1–4; 2 Cor. 8–9; James 1:27; 2:1–9, 14–26; 5:4–5; 1 John 3:16–17.
33. For a reflection on how our present social work will be incorporated eschatologically with God's new heaven and earth, see Miroslav Volf, "On Loving with Hope: Eschatology and Social Responsibility," *Transformation* 7, no. 3 (July/September 1990): 28–31.

being moved by compassion toward them. And being moved by compassion toward them begins with how we perceive them.

Now that we have traced some biblical and theological resources that clearly command us to love our neighbors, we must examine how we love our neighbors *well*. Part 2 of this book explores this theme and offers some principles to guide our redemptive service.

DISCUSSION QUESTIONS

1. What surprised you about the effect of Pentecost on the early Christian community?
2. How have you previously understood Jesus' life and mission with respect to the early Christian community's life and mission? Did you see them as connected and intertwined? If so, how? If not, why?
3. Think about the world around you. What are some situations of brokenness that you still see that have not yet been healed? What are some ways you can participate in bringing shalom to those areas?
4. Returning once more to the parable of the good Samaritan and the intersection of seeing and doing, how does the outpouring of the Spirit at Pentecost affect the way we see others? How does it affect the way we act toward others?

FOR FURTHER READING

Dempster, Murray W. "Evangelism, Social Concern, and the Kingdom of God." In *Called and Empowered: Global Mission in Pentecostal Perspective*, edited by Murray W. Dempster, Byron D. Klaus, and Douglas Petersen, 22–43. Peabody, MA: Hendrickson, 1991.

Kuecker, Aaron. *The Spirit and the "Other": Social Identity, Ethnicity and Intergroup Reconciliation in Luke-Acts*. New York: Bloomsbury, 2011.

Pao, David W. *Acts and the Isaianic New Exodus*. Grand Rapids: Baker Academic, 2000.

Turner, Max. *Power from on High: The Spirit in Israel's Restoration and Witness in Luke-Acts*. Sheffield, UK: Sheffield Academic, 1996.

Wenk, Matthias. *Community-Forming Power: The Socio-Ethical Role of the Spirit in Luke-Acts*. New York: T&T Clark, 2000.

Yong, Amos. *Spirit of Love: A Trinitarian Theology of Grace*. Waco: Baylor University Press, 2012.

PART 2

Principles and Practices for Serving Our Neighbors

In part 1 we noted that a distinguishing feature of the good Samaritan is that he truly saw the beaten man on the side of the road. But the biblical story does not end there. The second half of the parable relays how the Samaritan bandages the man's wounds, takes him to an inn where he can be looked after, and promises to return to pay any outstanding debts for needed care. The Samaritan's service begins with the act of seeing but ultimately is expressed in tangible actions. The actions are an expression of the Samaritan's compassion, as solidarity leads to entering into and taking on the man's suffering as his own in order to overcome it. The second part of this book takes up these issues and examines how we can work to mend our broken world.

This parable offers two further lessons. First, serving others requires something from us. The Samaritan delays his journey (at least long enough to take time to bandage the beaten man and bring him to an inn), inconveniences himself by placing the Samaritan on his donkey rather than riding it himself, and gives his own resources—oil, wine, and money—to ensure that the man is looked after. Being benevolent requires a sacrifice of time, comfort, and resources. In the twenty-first century such sacrifices are required of us as well as we participate in mending the brokenness of the world.

Second, we can use this parable to explore three means of serving others: relief, development, and advocacy.[1] In the story, immediate relief was required as the beaten man was on the brink of death and needed direct intervention. But presumably, at some point the man would begin to heal from his injuries. Should the Samaritan have kept paying his bills indefinitely? No! There would have come a day when the man would have been well enough to function again—even if only partially—which is when the work of development would be more appropriate. The narrative says the man's clothes were stripped, and so it is likely that any possessions he had with him were also stolen. This man had lost a lot (maybe everything) and needed help getting back on his feet again. But when he could contribute to his own well-being, he should be encouraged and allowed to do so. This is the work of development, in which a person or people do not remain beholden to the generosity of others but pursue their own well-being through their own labor. Yet from the perspective of service, this should not be the end of the story either. An even bigger question to attend to is why there were robbers on the road in the first place. This poor man fortunately receives help from the Samaritan, but what about the next traveler? What needs to be done to prevent this incident from continuing to happen in the future? An advocate looks at the place in the road where the incident occurred and wonders *why this road protected the robbers more than the travelers*. Advocates are able to see beyond the surface and identify the conditions that contributed to the problem. Advocates also possess the imagination to find a solution and the bureaucratic skills to effect change.

Just as the long-term well-being of the beaten man and his community depends on a multifaceted approach to service, cries for help in the world today must also be rightly discerned and answered according to the appropriate work of relief, development, and advocacy. For any lasting impact to

1. We are not suggesting that this parable is explicitly concerned with the acts of relief, development, and advocacy. However, it does offer an opportunity to integrate a connection to these three approaches in light of the situation found in the parable.

occur, we must carefully consider power dynamics, social structures, and cultural contexts at the start of any endeavor. This work requires personal humility so that genuine connections can be made with the ones we intend to help. When our service is redemptive, we realize that in the process of serving others, we have as much to learn as we have to give.

6

---•---

Poverty

Isolation and Exclusion

We Are All Poor in Some Way

The story of the good Samaritan provides a foundation for discussing poverty. The people in this story all occupied different social statuses. People have different levels of social prestige and status that impact how much influence, comfort, and ease of engagement with others they have in typical settings. Status is determined by a mixture of economic class, prestige, and political power based on a person's group memberships and occupation.[1] To illustrate this concept, imagine that you are invited to dine with international dignitaries at the White House. Would you have the appropriate clothes? Would you understand the protocol of the event? Would you be comfortable knowing which utensils to use at such a formal dinner? When you speak to offer your opinion, would the people at your table stop to listen or would they more likely disregard your thoughts?

This admittedly extreme example—not many people get invited to the White House—illustrates how social status can impact both confidence and self-consciousness. This idea helps us understand and identify which people inhabit the mainstream. Those who do are often referred to as the

1. Max Weber, "Class, Status, Party," in *Social Stratification: In Sociological Perspective*, 2nd ed., ed. David B. Grusky (Boulder, CO: Westview, 2001), 132–42.

majority (even if they are not the numerical majority, these people tend to have most of the social and economic power in a population); they set rules and enforce them. Social power, prestige, and economic position all reinforce one another. Having access to even one of those three domains makes it easier to acquire the others. Conversely, being denied access to these three domains makes it harder to accumulate any of them. Consider that it is easier for someone to make money if they already have it. The more money someone makes, the more social respect and influence they are likely to gain.

Other members of society occupy a different position, not having as much influence in their towns, communities, or nations. All too often, societies stigmatize these members of society with stereotypes, defining them by some imagined deficit or perceived otherness. These negative stereotypes are examples of the marginalized social statuses that are used to validate and perpetuate inequalities. A common example is how the Nazis systematically stigmatized Jewish people, depicting them with dehumanizing language and images. For the Nazi regime, this marginalization justified the displacement of European Jews and led eventually to the Holocaust.

In this chapter we focus on understanding poverty as a social force, as it is central to much of the work of redemptive service. This concept helps explain the aspects of poverty that extend beyond economic marginalization.

Social status and stigma help us understand discourses about poverty in the US. One dominant idea claims that someone who works hard enough will be able to earn enough to live well. This view leads to an ideology in which those who struggle financially just need to work harder. This conflates economic success with moral success and economic failure with moral failure. These unspoken rules in US society are still prominent discourses. However, while it is true that hard work can contribute to economic success, plenty of people work hard and still do not have enough money to live comfortably.

Narrowly focusing on personal attributes of poverty also tends to establish a dichotomy between the deserving and undeserving poor. Here, poverty is viewed primarily as an individual experience: some people will be hardworking and still have trouble, while others just need to go get a job. This is a dangerous practice for redemptive service, as God does not distinguish between who is and is not deserving of his grace. All have sinned, as Paul states in Romans 3:23. None of us are deserving. To take this idea further, in Matthew 25, Jesus expresses solidarity with groups of people who are socially marginalized. He lists widows, orphans, immigrants, and incarcerated people. Jesus does not say to give a glass of water and to help only those who have done no wrong or who are hardworking or who are law-abiding. He says to give to those whom society rejects and abandons.

People experiencing homelessness provide a relevant example of how these discourses of deserving and undeserving affect redemptive service. Many stereotypes drive popular conceptualizations of homelessness. As a result of these stereotypes, many say "get a job" or "stop doing drugs." These messages justify policies and practices that prevent redemptive service and turn those who are unhoused into the other. Rather than befriending people experiencing homelessness, learning their stories, and developing meaningful relationships, these stereotypes and discourses justify refusing to help. Many who are unhoused defy common stereotypes. The key idea here is that when engaging in redemptive service with people, determining whether someone's situation is their fault completely misses the point. The responsibility is to help and befriend. Hopefully, through reading later parts of this text, you will discover beneficial ways of helping.

Another potential pitfall of redemptive service is the rigid distinction between who is serving and who is served. All too often, this becomes the "haves" attending to the needs of the "have-nots." No one wants to be defined as a "have-not," for everyone has something beneficial to offer. Likewise, those who see themselves as the "haves" often enter the service project from a sense of superiority and paternalism. Regardless of our economic situation, we all experience some form of lack in our lives. Each of us knows heartbreak and has experienced pain. When we realize that we are all poor in some sense, we can better serve others from a place of solidarity. With this approach, we will think we are serving but we will also find ourselves learning from and being served by those we are helping.

Because service projects and missions outreach often focus on people or people groups who experience significant levels of economic hardship, it is vital to think deeply about what it means to have a limited income. Before thinking about practical ways to serve people in such a situation, it is necessary to understand more about being in poverty. This may seem on the surface like more theoretical than practical ideas. But for service to be truly redemptive, the practical work must be based on sound theoretical understanding. Our conceptualizations and explanations of poverty directly affect how we work to address and alleviate poverty.

Various Definitions of Poverty

Before defining "poverty," let's think about what defines "people groups." Poverty is a circumstance that a person might experience, and society does assign a status to it. Someone who experiences poverty could be called "poor." In this chapter we sometimes refer to people in these circumstances as "economically marginalized," as this terminology better expresses poverty as a circumstance that happens to people rather than a characteristic of people that can be (mistakenly) conflated with moral failure. This important distinction recognizes that no one is fully defined by their circumstances, and certainly not by their economic position. A person who does not have much money might still have a sharp intellect, a raucous sense of humor, skill with art, the capacity to love deeply, extreme generosity with others, and any other positive characteristic and virtue. Unfortunately, in focusing on those who are socially and economically marginalized, the tendency is to define people only by their lack. This deficit approach misses the fullness of people's humanity.

An example of this point comes from my (Ruthie's) experience with a church congregation of immigrants in rural Florida. In an attempt to understand the lives of these newcomers to Florida, I spent much time in their churches, fellowshipping with them, listening to their stories, and enjoying their hospitality. Most of the people in the churches worked in agriculture or the service industry. The people were similar to any other congregation. As a group, they were faithful, honorable, generous, compassionate, funny, frustrated, intelligent, kind, hardworking, hospitable, and so much more. Many of them also experienced deep poverty, and all of them shared stories of racism and social exclusion. For example, some told stories of spending long days picking fruits and vegetables that were destined for grocery stores while they themselves struggled to feed their own families. If the only description of this group of people had been their economic situation, they would be completely misunderstood. On the other hand, if the depth of their social and economic marginalization had been ignored, their story would not be accurately told. Redemptive service with this group, or any group, begins by wanting to know them through the lens of brotherhood and sisterhood while bearing witness to their social and economic situation.

Economic Poverty

While not all redemptive service pertains to economic marginalization, contemporary society is characterized by economic endeavors. Money certainly does not determine everything, but for those who do not have access to money, the lack thereof significantly influences their lives. Not having money often accompanies cascading problems. For example, many people in the US live month-to-month on their incomes, barely making enough to meet the costs of living. One setback like a car failure could result in a person losing their job because they are unable to get to work. This would trigger food insecurity and potentially even an eviction from housing. If there are children in this household, the housing displacement will potentially disrupt schooling and interrupt social networks. Those familiar with economic marginalization all too often experience extreme stress, as everything in life costs money and there just is not enough to survive.[2]

Poverty is brokenness. Both philosophy and science seek to understand abstract concepts, such as poverty, in clear terms that allow them to be defined, measured, and addressed. This process is called conceptualization, and it is a key aspect of any social scientific endeavor. How poverty is conceptualized determines how it will be measured, whether it is seen as a problem to be alleviated or just a fact of contemporary life. How a society defines poverty will affect the labels given to people and how those people are treated. Thinking about poverty as general brokenness is a helpful place to start. We are all broken in some way; we all experience poverty in some area of our lives. Yet one limitation of such a broad conceptualization is that it renders poverty difficult to measure.

Poverty commonly refers to economic lack. Closely linking poverty to money is rather narrow in scope, but it does make poverty straightforward to define and measure. Later in this chapter we will introduce multidimensional definitions of poverty that are broader than economic conceptualizations. We begin, however, with an important economic discussion. Money can be counted. As a result, economic definitions of poverty give us specific ways to address poverty in both programs and policies.

The history of poverty and public policy in the United States illustrates the connection between conceptualization, identification, and intervention. Poverty did not have a standardized definition or measurement until after President Lyndon B. Johnson declared the "war on poverty" in a State of the Union address in 1964. This speech established poverty as something that needs to be fought, and in order to do so it must be defined

2. Mark Robert Rank, *Confronting Poverty: Economic Hardship in the United States* (Los Angeles: SAGE, 2020).

and measured.[3] This new conceptualization launched an economic measure of poverty. Families whose incomes identified them as poor became eligible for material supports. Some of these supports are still important to communities. The Head Start program, for example, provides early childhood education, support, and nutrition for families whose income qualifies them for this service.

Economic definitions of poverty can be divided into absolute poverty and relative poverty. Absolute poverty is a standard measure of poverty applied to everyone regardless of external factors. It allows for relatively direct calculations of who has enough to survive and who does not. Relative poverty is also important because it takes into account context.

ABSOLUTE POVERTY: GLOBAL AND LOCAL

Absolute poverty is sometimes referred to as the poverty line. Once the poverty line is set, everyone is compared against it. Absolute poverty lines at the macro level provide an overview of how well people in a community are doing. At the micro level, they can also help determine whether an individual or family is eligible to receive certain services. A standardized measure for poverty gives a necessary indicator of vulnerability. Vulnerability helps describe and identify who is most at risk of harm or negative outcomes. If a hurricane tears through the Caribbean Sea, some communities are more vulnerable and have a greater risk of harm than others. Poverty is one way of identifying which communities are at greater risk. At the micro level, when a global pandemic upsets the service industry, as with COVID, some people are at greater risk of experiencing homelessness, and economic status is an important piece of identifying who those people are.

Globally, absolute poverty metrics are established by international agencies. The World Bank Group is one influential international organization that seeks to alleviate poverty. The World Bank was established in 1944 in the wake of World War II for the purpose of rebuilding an economically decimated Europe, promoting global economic stability, and preventing future world wars through economic interdependencies. The World Bank is expressly concerned with the economic status of countries. It funds development interventions that help countries improve their economic standing. The World Bank has established an absolute measure of extreme

3. John Iceland, *Poverty in America: A Handbook* (Berkeley: University of California Press, 2013), 20–21.

poverty in the form of the international poverty line, which as of 2022 is an income of $2.15 per person per day.[4]

Clearly, less than $2.15 per person per day is not much money. The establishment of a set measure across populations helps in comparing different places, programs, and policies. This absolute measure of poverty is invaluable in understanding and communicating the economic impact of disruptions.

Just like the World Bank sets the international poverty line, the US poverty line is an absolute measure of poverty that is set and adjusted each year by the US government. This is a determination of the minimum annual income that a household unit requires, based on how many people are living in that unit, to meet their basic needs. In 2023, the poverty line was $14,580 for a household with one person, and $30,000 for a household of four people. While the US poverty line varies by number of people in a household and is adjusted each year to account for inflation, it is still considered an absolute measure because it establishes the same standard across the US. Under this measure, $30,000 establishes the poverty line for a household of four regardless of cost of living, whether a family is living in New York City or Wichita Falls, Texas. Lack of consideration of external factors such as location is significant, as the cost of living—housing, taxes, utilities, and food—varies by location. Absolute poverty is not sufficient for describing the conditions of people living in poverty in these two areas because their experiences of poverty differ widely.

RELATIVE POVERTY: GLOBAL AND LOCAL

Absolute poverty, though a useful measure, is not without flaws. Relative poverty is an important way of measuring poverty that introduces comparison. Relative poverty is generally calculated by comparing a person's income with the median incomes in their area. A person living in relative poverty is defined as someone who earns less than half of the median income in any given locale. According to the US Census Bureau, the median household income in New York City in 2022 was $76,607. A household in NYC would thus be considered living in relative poverty if they earned less than $38,304. By contrast, the median household income of Wichita Falls, Texas, was $55,584.[5] A household earning less than $27,792

4. "Fact Sheet: An Adjustment to Global Poverty Lines," World Bank, updated September 14, 2022, https://openknowledge.worldbank.org/bitstream/handle/10986/34496/211602ov.pdf.
5. American Community Survey, "Median Income in the Past 12 Months (in 2022 Inflation-Adjusted Dollars)," United Census Bureau, 2022, table ID S1903, https://data.census.gov/table

in this area would be considered below relative poverty. As this example illustrates, there is a difference of $10,512 between household income in relative poverty in New York City and Wichita Falls. The relative measure of poverty considers other parameters when defining the minimum amount of income a household should earn to meet their basic needs.

One major benefit of the relative measure of poverty is that it introduces the idea of social isolation to an objective, quantitative measure of poverty. When a family earns less than half the median income of an area, they are excluded from many activities and amenities in that place. For example, while the US public school system was originally conceptualized to be the great equalizer, children from families that are earning less than half of the local median income cannot participate in many of the activities that their classmates can. In an elementary class, a child might be invited to a birthday party but not attend because their family cannot afford a present. Increasingly, early participation in sports in elementary school is necessary for children to develop the skills to compete on high school and college teams. These elementary school teams, however, are not free. Many children are excluded because their parents cannot afford the club fees, uniforms, and other costs. While relative poverty will not fully explain who gets to play and who is excluded, it is one way of looking at who is more likely to be excluded. Relative measures of poverty are used both in the US and by international agencies.

Using an economic measure to approximate social isolation and exclusion broadens the scope of poverty and reveals its effect on relationships and access to human capital, cultural capital, and social capital.[6] These are important to understand because they present a broader set of resources that people use to meet their needs. First, human capital is the set of skills, abilities, and credentials that a person possesses. A person with human capital can get a job or a position on a sports team. From the example above, early sports participation helps youths develop the human capital (skills) to be competitive on prestigious sports teams later in life. Second, cultural capital is the mastery of the unspoken rules and cultural norms of a context. Everyone has cultural capital, but not everyone has the cultural capital that is widely recognized by the institutions and dominant context. In the earlier example of attending a dinner at the White House,

---

/ACSST5Y2022.S1903?q=Wichita%20Falls%20city,%20Texas&t=Income%20(Households, %20Families,%20Individuals)&g=160XX00US3651000.

6. David Hulme, Karen Moore, and Andrew Shepherd, "Chronic Poverty: Meanings and Analytical Frameworks," *Chronic Poverty Research Centre Working Paper* 2 (November 1, 2001).

knowing the protocol and etiquette to interact with others comfortably and confidently is a person's cultural capital. Last, social capital refers to the networks of people and connections. When a child is not able to go to a birthday party because their parents cannot afford a gift and are embarrassed about it, the child misses out on more than just cake. They are also excluded from the stories and budding friendships that happen at the event. If parents also attend that party, it is a lost opportunity for that child's parents to develop social capital and connections that could be useful.

Relative poverty shows how economic limitations have a direct social impact on a person's life chances and capitals. Relative poverty can be thought of as economic isolation. Looking at any community, we must ask questions about inclusion and isolation. One way of intervening in these neighborhoods is to help people develop the human, cultural, and social capitals that are important for their context. Identifying where those interventions could be beneficial can begin by looking at which neighborhoods or communities are characterized by relative poverty.

Sometimes either relative or absolute poverty is prioritized over the other. But an understanding of relative poverty is not sufficient without an understanding of absolute poverty. They go together. A measure of economic isolation is incomplete without understanding the percentage of a population living in absolute poverty. If most of a community is living in absolute poverty, they are not living in economic isolation relative to one another. For instance, in Aleppo, Syria, 80 percent of the population lives below the international (absolute) poverty line.[7] As the conditions in Aleppo indicate, relative poverty is not the best way to describe the scope and magnitude of poverty in this location.

CONCLUDING THOUGHTS

The most widely used definitions of poverty are economic. A number of reasons account for this, but most importantly, economic measures are relatively easy to observe, calculate, and compare. Both absolute and relative measures of poverty are necessary for understanding the material deprivation (absolute) and social isolation/exclusion (relative) that people experience. Each of these measurements helps to address the limits of the

7. International Committee of the Red Cross, "Syria: Economic Crisis Compounds Conflict Misery as Millions Face Deeper Poverty, Hunger," Multimedia Newsroom, June 28, 2020, https://www.icrcnewsroom.org/story/en/1920/syria-economic-crisis-compounds-conflict-misery-as-millions-face-deeper-poverty-hunger.

other. There are also other economic measurements of poverty, such as the supplemental poverty index, that are helpful for understanding and describing economic outcomes, but absolute and relative measures are the most common and influential. Methodological differences in measuring economic poverty aside, all these conceptualizations share a basic underlying assumption: *money* is the best way to measure whether people have access to that which is required for a high quality of life (food, shelter, education, health care, etc.). Economists argue that focusing on money in defining poverty is ideal, because other indicators such as educational attainment and health outcomes are directly tied to the amount of money in circulation in a particular social system. However, this assumption is challenged by social scientists, who provide other ways of conceptualizing poverty.

Multidimensional Poverty Index

In part one, we argued for viewing salvation and redemption holistically. After the fall, our whole selves were broken, and alleviating that brokenness requires holistic redemption. This helps to explain why purely economic conceptualizations of poverty are insufficient. At its most basic form, money is the means by which we procure the goods and services that we need or desire. Knowing how much money someone has might tell us what they can purchase or consume, but it does not directly indicate whether someone actually has what they need. An undergraduate college student living in a dormitory with a meal plan might have little income but still have access to food, shelter, and other basic necessities. Conversely, someone who is diabetic might have an income above the poverty line, but because of the cost of insulin, transportation, and housing in their community, their monthly income does not extend far enough to cover their food costs. As both examples illustrate, the economic measure of income alone cannot sufficiently describe a person's ability to meet basic needs. In many situations, more than just economic disruptions have occurred. A more robust conceptualization of poverty is needed to address the weakness of income-based measures.

The multidimensional poverty index (MPI) quantifies what people are able to get and do.[8] This way of describing poverty is sometimes referred

---

8. Sabina Alkire and Maria Emma Santos, "Measuring Acute Poverty in the Developing World: Robustness and Scope of the Multidimensional Poverty Index," *World Development* 59 (2014): 251–74.

to as a "direct" measure of poverty, because rather than using money as a marker for the ability to access what is necessary, it directly measures the necessities of life. The MPI is broken up into three different categories, with individual indicators contained in each: health, years of schooling, and standard of living. These three areas have been identified as necessary for someone to lead a full and productive life. Just as the international poverty line of $2.15 per day (as of the writing of this text) focuses on extreme poverty, the MPI is primarily concerned with those who are living in conditions of acute poverty.

As a direct measure of who has what they need for a full and dignified life, the MPI provides specific descriptions of where the breakdown in basic needs is occurring. In education, for example, the MPI measures how many years of schooling people in a given area receive. When income alone is used as a substitute for overall well-being, boosting income does not necessarily translate into increases in education. The more detailed descriptions of the MPI, however, allow for more detailed interventions. With education, by looking at the direct indicators of the MPI in combination with demographic variables, analysts can understand with greater nuance who is not achieving desirable outcomes. For example, if gender is considered in conjunction with education, it is possible to describe how many years of schooling men versus women receive. Considering more nuanced indicators of poverty provides a more robust accounting of actual living conditions. With regard to redemptive service, this approach provides a better way of looking at who is more likely to be in poverty and offers better solutions. Before discussing how to address poverty, we want to first review basic understandings and common explanations for why poverty occurs in communities and in people's lives.

Various Explanations of Poverty

Whether using economic or multidimensional conceptualizations of poverty, both social scientists and the general public are interested in why poverty happens. Explanations for poverty are directly related to ideological beliefs. Whether we acknowledge it or not, we all have beliefs about what causes poverty. These beliefs come from a variety of places, including how we were raised, our political orientation, the beliefs of our parents and friends, the media sources we consume, and our personal experiences with poverty. These beliefs might not be based on facts or social science, which makes it vitally important that we critically examine our own beliefs about poverty and carefully consider other beliefs.

Research into beliefs about the causes of poverty finds that people have widely varying opinions. Our culture provides a prevailing, dominant schema or ideology about poverty and its causes—which is called cultural schema theory.[9] Research on poverty has found that some groups are more likely to believe there are personal, moral, or psychological causes for poverty at the individual level, while others are more likely to believe there are structural causes of poverty that are external to the individual.[10] A personal explanation of poverty can be dangerous, as it tends to blame poverty on the poor.

Most beliefs about poverty fit into one of three broad categories: individualistic, fatalistic, and structural.[11] Individualistic explanations of poverty focus on personal decisions, psychology, and morality. When discussing homelessness, for example, individualistic explanations might mention a person's laziness or susceptibility to drug addiction and alcoholism. These individualistic beliefs about poverty tend to blame the poor, even if that is not the intention. Fatalistic explanations attribute poverty to sickness and inability to work, natural disasters, or just bad luck. While these might seem similar to individualistic explanations, they differ in that they do not blame the person, because it is not someone's fault if they get cancer, for example. Structural attributions tend to look at society and systems as the explanations for poverty. This approach focuses on how certain policies favor some groups of people at the expense of others. Or it looks at how institutions such as education or the health care system push people into poverty or fail to provide the means for people to pull themselves out.

Because these explanations are rooted in belief systems, people hold them with great vigor. When discussing poverty or looking at events via the media, we tend to hold to that which affirms our positions and disregard opposing views. Psychologists call this confirmation bias. Everyone does it! We look for information that will confirm our beliefs and contradict other positions. This natural human tendency can cloud how we interact

9. Patricia Homan, Lauren Valentino, and Emi Weed, "Being and Becoming Poor: How Cultural Schemas Shape Beliefs about Poverty," *Social Forces* 95, no. 3 (March 2017): 1023–48.

10. Francis O. Adeola, "Racial and Class Divergence in Public Attitudes and Perceptions about Poverty in USA: An Empirical Study," *Race, Gender and Class* 12, no. 2 (2005): 53–80.

11. Matthew O. Hunt and Heather E. Bullock, "Ideologies and Beliefs about Poverty," *The Oxford Handbook of the Social Science of Poverty*, ed. David Brady and Linda M. Burton (New York: Oxford University Press, 2016), 93–116.

with people and deal with poverty. Failure to recognize our confirmation biases partially accounts for the difficulty in contemporary American culture to have meaningful discussions about social issues. To deepen our understanding of ourselves and poverty both locally and globally, we must understand two facts. First, many explanations for poverty are ideological and belief based. Second, we are biased toward the ideologies that we hold. Being aware of our own beliefs and the way our biases cloud our ability to think critically about social issues can help us do redemptive service more effectively. When working with people living in poverty, our hidden biases can cause us to treat people with less dignity than they deserve.

Each of these explanations for poverty is incomplete on its own. Focusing on structural causes without accounting for individual factors often causes people to be missed. Likewise, a myopic focus on individual explanations will miss the structures that reproduce inequality and perpetuate the problem. Someone going through hardship is often facing overlapping and interrelated individual and structural causes, as well as just bad luck. This is also true at the community level. If homelessness is a problem in a community, individual factors might be involved in why people are living unhoused. There could, however, also be structural factors, such as the lack of affordable housing, driving this problem. Seeing the structural as well as the individual factors is necessary when looking at programs to address the problem. Providing individual-level interventions such as job training or drug rehabilitation is helpful and necessary, but without the structural-level interventions of building low-income housing, the problem of homelessness will be unmanageable.

Responding to Poverty

The parable of the good Samaritan contrasts two ways to address poverty. The priest and Levite, the characters in the story who possess higher social status, glance at the man who had been stripped, robbed, and beaten up. They avert their eyes and cross to the other side of the street, putting as much distance as they can between themselves and the hurt man. The Samaritan, the marginalized character in the story, looks fully at the man, approaches him, and kneels to help. The actions and inactions we take when addressing people who are facing hardship are based on motivations, assumptions, beliefs, and justifications. What motivates the differences in response? What thoughts, assumptions, and justifications drive the actions of the priest and Levite versus the Samaritan?

Definitions of poverty and beliefs about the causes of poverty work together to drive our responses to people who are facing hardship. The plans, policies, and interventions that are put in place to alleviate poverty are directly based on what is believed to be its causes. Economic explanations of poverty, combined with individualistic explanations that poverty is caused by an unwillingness to work, will lead to policies that require a person to meet a minimum income, combined with proof of employment, to qualify for food stamps (the current policy in the US).[12] Conversely, approaches to poverty that focus on structural issues tend to lead to policies and systems that place the onus of people's well-being on institutions. An example would be the belief in the US that education can alleviate poverty at the individual level combined with the belief that education is a basic human right. These beliefs have driven US education policy to provide free public education for every child in the US between kindergarten and twelfth grade—regardless of ability, race, language, or documentation status.

Beliefs about the causes of poverty lead to justifications for either inaction or actions that address poverty. The danger in individualistic explanations is that they can blame people for their situation and then use that to justify inaction in helping those who are in need. In his highly influential book, *Evicted*, Matthew Desmond writes about his research with people who experience poverty and homelessness. Drawing from interviews, he discusses responses from various churches and religious leaders to unhoused people. When discussing poverty as an abstract concept, churches are more likely to address it as something to be treated with compassion. But when discussing specific poor people and the ways to help them, church members and leaders commonly discuss why it is a waste of time and money. These reasons are often based on the personal attributions made about the people who are suffering.[13] As someone who regularly engages with people on this topic, I've often heard statements such as the following:

- We can't give money, he'll just use it on drugs or alcohol.
- She has multiple children from different fathers.

12. Kathryn Edin and H. Luke Shaefer, *$2.00 a Day: Living on Almost Nothing in America* (Boston: Houghton Mifflin Harcourt, 2015): 29–33. A more current discussion of the work requirements for SNAP can be found at the USDA website, https://www.fns.usda.gov/snap /work-requirements. There are ways to be exempt from the work requirement; however, Edin and Shaefer point out that the bureaucracy that families must navigate to receive the benefits is so complex that it functions as a barrier even for those families who qualify for the support.

13. Matthew Desmond, *Evicted: Poverty and Profit in the American City* (New York: Crown, 2016), 127.

- He's a high-school dropout.
- She can't keep a job.
- What he calls "depression" is really just "laziness."

People in and out of the church use such responses as justification for not helping others. We tell ourselves this to excuse ourselves for seeing someone hurting, averting our eyes, and crossing the road—just like the priest and Levite.

From Poverty to the Poor

The measurements we use to calculate poverty determine who is poor, and so it is important to be deeply thoughtful about such measurements. These measurements allocate resources in a community and determine who will actually benefit from assistance. Yet even with the necessity of definitions and calculations, a problem persists: determining who is poor establishes an us-them relationship between those who are living in poverty and those who are not. This has the result of othering those who are identified as living in poverty, classifying them as inherently different and less. This can lead to a sense of superiority among those who do not receive the "poor" label. In the context of redemptive service, these labels and social definitions can demean those who are receiving help while elevating the helpers. Most people are understandably uncomfortable with the idea that they would bring an attitude of superiority to the practice of helping, but careful self-examination is necessary for humble service.

Having conducted decades-long longitudinal research, sociologists have found that 60 percent of Americans will spend at least one year in poverty at some point in their adult life.[14] These findings indicate that when speaking of the economically poor, for most of the adults in the US, this is a discussion of their own lives. The fact that economic deprivation will affect most people in the US for at least one year belies the notion that poverty is unusual or unlikely, which is a widespread misconception. These statistics challenge common stereotypes about ourselves and others. Understanding the frequency and widespread nature of poverty engenders a sense of solidarity with those who are economically isolated. As Jesus

14. Mark Robert Rank, Lawrence M. Eppard, and Heather E. Bullock, *Poorly Understood: What America Gets Wrong about Poverty* (Oxford: Oxford University Press, 2021), 9–16.

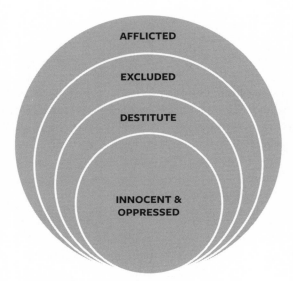

Figure 6.1 Different uses of the word "poor" in Amos
Based on Thomas John Finley, "An Evangelical Response to the Preaching of Amos,"
Journal of Evangelical Theological Society (1983): 411–20.

said in Matthew 25:40, "Just as you did it to one of the least of these brothers and sisters of mine, you did it to me."

One argument against Christians maintaining an us-them distinction about who is considered poor is similar to the idea of a multidimensional measure of poverty: if economic indicators of poverty are too narrow, then only thinking about people who are poor as those who experience financial poverty is also too limited. In describing who is identified as "poor" in the book of Amos, Thomas Finley presents an intriguing typology.[15] He says that four types of people are described as poor in Amos. First, innocent people who are victims of oppression (like slaves) are poor. Second, those who are destitute and do not have enough to meet their basic needs are poor, similar to measures of absolute poverty and the international poverty line of $2.15 per day. Third, those who are excluded and isolated are poor. Fourth, those who are brokenhearted or emotionally afflicted in some way are poor (see fig. 6.1).

By this definition, all of us at some time in our lives will be poor in one of these areas. And those who are poor in one area are not necessarily poor in all areas. People can have material lack but have high levels of

15. Thomas John Finley, "An Evangelical Response to the Preaching of Amos," *Journal of Evangelical Theological Society* (1983): 411–20.

community integration. Before engaging in redemptive service, we should reflect deeply on the ways that we ourselves are poor. We are all broken in some way. This awareness of our own lack and isolation is an important starting place for our giving. We give out of our lack and help others from our weakness. As the apostle Paul says, "Whenever I am weak, then I am strong" (2 Cor. 12:10). What better way to avoid a sense of pride and superiority? In doing this, we open ourselves to learning from those whom we are helping. A reciprocal relationship is healthy and necessary for meaningful service.

There is one inherent danger here in this conceptualization: if those who do not know what it means to be hungry treat poverty lightly, it could minimize others' suffering. There is very real physical and psychological suffering that comes from a lack of basic human needs, such as food, shelter, water, body autonomy, education, and basic health care. While it is necessary to view poverty through a multidimensional lens and identify how we are all poor in some way, each of these types of poverty brings its own struggles and feelings of hopelessness. Loving our neighbor as ourselves requires us to listen to others and think deeply about their situations while maintaining a perspective rooted in dignity and kinship with them.

So which is it? On the one hand, we are all poor. On the other hand, we do not want to minimize the suffering that comes with oppression and material deprivation. These arguments are in tension, but they do not negate each other. Maintaining both allows for an honest engagement with ourselves and others. Careful consideration of our own social position and that of others is a necessary foundational aspect of redemptive service.

Aboriginal leader Lilla Watson is credited with saying, "If you have come here to help me, you are wasting your time. But if you have come because your liberation is bound up with mine, then let us work together."[16] Joining in solidarity with the marginalized and acknowledging that we all benefit from the pursuit of shalom together is necessary before beginning a journey of effective redemptive service. Rather than seeing those we are serving as a different other whom we are trying to help, redemptive service engages in solidarity, fellowship, and mutuality. We share burdens as well as joys. We learn to see the strengths of others and weaknesses in ourselves.

16. Watson is widely credited with this saying, though sources indicate that she attributes its origin to a collaborative effort. See Theresa L. Petray, "Support vs. Solidarity: White Involvement in the Aboriginal Movement," *Social Alternatives* 29, no. 4 (2010): 69–72.

DISCUSSION QUESTIONS

1. What were the different social statuses of the characters in the good Samaritan story? How does social identity help us understand the parable?

2. In what times and settings have you been uncomfortable based on your social status? How did you handle that situation? Did anyone help you?

3. Create a list of explanations for poverty that you have heard and identify whether it is individualistic, fatalistic, or structural. Which explanations for poverty have you maintained? What has influenced you to subscribe to these explanations? Why is it important to think more broadly about these explanations and to consider all of them for redemptive service?

4. Describe the strengths and weaknesses of absolute and relative measures of poverty. Why do you think both are important?

5. Throughout this book, redemptive service is presented as service to others that promotes sustainable well-being and an increased quality of life for people while affirming the dignity and agency of those being served. Why might thinking about poverty through the lens of the multidimensional poverty index, which broadens the discussion of poverty to include more than economics, be useful for Christians who want to engage in work that is redemptive? Using the idea of a multidimensional view of poverty, what are some indicators that you might add?

FOR FURTHER READING

Desmond, Matthew. *Poverty, by America*. New York: Crown, 2023.

Edin, Kathryn J., and H. Luke Shaefer. *$2.00 a Day: Living on Almost Nothing in America*. Boston: Houghton Mifflin Harcourt, 2015.

Ehrenreich, Barbara. *Nickel and Dimed: On (Not) Getting By in America*. New York: Picador, 2011.

Rank, Mark R. *Confronting Poverty: Economic Hardship in the United States*. Los Angeles: Sage, 2021.

7

---•---

Relief

Short-Term Interventions as Redemptive Service

"Who is my neighbor?" This question prompts Jesus to tell the parable of the good Samaritan. And the actions of the good Samaritan show what it means to love our neighbors as ourselves. Loving our neighbors means seeing our neighbors' plight and acting to relieve their suffering. The Samaritan loved his neighbor by bandaging and cleaning his wounds, putting him on a donkey, and taking him to receive medical care. These actions represent a central aspect of redemptive service: offering immediate relief and care in a time of crisis.

Categorizing Interventions

This book has introduced redemptive service as a uniquely Christian activity that is intrinsic to following Christ. To effectively and ethically engage in redemptive service, it is important to understand the situations, people, and places we are seeking to help. In the previous chapter we conceptualized poverty from a variety of perspectives. In the next three chapters we offer a Christian perspective for understanding Christ's call to redemptive service for those who are in poverty—whatever form of poverty. These chapters focus on practical considerations when offering help to others. Short-term activities provide immediate care that solves a basic need right now: food pantries, homeless shelters, and disaster relief efforts. Ideally, people will not need to rely on these activities for long. Obsolescence (working yourself out of a job so that the work is no longer necessary) is the goal of any short-term or relief program. For a short-term project to make itself unnecessary, long-term programs often need to be implemented to fix what went wrong in the first place. Long-term programs, often referred to as development projects, seek to help people and communities become self-sufficient. In this chapter we look at short-term interventions, and in the following chapter we focus on long-term interventions.

"Give a person a fish and feed them for a day. Teach a person to fish and feed them for a lifetime." This saying alludes to short-term and long-term interventions. Giving a person a fish fills a short-term need by providing immediate help. Teaching a person to fish helps fulfill a long-term need by building self-sustainability. This proverb implies that short-term, immediate interventions are not as beneficial as long-term projects. But this is not true. When a person or community's system has broken down and outside help is essential, both short-term and long-term interventions are often necessary. In fact, they rely on each other. If a person is starving or does not have fishing gear, they are incapable of learning to fish.

Besides length of intervention (short term or long term), another important aspect to consider is the scale of the project. Project scale is important because micro-level work can directly benefit those who are being helped while macro-level projects can help prevent future problems from occurring. Services that help individuals or families are micro-level interventions, which are often seen in well-developed areas with populations that would benefit from outside assistance to meet basic needs. Micro-level projects can focus on short-term or long-term solutions. Food banks and homeless shelters are two common micro-level interventions that focus on meeting short-term needs. Housing projects like Habitat for Humanity or job-training projects are micro-level interventions that focus on meeting long-term needs. Habitat for Humanity and educational or vocational training programs are considered development initiatives.

Macro-level interventions focus on improving the general quality of life for communities or larger groups of people, typically in communities in which most people have reduced access to basic needs. These communities are found in countries all over the world, even the US, but most often in developing nations. The following table contains examples of short-term and long-term projects at the micro and macro levels:

**Short-Term and Long-Term Projects
at the Micro and Macro Levels**

	Micro Level	Macro Level
Short Term	Homeless shelter	Disaster relief
	Food pantry	Food aid
	Clothes distribution	
Long Term	Habitat for Humanity	Schools
	Job-training programs	Infrastructure building
	Adult literacy	Food co-op

Integrating Interventions

High-quality projects have some form of integration between short-term and long-term help for people and communities. In the fields of social work and nursing, the model for providing the best help is known as a continuum of care (CoC).[1] While a CoC will look different in the medical field than in social work, they both find ways to integrate care for a person or family. A CoC is a way of coordinating services for people from short-term, immediate needs through long-term self-sufficiency. For example, in the field of housing, applying the CoC model means that a person will receive immediate shelter but also have a coordinated care system to help them eventually move from the shelter to stable housing.[2] This can, and often does, take years. The result is a long-term solution.

For Christians who want to engage in redemptive service, coordinating long-term and short-term care can help determine which types of projects are worth contributing time and money toward. Finding the existing system of care in a community and contributing to those efforts maximizes the positive impact of resources. Many communities in the US already have a network of service providers along the CoC. These agencies coordinate their efforts to address both long-term and short-term needs in the community. These agencies are also staffed by people with comprehensive knowledge of the needs of the community. Professional social workers know which areas should be receiving services, as well as which groups are being missed. They know how to distribute resources where the need is highest.

1. Merry McBryde-Foster and Toni Allen, "The Continuum of Care: A Concept Development Study," *Journal of Advanced Nursing* 50, no. 6 (2005): 624–32.
2. Yin-Ling Irene Wong, Jung Min Park, and Howard Nemon, "Homeless Service Delivery in the Context of Continuum of Care," *Administration in Social Work* 30, no. 1 (2006): 67–94.

To put this into perspective, let's use a vital concern in many communities in the fall and winter: coat drives. When the weather gets cold, people need coats and other cold-weather gear. Many churches start collecting coats and other goods in their church lobbies. On the whole, this is valuable; it is an example of a short-term micro-level project that provides necessary help. As temperatures drop, conditions become life threatening for people who spend significant parts of their days and nights outside. There is a clear need for coats, blankets, socks, and hats to protect people from the harsh weather. Churches that engage in this activity often know that systems of distribution have already been developed by local agencies such as the Salvation Army. A church that wants to efficiently coordinate efforts to meet needs in the community will work with these agencies, funneling their donated resources to those agencies so those organizations can be responsible for distribution. The professionals who work in these agencies know where the needs are and how to most effectively meet those needs. In this example of cold-weather gear distribution, some people experiencing homelessness congregate in obvious places, but a significant portion of the population is hidden. The professionals, like those who work at Salvation Army, who have developed trust in the community are better able to access hidden populations.

Well-meaning churches that are gathering coats for their coat drive might understandably want to dispense those items themselves. Without the accumulated knowledge of distribution, they might simply distribute those items in the visible locations where people experiencing homelessness are known to gather. While this does provide goods to a few people, it misses the hidden groups. And when multiple organizations engage in coat drives and distribute their items to those people who are congregated in the most visible places, it is not uncommon for certain areas to be oversaturated with goods while other areas remain completely neglected. Such churches or organizations have noble intentions, but failure to coordinate the distribution efforts with a local service provider can significantly limit benefits.

Short-term projects are a necessary facet of redemptive service. When people are lacking immediate needs such as food, water, shelter, and warm clothes, it seems cruel to withhold those. There are obvious limitations to focusing on only this type of care. Serving communities exclusively in this way does not offer the long-term solutions that are key elements of the redemptive part of redemptive service. Disaster relief offers a model of intervention that helps showcase how both short-term and long-term projects are necessary.

Disaster Relief

Which natural disasters does your hometown have to prepare for? Do you live in a place that is prone to tornadoes, hurricanes, or earthquakes? Being at risk from these types of major natural disasters is a common human experience. While some places might be more vulnerable to certain natural disasters, most places have some type of emergency for which the residents need to prepare. Every year natural disasters decimate communities and neighborhoods. When these extreme events hit, church members are often the first to rally volunteers and donations to help those who are hurting.

Disaster relief takes place at both the macro and micro levels. When buildings and infrastructure are destroyed, whole communities are affected, and large numbers of workers are sent and dollars are spent on rebuilding efforts. Likewise, people whose homes and livelihoods have been disrupted need micro-level help. Food distribution, emergency shelters, water access, and sanitation are often at the forefront of these micro-level relief efforts.

Areas that are frequently affected might have safety protocols in place. These preparations can minimize the problems before the event happens. But preparations can only mitigate the impact. Nothing can prevent an earthquake or tornado. Disruptions to people's lives and livelihoods are inevitable. Effective disaster management response requires an understanding of the cycle of mitigation, preparation, response, and recovery.[3] Prepared communities recover faster, and so prevention and mitigation strategies are necessary for disaster relief.

Most redemptive service activities focus on the response portion of the disaster life cycle. When the crisis occurs, people in churches display empathy and run toward the crisis, embodying the Samaritan by helping their neighbor. If church members cannot go themselves, a multitude of Christian organizations have the infrastructure and mission to help. Major organizations such as the Red Cross, World Vision, Samaritan's Purse, and the Salvation Army engage in relief activities. To understand the role of the church in redemptive service and disaster relief, we now explore a specific example.

3. Richard Haigh, *Disaster Management Lifecycle* (Manchester, UK: Centre for Disaster Resilience, n.d.). Haigh presents a circular disaster cycle in which response is not the beginning. This conceptualization challenges popular notions of a typology of disaster-rehabilitation-relief in the international aid community. François Audet argues that this common continuum does more harm than good as it does not account for the mitigation and sustainability that precede relief. See Audet, "From Disaster Relief to Development Assistance: Why Simple Solutions Don't Work," *International Journal* 70, no. 1 (March 2015): 110–18.

Hurricane Katrina: A Disaster Relief Example

On August 29, 2005, Hurricane Katrina hit the city of New Orleans, Louisiana. New Orleans was the hardest hit by Katrina, but it was not the only place that the storm devastated. In all, Katrina took the lives of 1,836 people and caused more than $86 billion in damage (as of 2007 estimates).[4] Between one and two million people were displaced by the storm.[5] People around the world wondered how the US, a political and economic leader, could be so devastated by a hurricane. Immediate relief was desperately warranted.

Christians around the country responded. The Southern Baptist Convention, one of the largest evangelical dominations in the US, reported that their relief efforts for the survivors of Katrina constituted the largest response their denomination had ever mobilized. More than one thousand church members and one hundred mobile disaster relief units went to Louisiana, Mississippi, Georgia, and Alabama to help with cleanup efforts.[6] Many other Christian organizations were also involved in relief efforts. Looking at the Christian response to Katrina shows how the church is engaging in relief in meaningful ways. Measured by size and scope of response alone, it would seem that relief efforts for the devastation brought by Katrina is a story of relief done well. Much good was done by the people and organizations who went to the affected areas. Yet even though there is much to celebrate regarding the church's response to Katrina, looking closer points to some lessons on how to improve relief efforts. Self-reflection is critical when engaging in redemptive service at every level (relief, development, and advocacy). We can always reflect on our efforts and learn how to make them more effective in the future.

Disaster Relief Goals

Common objectives drive relief efforts regardless of the type of disaster. Frederick Cuny presents three primary goals of relief efforts: "(1) reduce or avoid the human, physical, and economic losses suffered by individuals, by the society, and by the country at large; (2) reduce personal suffering; and

4. Nicolas A. Valcik and Paul E. Tracy, *Case Studies in Disaster Response and Emergency Management* (Boca Raton, FL: CRC Press, 2013), 51–56.

5. Chester W. Hartman and Gregory D. Squires, eds., *There Is No Such Thing as a Natural Disaster: Race, Class, and Hurricane Katrina* (New York: Taylor & Francis, 2006), 1.

6. Tim Yarbrough, "Response to Katrina Largest Ever for Southern Baptists," Baptist Press News, 2005, https://web.archive.org/web/20080224142016/http://www.bpnews.net/bpnews.asp?ID=21495.

(3) speed recovery."[7] These can be applied to natural disasters or broad-scale disruptions such as global pandemics. Reducing losses and suffering while speeding up recovery are primary goals.

REDUCE OR AVOID LOSSES

Reducing or avoiding losses is consistent with Richard Haigh's life cycle of disaster management, which incorporates preparedness and mitigation. In New Orleans, Katrina itself was not directly responsible for the major damage to the city. Rather, the levees and floodwalls that made up the mitigation infrastructure were eroded and insufficient in materials, depth, and strength to support the inundation of water from the hurricane's storm surge.[8]

Relief begins before a crisis even occurs, with preparation and mitigation. Having a mindset of preparation and awareness of structural vulnerability gives Christians practical ways to engage in redemptive service. In our own neighborhoods and communities, we know the natural disasters for which we need to prepare. But we also have to think about who in our community is at the greatest risk of hardship. Take, for instance, two families living in neighboring houses, only one of which has a subterranean basement. The family with the basement could offer hospitality and refuge to their neighbors during tornado warnings. This shows the love of Jesus, and it is a mitigation strategy for relief. While a tornado might harm the house, safeguarding our neighbors' lives is of primary importance, even if we might not get along with our neighbors.

The definition of "neighbor" could also be extended more broadly and focus on towns. Some neighborhoods are at greater risk of damage from disasters because of a variety of factors, such as having older houses in need of repair that are more likely to be damaged. Imagine the impact that churches could have in their communities if church members adopted a neighborly attitude toward the people in those neighborhoods in which the built environments (schools, hospitals, houses, churches, sewage and septic systems, water and plumbing, cell towers, roads, sidewalks, high-speed

---

7. Frederick C. Cuny, "Introduction to Disaster Management Lesson 1: The Scope of Disaster Management," *Prehospital and Disaster Medicine* 7, no. 4 (1992): 400–409.

8. No amount of preparation can fully mitigate extreme weather events. But Katrina had weakened to a Category 3 storm when it hit on August 29. Reasonable preparations would have been strong enough to withstand winds and storm surge from such a weakened storm. Shirley Laska and Betty Hearn Morrow, "Social Vulnerabilities and Hurricane Katrina: An Unnatural Disaster in New Orleans," *Marine Technology Society Journal* 40, no. 4 (2006).

internet, etc.) have less structural resilience. These homes are more vulnerable to damage from severe weather events. Churches could consider these
vulnerabilities at the beginning of the heavy weather season and begin
their relief efforts before disasters occur. For example, at the beginning
of hurricane season, hurricane emergency kits could be assembled and
distributed to those who are at risk. In areas where cold weather can be
deadly, cold-weather kits can help in the event of power loss, which during
the winter could be life threatening if houses are not sufficiently insulated.
Relief starts with preparation.

REDUCE PERSONAL SUFFERING

The second objective for disaster relief that Cuny presents is to reduce
personal suffering. Reducing personal suffering takes on many forms.
These are the actions that typically come to mind when we think about
disaster relief: immediate medical help, search and rescue efforts, food,
housing, clothing, and basic human necessities. Often, the first action
that needs to be taken when natural disasters occur is to get people out
of immediate danger.

Reducing personal suffering can last longer than the immediate crisis.
Often, disasters impact every aspect of people's lives, such that they need
help and support for days, weeks, or even longer. This aid comes in the
form of shelter, drinkable water, food, sanitation, health care, and a variety of other physical needs that displaced people have. With Hurricane
Katrina relief efforts, thousands of people in New Orleans took shelter
in the Superdome, a football stadium. Referred to as a "shelter of last
resort," the Superdome possessed insufficient services for the people who
stayed there. People had limited access to food, water, sanitation, privacy,
and other needs, like a place to sleep. When the storm passed, people
were relocated from the Superdome to shelters around the country while
waiting for reconstruction efforts. Some people returned to their homes;
others never did.

Besides physical needs, there are emotional and spiritual needs for
people whose lives have just been thrown into chaos. Reducing personal
suffering encompasses emotional suffering as well. Trauma-informed mental health care is a vital part of this endeavor. Likewise, giving attention to
the spiritual lives of people helps them begin to cope with their suffering.
The people who were displaced from New Orleans after Katrina were
sent to shelters all over the US. For these displaced people, prayer often

became a primary, effective coping mechanism.[9] The hope that comes from connecting to God and the fellowship of other believers can help people begin to recover.

Reducing suffering for people after a disaster requires multidimensional responses when viewed as redemptive service. In this context, prayer that helps people connect to God and reminds them of the hope that lies in a relationship with Jesus is vastly important, and the church is uniquely prepared to offer it. But this spiritual intervention does not replace practical physical matters. People need safe places to live and sleep. Physical needs cannot be ignored for an emphasis on the spiritual.

We close this section with an example of relief from Kenya in the 1980s. An American missionary couple named Bob and Murriell McCulley were living in Kenya. They had been there for about seventeen years building a network of small rural churches throughout the countryside, primarily working with Masai people, as they were able to speak both Swahili and Maa. When a famine came to Kenya, one of the Kenyan pastors that the McCulleys worked with was quoted in a newspaper article, lamenting that "the children in his village were dying and the church was unable to intervene."[10] Bob traveled to Nairobi and spoke with anyone who would listen to him about the problem. Finally, he was invited to an interagency meeting at the United Nations. Because the McCulleys had active networks with the rural villages, they had the infrastructure to lead and manage the food distribution programs of the United Nations Food and Agricultural Organization and the United States Agency for International Development. Murriell had trained in the US as a nurse, and the couple knew a pediatrician in the area who worked closely with the distribution efforts.

The churches the McCulleys had built were used to store corn, beans, and vegetable oil. While they had the most well-developed network in the region, there were still villages that needed food distribution centers and that did not have churches, so distribution centers were built. In the end, the lament of the pastor was answered, and the church was able to help the hungry in that region. Through this endeavor, new churches were formed and existing churches grew. Feeding the hungry and praying for the sick is powerful work, building the kingdom of God. But the work that Bob and

9. Patric R. Spence, Kenneth A. Lachlan, and Jennifer M. Burke, "Adjusting to Uncertainty: Coping Strategies among the Displaced after Hurricane Katrina," *Sociological Spectrum* 27, no. 6 (2007): 653–78.

10. Bob McCulley and Murriell McCulley, *Faithful: Stories of Living with Our Incredibly Faithful God* (Springfield, MO: Africa's Hope, 2019), 175–81.

Murriell did was not without criticism. In telling the story, Bob writes, "One well-meaning friend accosted me with the charge that we had abandoned the 'best' (preaching the gospel) for the 'good' (feeding the hungry)." Now, many years after the famine ended and rains have returned to rural Kenya, there are still vibrant churches at the former distribution sites. In relief efforts of redemptive service, the "best" and the "good" are not in conflict with one another. Feeding people and praying for them go together. On the one hand, prayers without food or other practical interventions seem hollow to those who are suffering. On the other hand, providing practical interventions without also offering (but not requiring) spiritual connections like prayer does not provide the hope and connection that makes redemptive service distinctive from secular endeavors. In redemptive service, practical and spiritual responses to crises rely on each other.

SPEEDY RECOVERY

The third stage of disaster relief in redemptive service is working for a speedy recovery. This relief effort is designed to be short term. A speedy recovery helps people get back to their homes, communities, and lives as quickly as possible. When disasters are all-encompassing, recovery must occur at every level of a community. The recovery must take place in the environment, institutions, economies, personal and social lives, and the built environments of a community.[11] While it is outside the scope of this chapter to discuss each of these types of recovery in depth, it is important to acknowledge how wide-ranging and interconnected these types of recovery are. For example, recovery of built environments includes repairing roads, houses, electrical systems, public buildings, stores/restaurants, water, internet, and so much more. Rebuilding these physical structures is necessary if the economy of a community is going to recover. For some disasters, it takes years for a community to truly recover.

The extent of disruption from a disaster is measured in the time it takes for a full and substantive recovery. When a disaster is getting a lot of attention on the news, people are motivated to volunteer time and effort to aid relief and recovery efforts. Months and years after the event, though, when the world has moved on to another crisis, the people who were affected are still working on the rebuilding efforts but often doing so on their own.

---

11. These are not the only types of disaster recovery, but they cover most of the forms. More information about recovery, including over twenty models of disaster recovery, can be found in Ian Davis and David Alexander, *Recovery from Disaster* (New York: Routledge, 2016).

Ten years after Katrina hit New Orleans, the US Department of Housing and Urban Development (HUD) was still providing aid in the form of housing redevelopment, infrastructure rebuilding, tourism development, and other projects.[12] As beneficial as HUD was, God is more effective. His resources are not finite, and he does not have to cut assistance in one area to address another crisis elsewhere. He stays and works with us to rebuild broken places for as long as we need it. Finishing a job is imperative for doing effective relief and recovery work.

Redemptive service also involves helping people cope with disruption and a recovery process that could take years. In the aftermath of Katrina, prayer was found to help people reduce stress and cope with loss.[13] Redemptive service that helps others in the name of Jesus—offering not only physical and practical help but also the hope of communion with our Savior through prayer—can truly be helpful to people and communities.

When looking at redemptive service, disaster relief is not so dissimilar from the types of care discussed earlier in the chapter. Reducing or avoiding losses, reducing personal suffering, and preparing for a speedy recovery are important stages of disaster relief that can also be applied to other forms of short-term help discussed in this chapter. For example, those who are homeless, whatever the reason, need these three aspects of relief just as much as a community devastated by a hurricane does.

Practical Suggestions for Short-Term Volunteers

Christians wanting to do the work of redemptive service often focus on short-term care. We have focused thus far on important considerations of effective short-term projects. Volunteers should identify projects that are run by locals within a community and that are networked with others in a continuum of care, which will lead to the best outcomes. Likewise, with relief efforts, the work begins by recognizing the most important needs and vulnerabilities. Whatever type of short-term intervention—food distribution, homeless shelter, or disaster relief—there are some important actions to avoid and others to adopt to do this work well.

First, when volunteering for a short-term intervention, treat the volunteer work as if it were a paid position. Most often, professionals are

12. Todd M. Richardson, "A Look Back at Hurricane Katrina," PD&R Edge, September 21, 2021, https://www.huduser.gov/portal/pdredge/pdr-edge-frm-asst-sec-092121.html.
13. Spence, Lachlan, and Burke, "Adjusting to Uncertainty," 671–72.

leading the projects and have put a considerable amount of effort into ensuring their effectiveness. Professional staff at a nonprofit organization will become frustrated with unreliable volunteers. Service providers who rely on volunteer support often struggle because unpaid workers do not seem to take the job seriously. While it might be inappropriate to wear business attire while stocking a food pantry, that does not mean that behaving professionally is unimportant. For example, when doing food distribution service, acting professionally means showing up early for the shift, paying close attention to training provided by the staff, and doing tasks as if being paid for them. A volunteer with a haughty attitude reflects poorly on the work being done. Treating people with kindness and working hard are important aspects of volunteering.

A second consideration is motivation for the work. People volunteer at nonprofits for a variety of reasons. Some people are motivated by generosity and altruism,[14] while others see job potential and an opportunity to add to their résumé.[15] College students often volunteer to fulfill a service requirement in order to graduate. Whether the motivations are intrinsic or extrinsic, serving well begins with being honest about why we are volunteering. Our motivations will affect how we work. Internal motivations are a noble reason to engage in this work, but if they are based on emotions, the work will stop being interesting when the emotions fade. Likewise, if a person is only trying to meet a graduation requirement and does not believe in the work, they might be unengaged or even resentful of being required to work without compensation. Whatever we do, we must see the work as being done for the Lord. Our work is an act of worship, even when it is not glamorous.

Matthew 25 says that whatever we do to help those who are suffering, we do for Jesus. The work needs to reflect Jesus as the recipient of our efforts. With food preparation, for example, taking this attitude can inform the type of food that is purchased and prepared. Perhaps one general rule would be to purchase and prepare food for others that we ourselves would be willing to eat or serve to our loved ones. If we are using goods

14. Marisa R. Ferreira, Joao F. Proenca, and Teresa Proenca, "Motivations and Management Factors of Volunteer Work in Nonprofit Organisations: A Literature Review," in *Eighth International Congress of the International Association on Public and Nonprofit Marketing* (Eighth International Congress of the International Association on Public and Nonprofit Marketing, 2009).

15. Takashi Yamashita, Jennifer R. Keene, Chi-Jung Lu, and Dawn C. Carr, "Underlying Motivations of Volunteering across Life Stages: A Study of Volunteers in Nonprofit Organizations in Nevada," *Journal of Applied Gerontology* 38, no. 2 (2019): 207–31.

for others that are lower quality than the goods we consume ourselves, are we loving them the way we would love Jesus? Whatever the pragmatic situation, redemptive service is distinct from secular work in its motivations. Taking Jesus at his word, service is a partnership with our Savior to mend the world's brokenness.

Third, it is vital to be attentive to the impact of our work. The most effective volunteers are motivated by the desire to help people in a broken world. Unfortunately, intent alone is not sufficient. Well-meaning people who are genuinely motivated by kindness might end up doing more harm than good. We have to distinguish *intent* from *impact*. A striking example of this was a young woman from Virginia who went to Jinja, Uganda, to start a Christian nonprofit that worked with children and babies. The young woman did not have medical training, nor did she hire doctors in her organization. Still, she administered medical care herself to undernourished babies and children who were brought to her, rather than finding them beds in a local facility that could provide appropriate care. More than one hundred children died receiving services.[16] Despite her noble intent, this young woman devastated the families of those children. Good intentions will not restore those families. When engaging in redemptive service, it is necessary to be mindful of both intent and impact.

Though there are many devastating stories of redemptive service efforts gone wrong, there are also many stories of these efforts being successful. The McCulleys are a notable example of this work done well. Likewise, social workers in communities throughout the US are doing quiet, often thankless, work to help people find housing, food, medical care, and other basic necessities. With care and consideration, the work of compassion can be truly redemptive.

DISCUSSION QUESTIONS

1. Would you rather be the one getting free food or giving free food? Why?
2. Why is it necessary to "give a fish" (meet short-term needs) before "teaching to fish" (address long-term goals)?

16. Whitney Hammel Anny, "White Saviorism: Lessons Learned and Continued Reflections," in *A Scientific Framework for Compassion and Social Justice: Lessons in Applied Behavior Analysis*, ed. Jacob A. Sadavoy and Michelle L. Zube, 309–14 (New York: Routledge, 2021).

3. Why might services need to be integrated across short-term and long-term goals in order for the benefits to be maximized?

4. The key elements of disaster relief are reducing or avoiding loss, reducing personal suffering, and promoting a speedy recovery. Which of these three have you participated in, or which would you be most interested in if a disaster happened near you?

5. The chapter closed by discussing behaviors to avoid when volunteering. While most of these might seem like common sense, do you think that nonprofit organizations and service providers struggle with substandard work from volunteers? Why might this be?

6. How would you explain the difference between *impact* and *intent* in redemptive service? Is working with selfish intent but having a positive impact more desirable than working from good intentions but ultimately doing harm? Why or why not?

FOR FURTHER READING

Corbett, Steve, and Brian Fikkert. *When Helping Hurts: How to Alleviate Poverty without Hurting the Poor . . . and Yourself.* Chicago: Moody, 2014.

Lupton, Robert D. *Toxic Charity: How Churches and Charities Hurt Those They Help (And How to Reverse It).* New York: HarperOne, 2011.

Scales, T. Laine, and Michael S. Kelly, eds. *Christianity and Social Work: Readings on the Integration of Christian Faith and Social Work Practice*, 6th ed. (Botsford, CT: North American Association of Christians in Social Work, 2020).

8

Development

Long-Term Interventions as Redemptive Service

Having focused on short-term interventions and the importance of meeting basic needs in the previous chapter, in this chapter we focus primarily on long-term interventions that seek to bring about change and build the abilities of people groups. The goal of most development initiatives is poverty alleviation. Poverty and economic isolation can be found in communities everywhere. As mentioned in chapter 6, narrowly focusing on economics can be limiting, and yet economic poverty often contributes to the problems that developers are trying to address.

Defined

In this chapter we present four types of development. Development often targets macro-level changes; however, there certainly are micro-level interventions that integrate into the overall process. Development is also both a process and an outcome.[1]

Development is a process that seeks to enhance a group's ability to act collectively for themselves. When performed well, development is not

1. Rhonda Phillips and Robert H. Pittman, "A Framework for Community and Economic Development," in *An Introduction to Community Development*, ed. Rhonda Phillips and Robert H. Pittman, 25–43 (New York: Routledge, 2014).

something done *to* people. Rather, it is done *with* people. As with relief, one goal of many development initiatives is obsolescence. With development, though, obsolescence does not mean that whatever problems a community faces are necessarily fixed. Rather, obsolescence means that the people no longer need outside intervention. They can work together to fix problems themselves.

Development is also an outcome of actions that are implemented for improvement in a community, whether spiritual, physical, environmental, cultural, social, political, economic, or other. Development is closely tied to long-term redemptive service that works with people to bring healing. Development projects often identify places of brokenness in communities and creatively work with community members to fix broken systems or to implement new systems that provide long-term solutions. Returning to the fishing adage, development is more like the long-term solution of teaching a person to fish. By learning to fish, that person has developed capacities and skills. Their personal freedom is enhanced. What's more, they can teach others in their community, even their children, to fish. The problem of hunger is addressed not just for that person but for anyone that person can share knowledge with.

Types of Development

The word "development" is widely used in nonprofit and international circles, even to label and differentiate countries. Some countries or regions (like Western Europe) are considered to be "developed." The "developed world" refers to countries that have achieved some measure of economic self-sufficiency. Other countries, called "developing," are viewed as needing outside help to achieve the same progress as the "developed" nations. Depending on the context, "development" can mean very different things.

One type of development is economic development. This conceptualization emerged in the 1940s after the economic devastation of World War II. The world had just endured two massive wars in a short period of time. Nations came together with the purpose of helping each other meet needs and develop economic interdependence to prevent another world war. W. W. Rostow's theory of modernization provides a typology of countries based on their level of industrialization and type of economic output. In this model, development refers to a nation's ability to meet its own production needs through either industrialization within that country or importation from other countries. In this case, a developed nation has high mass consumption, with strong levels of production as well as consumer demand. The US, South Korea, Japan, France, and Germany, among others, fall into this category. On the other end of the spectrum are countries with elevated levels of poverty. Examples include Yemen, Liberia, and Afghanistan. Gross domestic product (GDP) determines where a country falls in the continuum of economic development. The World Bank uses GDP to classify countries along these lines for the purpose of funding development initiatives to alleviate poverty. The goal of many of the projects funded by the World Bank is to increase GDP.

Linking development with GDP is a macroeconomic approach. Proponents of economic development also take a microeconomic approach that focuses on the economic independence of individual families. One popular iteration of this approach is microlending programs that provide funds for individuals or small groups to start businesses and grow toward economic independence. Muhammad Yunus and his organization Grameen Bank in Bangladesh popularized microcredit. Yunus won a Nobel Prize for his work with microlending, which has been widely adopted by nonprofit organizations all over the world as a tool of poverty alleviation at the individual level. Microfinance or microlending programs tend to prioritize lending to women as a way of empowerment. While these programs have helped many people, some analysts have argued that they have failed to live up to their promise in the big picture. Individual families might have more money to use on food and education, but this does not help whole communities to be lifted out of poverty. Likewise, a household view of economic success might not fit with the cultural context of many of the people who benefit from microcredit.[2] Another problem is that some microlending organizations charge interest in the repayment of the loans, profiting from the poorest people in the world. Finally, households can be left worse off when they take a loan but cannot repay it.[3] While microcredit is a promising practice of development at the household level, it has had some problems that suggest it may not be the best way to help.

Whether at the macro or micro level, viewing development as economic independence has some strengths and weaknesses. Because money is central to how the world operates, it makes certain sense to link economic

2. Philip McMichael, *Development and Social Change: A Global Perspective*, 6th ed. (Los Angeles: SAGE, 2017), 169, 225.

3. Anu Muhammad, "Grameen and Microcredit: A Tale of Corporate Success," *Economic and Political Weekly* (2009): 35–42.

status with outcomes such as access to schools, sufficient food, and medical services. Indeed, it takes money to build schools or to provide medical care. Yet economist and philosopher Amartya Sen challenged the idea of a direct link between GDP and development. Beginning his work with famine relief in India, Sen wrote in his book *Development as Freedom* that the famine in India was a problem of policy not plenty.[4] Speculations about scarcity led to policies that misappropriated resources, leaving those who were poor without food. For Sen, development means increasing people's capacity to choose for themselves. He argues that democratic governance and a free press are necessary for equitable systems.

Sen popularized a more nuanced conceptualization of development with the notion of human development. He worked with the United Nations Development Program to create the human development index, which looks at quality of life globally. While economic outcomes are important, they are not the only measure. Also included in human development are measures of education and health outcomes. Human development focuses on overall measures of quality of life. Narrowly focusing on production is reductionistic; it is possible to have increases in quality of life without increases in economic production. Economic development says that making more money will lead to better schools. The human development approach instead says that providing better schools and hospitals will improve people's lives and give them more freedom to choose. If they want to engage in economic systems and make more money, they will have the freedom to do so. However, that will not be forced on them. Sen says that development should give people the freedom to make those choices for themselves. He contrasts a person who is starving with a person who is fasting for religious or health reasons. In both cases, the person's body is deprived of food. The key difference is the freedom to choose. The fasting person has access to food but chooses not to eat it, while the starving person would eat if given the opportunity. Sen's work has driven much of the effort of the United Nations over the past three decades.

A third conceptual understanding of development is sustainable development. Sen's work in human development has been refined by some who claim that it does not include measures of environmental sustainability. People cannot be separated from the places they inhabit. Currently, most global development projects focus on sustainable development, which refers to any help or change that will give as much to the systems as it takes

4. Amartya Sen, *Development as Freedom* (New York: Knopf, 1999).

so that the systems will not deplete themselves. Rostow's modernization system, which links development to consumption, does not consider the impact on the environment. In many places that are considered "developed," the environment cannot sustain the lifestyle of the people who live there, which is called the "development paradox."[5] The United States is one example of the development paradox. If every country consumed resources at the rate of the US and other developed nations, the earth's resources would be depleted. While the US and other developed nations have achieved high material quality of life, many scientists argue for a re-alignment of resources if we want to maintain current standards of living for future generations.[6] When looking at nations that are still in the process of developing, the international community sees the opportunity to approach issues of development and poverty alleviation without adopting the model of the West. The United Nations Development Program uses the sustainable development goals (SDGs) that drive development initiatives.[7] These goals situate people's quality of life and economic outcomes in their environments. Any solution has to be a solution for the entire system.

Community Development

Community development is a practical implementation of economic development, human development, or sustainable development. It is inherently practical in nature. Community development initiatives will often be designed from an ideological perspective of economic, human, or sustainable development. Often, discussions of development imply an international context. But development projects in the US are often called "community development." These projects happen in almost every community, as improvement is possible everywhere. Note, however, that community development initiatives are also found across the globe. Parsing community development from economic, human, and sustainable development

5. Philip McMichael and Heloise Weber, *Development and Social Change*, 7th ed. (Los Angeles: SAGE, 2020), 16–17, 23.

6. Julia K. Steinberger, William F. Lamb, and Marco Sakai, "Your Money or Your Life? The Carbon-Development Paradox," *Environmental Research Letters* 15, no. 4 (2020): 044016.

7. Much discussion of development in the international community follows the model presented by the United Nations Development Program. These sustainable development goals (SDGs) combine human development with environmental concerns for long-term, sustainable development. Additionally, the SDGs attempt to remain sufficiently robust as to be implemented in ways that are culturally relevant to global nations. To learn more, see "Sustainable Development Goals," United Nations Development Program, https://www.undp.org/sustainable-development-goals.

is somewhat artificial, as those are just different types of community de-velopment. One difference between community development and other types of development is scale. Community development initiatives try to improve communities or neighborhoods. They implement change between the micro-level change for individual families and the macro-level change of nations. For the remainder of this chapter, we use the terms "commu-nity development" and "development" interchangeably. They both refer to community development initiatives and apply to both international and domestic settings.

Community development initiatives focus on people, resources, chal-lenges, and structures within communities. They vary based on the ap-proaches, beliefs, and training of the people who undertake them, as well as the type of initiative. Some seek to increase access to housing. Others might look at food access, studying food insecurity, cost of foods, whether a grocery store selling fresh produce exists within a mile, and how many households in that area are without transportation. Initiatives might focus on education, schools, tutoring, adult professional training, adult literacy, English classes, or any number of ways to increase the skills, knowledge, and capacities of community members. Urban and rural community development also can take different forms. Transpor-tation, for example, is much different in densely populated cities with public transportation than in rural places, where people are spread apart and transportation can be a significant barrier to food, work, health care, and other resources. Each initiative is tailored to help people and address barriers to success.

Principles of Development

In the first part of this chapter we provided a brief history of international development and how it has been conceptualized for the past eighty years, and we raised concerns about various strategies. For example, micro-lending programs are still popular. Before working with or supporting an organization that does microlending, though, we should be aware of the potential damage that they do. What are the long-term effects on the people who receive loans? What percentage do not repay the loans? What happens to those who were already resource-strained and now have to repay a loan that was intended to help? These questions can help evaluate a program of this type to see whether it is consistent with redemptive service.

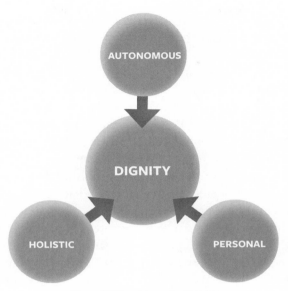

Figure 8.1 Development principles

Redemptive service is a way of thinking about helping others. The principles of development should guide redemptive service. Figure 8.1 shows a model of development principles that align with redemptive service. These principles are helpful in building programs that will benefit the people who are being served. This model can likewise be used to evaluate strengths and areas of growth for programs that are already in progress.

Autonomous

Autonomy is the idea that the people being served are the foundation of any program; they have ownership and influence over the program as it is being developed; and their activity and direction fuel the project execution and completion. Their autonomy is an important priority in development projects. If community members are not involved in the ideas and project development, if they are not involved in the project implementation, and if their ultimate control over the project is not the long-term goal, then the project does not promote the autonomy of the people. Centering the community at every step of the development initiative, giving them control over the goals as well as the activities, is called participatory community development. A participatory approach is development done *with* a community rather than *for* a community.

A participatory approach contrasts with how community development has largely been done since the 1940s. Traditionally, community development has taken a top-down approach. The United Nations' sustainable development goals, for example, seek to include individual communities; but being a large, multilateral organization, they are emblematic of a top-down vision of development. When outsiders diagnose problems in a community and determine how to fix them, these ideas will often not fit with the goals, needs, and culture of the people living there. This top-down, outside-in approach yields limited benefits.

Projects that ignore cultural contexts typically are not successful. Every community has its own culture with values, beliefs, and norms, yet these norms are difficult for outsiders to ascertain. They become barriers to development initiatives. In a participatory approach, local stakeholders—the people who make up the community—are involved and perhaps even directing the initiative. They can interpret the project within their cultural context, consistent with their cultural values, beliefs, and norms. Using this approach, the initiative is more likely to be relevant to the people and lead to sustainable, lasting change.[8] In a successful project, the outsiders leave and the communities continue to reap the benefits of the work.

Redemptive service means going to others and helping when something is broken. A participatory approach does not blame the people for the brokenness. Nor do the ones offering help, who do not experience brokenness in that way, assume they have all the problems figured out. Everyone is broken in some way, and we seek to help others because of the brokenness we've also experienced in our lives. If someone believes they have it all together, they will not have the humility to look at the situation of those being helped, understand their contexts, and partner with them, allowing them to own the service. Autonomy as a principle requires that those who are serving be aware of their tendency to consider themselves better than those being served. Those doing redemptive service should view themselves and others from a place of humility and be willing to learn from those whom they are serving, acknowledging that the community members are the experts in their context.

Maintaining autonomy keeps the participants and the community central to the work. In the 1970s, sociologist Herbert Gans wrote a scathing article about how poverty is treated in contemporary society. Gans

8. Krittinee Nuttavuthisit, Pavitra Jindahra, and Pattarawan Prasarnphanich, "Participatory Community Development: Evidence from Thailand," *Community Development Journal* 50, no. 1 (2015): 55–70.

argues that poverty has not been alleviated because it benefits those in the dominant groups.[9] One of the "positive" functions of poverty that Gans discusses is the creation and maintenance of the human service industry (social workers, homeless shelters, food banks, etc.), which provides jobs and career opportunities for people who are not in poverty. According to Gans' critique, any development organization whose goal is not autonomy for those being served is ultimately feeding itself and its own interests. While we cannot blame poverty on the workers and organizations that are at the forefront of helping people (often at great cost to themselves), Gans' criticism is instructive as a way to refine and perfect development initiatives and to center people and communities in projects, processes, and outcomes. This criticism questions whether development initiatives are altruistic or self-interested. Affirming the autonomy of those who are in need is a protection against Gans' critique.

By building the capacities of people in communities, the interests of the community are centered. Developers work themselves out of a job. In this way, development is both a process and an outcome, which the participatory approach emphasizes.[10] As a process, autonomy emphasizes that the project will be informed, if not led, by the community members themselves. As an outcome, autonomy highlights the temporary nature of the outside support. By prioritizing autonomy, even a development project that takes decades to finish has an end goal of a stable community that no longer relies on outside interventions.

Holistic

Redemptive service is also holistic. A holistic approach to development realizes that people and societies operate in systems. A community thrives when all of the systems are working well: education, health care, justice, food, infrastructure, government, religion, economics, housing, and more. A holistic approach to community development avoids focusing on just one of these areas. While nonprofit organizations might specialize in one, many collaborate across different systems to maximize the benefit to the people they serve. Jane Addams and Hull House in Chicago, which was founded in 1889, is one example of a holistic approach to community development.

9. Herbert J. Gans, "The Positive Functions of Poverty," *American Journal of Sociology* 78, no. 2 (1972): 275–89.

10. Rhonda Phillips and Robert H. Pittman, "A Framework for Community and Economic Development," in Phillips and Pittman, *Introduction to Community Development*, 25–43.

Jane Addams was unique in that she believed poverty alleviation could not happen without living with the community she served. She bought space in an impoverished area and slowly began to build trust among the neighborhood members. The programs that she put into place addressed systemic issues. Services offered to the residents by Hull House included housing, job training, food distribution, and building a public park.[11]

Holistic development highlights the effects of brokenness on the whole system, while showing that people and communities are not defined solely by whatever problem exists in their system. If a person breaks an arm, they go to the doctor and get it set in a cast, but their whole identity is not determined by the broken arm. They still go to work or school. They still engage in everyday activities. If this person is an athlete, they must take a break from sports, but even injured athletes might still wear their uniform and cheer from the sidelines. They can certainly still spend time with friends or loved ones. They are still capable of using their mind in work or school. They still have athletic capacity, though it is temporarily dormant. They can still reach out and be a friend. The broken arm affects them, but it does not define them.

It is important that we think holistically about the people we serve. Rather than referring to people as "homeless people" or "the homeless," a holistic approach might refer to these members of our communities as "people experiencing homelessness" or people who are "unhoused." This small but significant change places the person first, acknowledging that they are a person with skills, abilities, personality, and all the complexity of being human. Condition-first language such as "homeless people" can be demeaning, conveying that their stigmatized status is the most important identifier. Such an approach fails to look at a person holistically and see in them the *imago Dei*. It sees only the brokenness.

Identifying someone as a whole person with strengths and abilities as well as significant struggles is a micro-level perspective. But a holistic view is not limited to just individuals. Whole communities can be appreciated for their strengths and assets, as opposed to seeing a community only for its problems. This approach is called asset-based community development (ABCD).[12] One benefit is that it allows for micro-macro integrations,

---

11. Patricia Madoo Lengermann and Gillian Niebrugge, *The Women Founders: Sociology and Social Theory 1830–1930, a Text/Reader* (Prospect Heights, IL: Waveland, 2006).

12. John P. Kretzmann and John L. McKnight, *Building Communities from the Inside Out: A Path toward Finding and Mobilizing a Community's Assets* (Evanston, IL: Institute for Policy Research, 1993).

whereby individual people of a community contribute their strengths and capacities to benefit the whole community. Every community has problems and difficulties, but every community also has strengths. Focusing on a community's resources to develop initiatives links well with the previous idea of autonomy in that the community itself is driving the project. Another benefit is that creating change using existing assets is more sustainable, as growth does not depend solely on outside input. Solutions tend to be more stable and lasting when the capacities of the people and the community are the foundation to problem-solving.

Personal

The third characteristic of development that is important for redemptive service is that the work is personal. After all, God is personal with us. Jesus says that God knows how many hairs are on our head (Luke 12:7). God meets each of our individual and personal needs. Redemptive service maximizes positive outcomes when that work is also personal. Personalized development initiatives avoid a one-size-fits-all view of problems and solutions.

Personalizing begins with identifying the root causes of issues. Root causes are the underlying, often structural, issues that cause and perpetuate problems. While many different communities have similar problems, they often have quite different root causes. A root cause analysis allows development initiatives to move beyond merely addressing the symptoms of a problem and actually seek sustainable solutions.[13] Consider the following example: Three different people have a fever. A reasonable response might be to give each of them an over-the-counter fever reducer. Fevers, however, are generally only the symptom. On closer examination of the individuals, its turns out one has stepped on a nail, leading to an untreated, infected wound. The second person has contracted influenza. And the third person has heat exhaustion. All three of these conditions yield a fever, yet the medical response differs for each. Left untreated, an infected wound can cost a limb, or even a life. Just addressing the fever won't improve the overall condition. Similarly, a root cause analysis is a necessary tool for personalized development initiatives, individualizing the development project to that context. Developers can then focus initiatives at the level of the cause rather than just the effects.

13. John (Jack) W. Vincent II, "Community Development Assessments," in Phillips and Pittman, *Introduction to Community Development*, 133–54.

A root cause analysis is not necessarily antithetical to a discussion of ABCD. Identifying the root causes of a problem will often happen through a systematic inventorying of the assets and strengths of a community. An asset-oriented approach does not ignore existing problems. Indeed, it is often the assets in a community that are used to identify and implement solutions to root causes.

An individualized approach to development gets to know the people in a community. Developers learn people's names and occupations, but also their likes and dislikes, abilities, strengths, personal goals, concerns, hopes, and interests. This can happen only through the development of relationships, which are vital to redemptive service. If God knows how many hairs are on our heads, he must know us deeply and personally. Likewise, our work with others in redemptive service will also be characterized by personal connections. An impersonal approach reduces a person to their need, taking a one-size-fits-all approach, instead of tailoring the plan to meet the needs of the person and the community.

Personalization, as it relates to ABCD, relies on people within the community to address the challenges faced by the community.[14] People are the essential building blocks of communities and neighborhoods; they are every community's biggest asset. Recall the earlier discussion on human, social, cultural, and economic capital. These types of capital are assets. Everybody has some strengths, but nobody has the same set of strengths. Likewise, no community has the same strengths, because no community has the same people. A personalized view of a community necessitates getting to know people and building relationships. This approach still recognizes root causes and needs; however, a root cause analysis of a particular problem will see the strengths of the individuals and find how they can identify solutions. This deeply individualized and personalized view of community development means no two projects will be the same.

The relationship building that happens in ABCD is a form of developing community members' social capital, which refers to the people someone knows and the relationships they have. If someone's car breaks down and they ask a friend for a ride to work, they are using their social capital. If a single mom gets called into a shift at work but does not have childcare, social capital will allow her to call on neighbors and friends to find someone to watch her children. Social capital is useful in finding resources to

---

14. Kretzmann and McKnight, *Building Communities from the Inside Out*.

overcome life's everyday obstacles.[15] Community developers seek to build two main forms of social capital. The first is bonding social capital, which connects members within a community. Activities such as block parties help people get to know and hopefully become friends with others who live nearby. They can then become resources for each other and create community bonds that help them develop resilience and a shared sense of identity. The other form of social capital is bridging social capital, which connects communities and neighborhoods with people outside their circles. Bridging social capital is useful when communities want to mobilize resources or advocate for change among policymakers. Developing social capital is a direct result of personalization in community development because it focuses on relationships both within and across communities.

Personalization in community development happens at the individual and community levels. ABCD is one form of this place-based approach. Emphasizing place in community development is vital for several reasons. First, groupings of homes and the institutions that support them—whether neighborhoods, villages, or cities—are all located in a specific geographic context.[16] Climate, landscape, availability of green space, growing conditions, and other features of the natural environment are unique to each place. Increasingly, community development initiatives account for these environmental factors, as the longevity and health of the project requires that developers not take more resources than they put into a community. For example, international agricultural development projects work best when they focus on food products that are already part of the local environment. Importing a foreign grain or animal that might not grow in that area or that the local people might not even find desirable will waste resources, and the project will last no longer than the outsiders who are supporting it. When they leave, the project will die. This approach does not personalize the project to the physical and cultural context.

A place-based approach looks at the physical environment as well as the institutional assets found in that area. Neighborhood or village associations are groupings of people who already come together to discuss local events and solve problems. A place-based approach might identify other group-level assets in local businesses or nonprofit agencies. These assets form the building blocks for future growth. A place-based approach

15. Paul W. Mattessich, "Social Capital and Community Building," in Phillips and Pittman, *Introduction to Community Development*, 38–49.

16. Anna Haines, "Asset-Based Community Development," in Phillips and Pittman, *Introduction to Community Development*, 38–49.

to community development incorporates local culture, norms, strengths, people, and institutions, harnessing them as the foundation of the work that solves the community's problems.

The aspects of community development discussed in this chapter—assets, capitals, participatory approaches, root causes, and sustainability—are all components of something called "capacity building." A capacity is an ability. Capacity building focuses on enhancing the community's own ability to identify its strengths and areas of concern, assess how to work together to solve the problems, and act together to realize those solutions.[17] Capacity building is crucial because it helps determine both the necessity and the limits of external help. Such external help could come through economic support or manpower from volunteering or nonprofit agencies that have moved into a community.

Understanding the limits of outside input is especially relevant for development initiatives that seek to alleviate poverty. One criticism of ABCD is that focusing on assets in a resource-constrained environment increases stress on people. The suggestion is that communities that are already struggling should not have to bear the burden of their own development; they need help. One problem with this criticism is that it presents a deficit approach to communities. It views them only as being needy. Another way to respond to this argument against ABCD is to focus on capacity building. Capacity building can be used to recognize strengths and acknowledge limits, and external supports can give people the ability to help themselves. Outside help comes, but at the end of the project, people no longer rely on that help because their capacities have grown such that they are able to address concerns themselves.

Dignity

The three characteristics of development for redemptive service—autonomous, holistic, and personal—all point to a central factor: dignity. Development and redemptive service always affirm the dignity of the people being served. If not, development initiatives detract from and harm people and communities. Without dignity, development is at its worst. To ask whether an initiative or project will benefit a person or group of people is to ask whether it will be inherently dignifying to them.

17. Selma C. Liberato, Julie Brimblecombe, Jan Ritchie, Megan Ferguson, and John Coveney, "Measuring Capacity Building in Communities: A Review of the Literature," BMC *Public Health* 11, 850 (2011).

Earlier we discussed human development through Amartya Sen's research on the necessity of people's freedom to choose for themselves.[18] For Sen, two factors are required for freedom: people's capabilities and their functionings. Capabilities are a person's opportunities to do or be what they want: to be fed or educated or receive quality health care. Capabilities become functionings when they are actualized. Building a school and educating children are not always the same thing. Consider the difference between teaching and learning. Teaching focuses on the actions of the teachers, while learning focuses on what a student does. Any teacher will admit that there can be a wide gap between what they are teaching and what students are learning. Likewise, building a capability increases access to what people need in a community while building a functioning allows people to choose whether they use those goods, services, or opportunities. For Sen, freedom is in having the choice. To illustrate his point, Sen contrasts a person who is hungry due to lack of food with a person who is hungry because they have chosen to fast for personal or religious reasons. If there is no food, there is no choice to eat or not. This detracts from people's dignity at a fundamental level. Conversely, the principle of dignity also means recognizing that there might be reasons why someone might refuse to take food that is offered. This is freedom.

Development projects that build people's freedoms (access plus choice) prioritize dignity, consistent with how God interacts with creation. God affirms our dignity by giving us access to him through Scripture and the presence of the Holy Spirit because of Jesus' sacrifice on the cross. However, God never forces us to accept him or walk with him. God shows dignity and respect for us by giving us free will to choose whether or not to follow him. Our personal development benefits in every way if we choose the relationship that God wants to have with us, but even still God values our dignity. If our Creator has established this pattern, we too must treat others that way. Redemptive service that loves our neighbors as ourselves focuses on building capabilities and access to those parts of life that are necessary to live with dignity, and it allows our neighbors to choose whether and how they want to use those goods and services.

Conclusion

In this chapter we have presented an overview of development according to a variety of perspectives. We also introduced key components of

18. Amartya Sen, *Development as Freedom* (New York: Knopf, 1999).

community development in both domestic and institutional settings. People who want to give their time, talents, and money to an initiative usually want to do excellent work that will help others. Not all projects and opportunities have the same benefit for people, though. Many organizations are quite skilled at marketing themselves to church members, preying on people's emotions as they bid for donations and volunteers. It can be difficult to assess the quality of those projects or organizations when their emotional appeals are so compelling. The model presented in this chapter can be used as a tool for critical thought and engagement with different projects. These considerations are a good starting point for those who are not professionals in the development field but who want to engage in service in a way that is ethical and honoring to God and others.

Solid community development activities are built on a foundation of giving people autonomy, viewing lives holistically, being personal in interactions, and always affirming and amplifying the dignity of others. It's a tall order. Many people at the beginning of their journey of redemptive service do not have control over the projects in which they participate. The information in this chapter, then, can be used to determine a project's worth. Fundamentally, redemptive service requires humility and a willingness to learn. This work can be messy because people are messy. The beauty of the model presented in this chapter is that if the work is personal, if relationships are being developed, if the approach is participatory, and if everyone involved is valued, then there will be grace and understanding for the inevitable mistakes and missteps. And the learning and development will be bidirectional. Everyone will benefit. This robust process results in lasting positive change.

DISCUSSION QUESTIONS

1. In this chapter, "development" is defined as both a process and an outcome. What are some ways that the chapter described development as a process? How did the chapter show development to be an outcome?

2. Compare and contrast the three conceptual approaches to development: economic, human, and sustainable. What are strengths and weaknesses of each approach?

3. In your own words, define each of the four principles of development as they relate to redemptive service. Why is each important? Is there one that stands out to you as the most significant? Why?

4. What are some key ways that short-term interventions differ from long-term development projects? How are both important?

5. Go online and look at different development programs from organizations such as World Vision, Samaritan's Purse, or another nonprofit Christian organization that does development initiatives either in the US or abroad. Use the model of development that is presented in this chapter to evaluate the program. What are the strengths and potential areas to be strengthened?

FOR FURTHER READING

Corbett, Steve, and Brian Fikkert. *When Helping Hurts: How to Alleviate Poverty without Hurting the Poor . . . and Yourself.* Chicago: Moody, 2014.

Gordon, Wayne, and John M. Perkins. *Making Neighborhoods Whole: A Handbook for Christian Community Development.* Downers Grove, IL: InterVarsity, 2013.

Green, Gary Paul, and Anna Haines. *Asset Building and Community Development.* Los Angeles: SAGE, 2015.

Lupton, Robert D. *Charity Detox: What Charity Would Look Like if We Cared about Results.* New York: HarperOne, 2015.

Myers, Bryant L. *Walking with the Poor: Principles and Practices of Transformational Development.* Maryknoll, NY: Orbis Books, 2011.

Nussbaum, Martha C. *Creating Capabilities: The Human Development Approach.* Cambridge, MA: Harvard University Press, 2013.

Padgett, Deborah, Benjamin F. Henwood, and Sam J. Tsemberis. *Housing First: Ending Homelessness, Transforming Systems, and Changing Lives.* Oxford: Oxford University Press, 2016.

Perkins, John M., ed. *Restoring At-Risk Communities: Doing It Together and Doing It Right.* Grand Rapids: Baker, 1995.

Shook, Jill Suzanne, ed. *Making Housing Happen: Faith-Based Affordable Housing Models.* 2nd ed. Eugene, OR: Wipf & Stock, 2012.

9

Advocacy

Prevention as Redemptive Service

Having focused on the principles of short-term intervention (giving a person a fish) and long-term development (teaching a person to fish) in the previous two chapters, we now move to advocacy, which can be thought of as attending to the conditions of the pond. If the pond has no fish or if the water is toxic to the fish, teaching a person to fish will not help. Advocacy focuses on identifying underlying issues that perpetuate problems and then influencing those in power to provide structural solutions.

Advocacy is important to redemptive service because it acknowledges that in relieving suffering for others, sometimes the change needs to take place outside the community. Advocacy has not always been a part of redemptive service. Direct relief or development efforts are sometimes considered more relevant than an indirect approach that focuses on structural change. This, however, is a false dichotomy. Advocacy is an aspect of charitable action.[1] Advocacy efforts are an invaluable part of redemptive service, and when done well, the effects are long-lasting and deep. An advocate uses their voice and influence to change structures and reduce

1. Winnifred R. Louis, Emma Thomas, Cassandra M. Chapman, Tulsi Achia, Susilo Wibisono, Zahra Mirnajafi, and Lisa Droogendyk, "Emerging Research on Intergroup Prosociality: Group Members' Charitable Giving, Positive Contact, Allyship, and Solidarity with Others," *Social and Personality Psychology Compass* 13, no. 3 (2019): e12436.

suffering. The Bible is full of people who acted as advocates. The story of Moses offers several powerful examples of advocacy throughout Moses' life.

Moses was born amid infanticide. Baby boys were being systematically killed. Moses' mom advocated for him by hiding him. When he was in the basket in the Nile and Pharaoh's daughter found him, Moses' sister Miriam advocated for him by offering to find someone (his mom) to care for him. These examples of individual advocacy illustrate the interruption of systems. Individual advocacy occurs at the micro level. Pointing out how a system is failing a particular person and then advocating for that person's well-being is individual advocacy. While this often does not extend beyond the person, it can be an important first step to other types of advocacy that are broader in scale. One benefit of individual advocacy is that it can establish a discrete case that shows how the broader system is broken. Sometimes broader change comes with the accumulation of multiple small wins. While the individual advocacy of Moses' mother and Miriam only challenged the system for Moses, they did keep him alive, allowing for the broader examples of advocacy later in Moses' life.

After Moses had grown up and received God's call in the burning bush, he returned to Egypt to convince Pharaoh to let the people go. Moses was an advocate for the people to Pharaoh. As someone familiar with the Egyptian court, Moses spoke to Pharaoh on behalf of the people, even though he was not a slave himself. Later, after the crossing of the Red Sea, while Moses was with God receiving the Ten Commandments, the people built a golden calf and worshiped it, which angered God. But again, Moses acted as an advocate, convincing God not to wipe out the people. Moses' actions with both Pharaoh and God represent group advocacy. With Pharaoh, Moses called out the people's suffering and asked for respite. With God, Moses asked for mercy for the people. In both instances, Moses used his relationship and influence to change the minds of those in power, to sway them for the people. Moses' social location highlights an important aspect of advocacy: power differences.

Power is the ability of someone (or a group) to accomplish their goals despite the resistance of others. Pharaoh wielded power by forcing the Hebrews into slavery. He exercised his power when he ordered the Hebrew baby boys to be killed. Sometimes, people in power use their position to harm and exploit others, as Pharaoh did. Other times, people in power are not necessarily taking advantage of others, but they might be ignoring certain groups and diverting resources away from them. In both instances, power is connected to resource allocation. In an exploitative model, the people are the resource being exploited by, for instance, the powerful Pharaoh. In the second instance, people in power decide where resources should go and who should benefit from them. An advocate sees the big picture and understands the relationship between power and control over resources, and they see the effect this has on a subordinate group of people in a community. Advocates stand in the gap. They take the position between the powerful and the ones who are excluded from consideration. Moses stood between Pharaoh and the Hebrew people. He went to the source of power and asked for leniency.

Moses was unsuccessful, and repeatedly so. His advocacy irritated Pharaoh, causing Pharaoh to increase his harsh policies, yet Moses persevered. He knew what was needed, and he did not give up. Usually, people who are in power want to maintain that position. Every group wants resources. Changing minds about how to spend money and whom to support in a community will mean that the money does not go to other (sometimes more influential) groups. Advocacy for a marginalized group will often be a long endeavor, changing minds and hearts and challenging comfort zones. The work of advocacy does not always yield fast results; advocates are often refused. Successful advocates understand that the struggle for change will be long; they adjust their techniques and arguments as they go, and they keep trying.

Advocates have a nuanced relationship with power. They hold power but do not want power for themselves. Instead, they seek to influence the decisions of those in power. If advocates seek any personal benefit, they are not really working for the good of those they are trying to help. Moses did not want to be Pharaoh; he just wanted the people to be free. Rather than seeking personal gain, advocates combine their voice and influence with the voices of those who are marginalized to help them while always working to preserve their dignity.[2]

Types of Advocacy

The earlier discussion on dignity for development initiatives also applies to advocacy. In redemptive service, often the work is done with people groups that one does not belong to or in neighborhoods that one does not

2. Michael Schwalbe, *Making a Difference: Using Sociology to Create a Better World* (Oxford: Oxford University Press, 2020), 69–78.

live in. Outsiders can take one of three positions: advocating for people, advocating with people, and supporting self-advocacy by those people.

Advocacy for People

Sometimes a people group does not have the ability to advocate for themselves or does not feel safe doing so. Advocacy is done *for* people when the barriers to accessing power structures are so high that people cannot or do not want to advocate for themselves. Outsiders need to discuss advocacy plans with the people and accurately represent their interests and values. Advocating for people can be problematic when advocates are not members of the people group for whom they are speaking. Outsiders must stay true to the needs and aims of the people group and represent them as if they were representing themselves. The participatory method discussed earlier also applies to advocacy for communities. The participatory approach centers the voices, aims, processes, and outcomes that are developed by the people who are being served. They direct the activity that will improve their quality of life and promote dignity.

One example of advocacy is promoting low-barrier housing for people experiencing homelessness. Low-barrier housing, similar to a policy called "housing first," seeks to remove any qualifications for receiving shelter, such as sobriety, proof of identification, a completed background check, and so on.[3] Housing-first advocates believe that people who are living outside need to have stable housing before they can address other problems such as drug addiction or mental health issues. While these problems are not experienced by everyone who loses their housing, they are common challenges faced by people experiencing homelessness. Furthermore, these tend to be the most visible challenges to the unhoused residents of a community. Added to this, society deeply stigmatizes addiction and mental health conditions.[4] All of these factors converge and present barriers for people experiencing homelessness who struggle with mental health or addictions to effectively advocate for themselves. Social workers and other service providers work closely with these community members as their advocates. They seek to change public perception that blames people for these conditions. Blame does not support recovery, nor does it promote

3. Deborah Padgett, Benjamin F. Henwood, and Sam J. Tsemberis, *Housing First: Ending Homelessness, Transforming Systems, and Changing Lives* (Oxford: Oxford University Press, 2016).

4. Joanna Ruth Fox, "Exorcising Memories of Internalised Stigma: The Demons of Lived Experience," *World Journal of Psychiatry* 11, no. 3 (2021): 63.

the types of intervention that can improve people's lives, such as housing-first programs.

When advocating for someone else, we must take care not to insert outside opinions or advocate for plans or policies that are contrary to the wishes of the community. The adult autistic community has a long history of examples of neurotypical people advocating for them in ways that support ableist messages that do not benefit them, and in many cases harm them. One common slogan in the autistic community is "nothing about us without us."[5] Autistic people are best positioned to advocate for themselves.[6] Though parents must advocate for their autistic children, there is a long and tragic history of outsiders speaking for the autistic community in ways that have been dehumanizing. One example is the puzzle piece icon used by well-intentioned people to represent autism awareness. Some in the autistic community reject this image, as they do not feel like they are a puzzle to be worked out. This example highlights the complexity of outsiders advocating for a group. Now, we should not let the nuances of this example overwhelm us as we interact with and advocate for others, unable to make a decision due to overthinking a problem. The way forward is to focus on people, building bridges, learning, and being willing to apologize and change. When engaging in redemptive service, we are entering painful and difficult situations. There is a sacredness to people's pain, and sharing it is not supposed to be easy or comfortable. We do so with humility and a willingness to learn and grow.

Advocacy with People

Advocating *with* people adds the advocate's voice, energy, talents, and various capitals to the efforts that are already being done or will be done by the community members who are disenfranchised. Consider the concept of allyship. Allies have an advantageous social location, but they seek

5. Steven K. Kapp, *Autistic Community and the Neurodiversity Movement: Stories from the Frontline* (Singapore: Springer Nature, 2020), v–vi.

6. There is some debate about using person-first language ("person with autism") or identity-first language ("autistic person"). While these arguments are nuanced and complex, identity-first language has wide acceptance within the autistic community, and we follow their lead in this text. At the individual level, it is always best to identify which approach an individual person prefers and use that. Patrick Dwyer, "Stigma, Incommensurability, or Both? Pathology-First, Person-First, and Identity-First Language and the Challenges of Discourse in Divided Autism Communities," *Journal of Developmental and Behavioral Pediatrics* 43, no. 2 (2022): 111–13.

to challenge the system that determines those advantages. Allies come alongside those who are marginalized and use their position of influence to amplify those marginalized voices, which are too often ignored. One example of an ally can be found in the story of the Freedom Riders. These Black and White student activists protested together in bus rides across the southern United States during the civil rights era. Everyone on the buses joined together in solidarity and dedication to Black liberation and equality. Everyone was willing to put themselves at risk of harm for the cause. But the heroes of the civil rights movement were not the White allies, and the focus rightly remains on Martin Luther King Jr. and the many African Americans who marched, sang, and protested. King's "Letter from Birmingham Jail" details the failure of White Christians to ally with Black civil rights leaders in significant numbers.

Redemptive allyship has four steps.[7] First, allies become aware that some form of systemic, structural oppression and exclusion exists. This exclusion is based on categorization and injustice. Allies seek to challenge the stereotypes and stigmas faced by marginalized social groups. The Jim Crow laws of the US are an example of marginalization and systematic injustice purely on the basis of race.

Second, allies realize that through no merit of their own, they receive certain benefits just because of group membership. There are two sides to injustice: if some people are pushed to the margins of society, others are in the center. Allies see that they are at the center and that they benefit as a result. Unsatisfied, they seek to change this arrangement. Think of a playground where some children are allowed to play while other children must stand outside the fence and look in. The children who are on the playground become allies with the children outside when they first become aware that the other children are excluded. They also become uncomfortable playing when others are excluded. The children on the playground find that they cannot enjoy the benefits of the playground equipment without sharing it with the children who are on the periphery. There is room for everyone on the playground.

Third, allies acknowledge accountability and commit to promoting change. The structural changes that promote inclusion and equality never happen quickly. They require extended, dedicated efforts. The work of civil rights is ongoing even today. Personal accountability is not the same as guilt. Guilt, in this context, is an emotion that focuses too much on

7. Louis et al., "Emerging Research on Intergroup Prosociality," e12436.

the advantaged position of the person. Hyperfocus on the self will not result in action that promotes change.[8] The analogy of the playground is relevant here: the children who are included have this position through no fault of their own. Dedicating themselves to sharing the benefits of the playground with the excluded children is not the same thing as feeling guilty for being able to use it.

Fourth, allies build solidarity with disadvantaged groups. This solidarity pushes allies out of the us-them mindset and affirms a sense of *we* that transcends group distinctions. We don't want to erase group distinctions, but we do want to actively resist the hierarchy that exists between those distinctions. Revelation 7:9 emphasizes that every tribe, tongue, people, and nation will worship God together. Their differences are still evident; they are not erased. But those differences are not used to stratify who gets to stand closer or farther from God. Everyone stands and worships at God's feet. Solidarity acknowledges difference while delegitimizing the hierarchies that are imposed on those differences.

These four stages of allyship are necessary but not sufficient for redemptive service. Allies must constantly reflect on how they position themselves. Do they avoid virtue signaling or presenting themselves as a savior? Virtue signaling occurs when people who might be well-intentioned publicly announce their allyship to gain status. As with guilt, this shift to the self centers allies rather than issues and injustices. A savior mentality occurs when allies consider themselves to be liberating or rescuing people who are different from themselves in some way. Challenges to this mentality are uncomfortable but important. Helping others can lead the helper to believe they are better than the person being helped. Recall from chapter 6 the importance of knowing our limits and acknowledging self-poverty as a foundation for engaging in redemptive service. Doing so challenges the superiority that sometimes accompanies advocacy or other forms of redemptive service.

Self-Advocacy

Self-advocacy refers to the efforts of groups or communities being helped. With self-advocacy, marginalized groups are empowered to be their own advocate. The role of the outsider moves completely to the background,

---

8. Aarti Iyer, Colin Wayne Leach, and Faye J. Crosby, "White Guilt and Racial Compensation: The Benefits and Limits of Self-Focus," *Personality and Social Psychology Bulletin* 29, no. 1 (2003): 117–29.

providing support and encouragement where needed but not taking credit or seeking attention.

Self-advocacy means that disregarded people and groups should represent their own interests and positions.[9] Self-advocacy can be deeply empowering, as it affirms the agency of people to change their own situations. Self-advocacy is also beneficial in that the representations of people or groups are not filtered through the lens of outsiders; people groups represent themselves and their goals. Self-advocacy maintains focus on the groups that experience injustice. With self-advocacy, outsiders accept a position on the sidelines, a supportive role in the advocacy efforts. This role can be difficult for them because the helpers have not often occupied a peripheral position.

Centering the marginalized and moving outside helpers to the sidelines is a key aspect of redemptive service. Recall the concept of capacity building from the chapter on development, in which people identify their community's problems and the structural barriers to achieving solutions to those problems, followed by working on the front lines to change those structures that limit success and growth. Redemptive service can lead to that kind of transformation.

In our discussion on advocacy, we have repeatedly mentioned context and structures. All three forms of advocacy address the problematic structures that keep groups marginalized. Amartya Sen identifies two questions that are important in development that are relevant here: "What do you want to achieve?" and "What can you achieve?" The difference between what people want to achieve and what they can achieve will highlight structural limitations that keep people from actualizing their potential.[10] For example, in community development, food access is a frequent problem. Applying these two questions, community members might say that they want access to local sources of fresh food, but they do not necessarily see how they could build or bring a grocery store into their community themselves. Costs of building, regulations, and a lack of knowledge in food distribution systems all converge to place structural limits on a community building a grocery store themselves. They have the desire, but they do not have the capability. Advocacy addresses those structures and seeks to remove any barriers to food access.

9. Barry Gray and Robin Jackson, *Advocacy and Learning Disability* (Philadelphia: Jessica Kingsley, 2002).

10. Martha C. Nussbaum, "Creating Capabilities: The Human Development Approach and Its Implementation," *Hypatia* 24, no. 3 (2009): 211–15.

Advocacy and Structures

Structures promote growth or constrain human development. To help define this somewhat abstract concept, imagine a tomato plant. Tomato plants have a cage that provides support for the stalks, allowing them to grow tall without falling over. Without cages, tomato plants will not flourish. The cage (a structure) provides rigid strength, without which the tomatoes will grow into the dirt and be quickly eaten by bugs. People need structures to grow and develop as well. We need rules to keep our behaviors in line. We need some form of home to protect us from outside elements and keep us safe. We need rules that help us know how to act and get along with each other. Structures are necessary for society.

While structures are essential, they can cause harm. Not every structure is beneficial. Because structures are built by people, they are imperfect. Again, an example of harmful structures are the Jim Crow laws of the nineteenth and twentieth centuries in the US. These laws explicitly and deliberately oppressed people of color, especially Black people. Segregation permeated every aspect of society and reinforced racial and ethnic inequalities. For people of color, access to health care, education, food, housing, jobs, recreation, and every part of their life was influenced by structural limitations that dictated what they could do and where they could go. In these situations, advocacy in redemptive service identifies the costs of harmful structures and human suffering.

Three specific types of structures are relevant to advocates who seek to engage in redemptive service: built environments, policies, and norms. All three work together to explain how context affects people's outcomes and life chances. Built environments, policies, and norms are the context in which communities operate. Advocacy promotes equitable social systems.

Structure as Built Environment

The most obvious structure is built environments, those things that are materially and physically constructed by human endeavor. These can usually be seen. The built environment is related to the materiality of people's lives. Built environments include buildings such as schools, hospitals, houses, and churches. They also consist of hidden infrastructure such as sewage and septic systems, water and plumbing, cell towers, roads, sidewalks, high-speed internet, and other physical structures. Built environments physically shape how people live and interact with the world.

Making physical improvements can go a long way in reducing suffering and promoting capacity building and long-term development. For example, in the book of Nehemiah, the nation of Judah has been in exile. Some are being permitted to return to Jerusalem, but the city is in shambles. In particular, the walls are in ruins, ineffective at protecting the people. Those who have returned to their homeland are vulnerable to outside attack. In learning of this, Nehemiah, Jewish by ancestry and cupbearer to the foreign king, advocates for the rebuilding of Jerusalem. The king permits him to do so, even providing funding and protection as Nehemiah returns to Jerusalem and organizes the people there to rebuild the walls. Nehemiah was an advocate, working under the direction of God to rebuild the city.

A more recent example of advocating for built environments involves access to high-speed internet amid school closings due to the COVID pandemic. When schools closed and instruction went online, variability in access to high-speed internet created a difference in access to education. Families living in rural areas had less access because cables and lines had not been installed. Families living in low-income neighborhoods were also more likely to be without access. And families that had lost their income also sometimes lost access to internet service. This lack of access was disproportionately experienced by non-White families that were poor.[11] Understanding the built environment for different people groups helps us understand people's lives and experiences. Built environments are not erected based on whim or happenstance. Policies dictate how and where resources will be spent in creating and improving buildings and infrastructure.

Advocates must think deeply about the built environment and the impact of physical structures on people's lives. Some problems might have relatively straightforward solutions, but that does not make the work easy. Advocating for physical building projects can be a long and hard process of developing campaigns and organizing people around a common cause to raise money to meet construction costs. But there is a simplicity about advocating for physical structures. They are observable, and people understand the need. A relevant example of advocacy for built environment and racial justice can be found in Lowndes County,

11. Ananya Sen and Catherine E. Tucker, "Social Distancing and School Closures: Documenting Disparity in Internet Access among School Children," Social Science Research Network (SSRN), April 10, 2020, http://doi.org/10.2139/ssrn.3572922.

Alabama.[12] Decades of disinvestment of resources in rural areas of the South, particularly those populated predominantly by African Americans, had resulted in an environmental justice crisis for many residents of Lowndes County. Because the population density had been too low to fund a municipal sewage system, sanitation was handled by septic systems. One key difference between septic and sewage systems, however, is that individuals—rather than the municipality—are responsible for maintaining septic systems. However, when people have been economically isolated for generations, this maintenance can be prohibitively expensive, which was the case for many in Lowndes County. In this area, weather and soil conditions caused raw sewage to back up into front yards and even into homes. This was not a new problem; people had been advocating for state intervention for years. Even though the process of advocacy and recognition was long, the solution was relatively simple: improve the sanitation infrastructure. In 2023, there was finally hope for change for the people of Lowndes County as the US Department of Justice came to an agreement with the Alabama Department of Public Health, which agreed to improve facilities for residents. One unintended consequence of this case is that sanitation—alongside water and education—is being viewed as a human right. This illustrates how advocating for physical structures might also involve advocating for policy changes.

Structure as Policy

Structures also include policies that are relevant to the work of advocacy. Policies are explicitly stated or written rules or laws that govern social interaction. Policies drive the systems that overtly dictate processes such as distribution of resources and patterns of social interaction. Policies have a direct influence on people's lives. Many policies discriminate against people based on their social location. Again, the Jim Crow laws are a concrete historical example of a system of policies that discriminated against people on the basis of race and ethnicity. These policies established that Black people had to sit in the back of buses and could not eat in White-only restaurants. Other policies included housing discrimination and the federal lending program that provided loans to White families but denied

---

12. Elizabeth A. Albright, Catherine Coleman Flowers, Randall A. Kramer, and Erika S. Weinthal, "Failing Septic Systems in Lowndes County, Alabama: Citizen Participation, Science, and Community Knowledge," *Local Environment* (2023): 1–8, https://doi.org/10.1080/13549839.2023.2267066.

them to Black and Latinx families. These policies led to the segregation of housing with social and economic consequences that are still felt today.[13] Policies have material consequences.

While it might seem like ancient history to imagine public policy that would explicitly exclude a racial or ethnic minority, the US Food and Drug Administration refused to allow anyone from Haiti to give blood even into the 1990s. This policy discriminated against people based on nationality and contributed to ongoing widespread marginalization of people who are from Haiti.[14] We recognize that specific policies that are still relevant today are bound to be deeply political and cause controversy. And while a dominant value in the US is to maintain comfort and avoid conflict, perhaps a little tension would be beneficial.

The story of Esther provides a biblical example of a policy directly harming an ethnic group. The king had signed a law stating that all Jews could be killed on a certain day. Esther acted as an advocate for them, using her voice to speak against this harmful policy. The first law could not be revoked, so the king wrote a new law—a new policy—saying that the Jewish people could defend themselves. Policy solutions to people's problems can be quite powerful.

Esther's story provides a biblical example of policy advocacy. Both the problem and the solution were enforced at the policy level. Analysis of policies today might not reveal such explicit examples of discrimination, yet it is important to question whether a public policy is unjust. One major recent policy change that has had bipartisan support has been in how to label children who are victims of sex trafficking. Before the early 2000s, these children were called "prostitutes" in legal statutes without identifying them as people who are trafficked.[15] This label seems to blame the children for the work they were forced into when in fact they were powerless and exploited. The advocacy and awareness-raising campaigns that redefined sex trafficking as a local, pervasive problem have been deeply important and have shaped discussions and legislation today. Tension often accompanies critical discussions of current policies that question whether they are just in how they are interpreted, applied, and enforced.

13. For more information on federal policy and housing discrimination, see Richard Rothstein, *The Color of Law: A Forgotten History of How Our Government Segregated America* (New York: Liveright, 2017).

14. Charlene Galarneau, "'The H in HIV Stands for Human, not Haitian': Cultural Imperialism in US Blood Donor Policy," *Public Health Ethics* 3, no. 3 (2010): 210–19.

15. Wendi J. Adelson, "Child Prostitute or Victim of Trafficking?," *University of St. Thomas Law Journal* 6 (2008): 96.

The work of advocacy in redemptive service involves standing in the gap and moving into that tension. Just like Esther took a risk to stand against unjust policies for her people, redemptive service can be risky. Though we want to think that policies are neutral, they often reflect the innate biases of those who wrote them. Policies both drive and reflect dominant norms.

Structure as Social Norms

Structure might also take the form of social norms. These unspoken rules govern behavior. Norms establish the often-tacit patterns of interaction that people live and work by. Norms are frequently invisible because they are viewed as being normal or the way things are or the natural way. One example of this is the traditional division of labor in the home. In the dominant culture of the US, women were traditionally responsible for the majority of the housework, childcare, and other forms of unpaid labor at home. Men were primarily responsible for being the breadwinners, doing the paid labor, and perhaps caring for the yard and car maintenance. This gendered division of labor was the norm of past generations in the US, yet it is not a set rule today. It is becoming more common to find single-parent households or two-parent families in which men routinely do laundry or wash dishes and women mow the lawn and take care of automobiles. Women are more likely to work outside the home and be paid than they are to stay at home, even after they have children.[16] At a deeper level, the norms that govern family structures have changed. Families today are quite diverse and characterized by divorce, remarriage, cohabitation, single parents, and other varieties.[17] This pluralization of families is the result of changing norms in our society, and it is also the cause of new changes to other norms.

The changing norms of family division of labor show the importance of ongoing advocacy. For example, when norms dictate that the mother rather than the father will stay home with sick children, women's careers are negatively affected. Even the most understanding employers are put under stress when workers are frequently absent. Women who are more

16. Cheridan Christnacht and Briana Sullivan, "About Two-Thirds of the 23.5 Million Working Women with Children Under 18 Worked Full-Time in 2018," US Census Bureau, 2020, https://www.census.gov/library/stories/2020/05/the-choices-working-mothers-make.html.

17. Merike Blofield, Fernando Filgueira, and Carmen Diana Deere et al., "Pluralization of Families," in *Rethinking Society for the Twenty-First Century: Report of the International Panel on Social Progress*, vol. 3, *Transformations in Values, Norms, Cultures* (Cambridge: Cambridge University Press, 2018), 677–712.

likely to miss work will also more likely be passed over for promotion and advancement. These are not explicit policies but the result of social norms that tend to advantage men in the workplace at the expense of women. Employers often do not see gender as part of the equation in making this determination; they merely promote the most reliable worker. The result is that any question of gender-based bias is often emphatically denied by employers because it was done unconsciously. Analyzing the fairness and justice of certain norms can lead to tension and pushback. Norms are the default way of being in a society, so questioning norms is tantamount to questioning society itself. But what is natural and normal for one group is not viewed as such for others. Norms reflect the beliefs and values of the dominant group. The advocate who speaks out against unfair norms does significant work. Seeing that unfair treatment has become internalized into a set of behavior patterns and speaking out against that normalization begins the process of changing those behavior patterns.

Throughout his ministry, Jesus spoke against norms that prevented people from seeing their neighbors as themselves. He challenged the norm that said the wealthy are better and have stronger moral character because of their material condition. In Luke 21, a widow puts two coins in an offering after rich people have put in a lot more, and Jesus tells his disciples that her offering was greater because she gave everything she had. Jesus also challenged norms about gender and ethnicity when he reached out to the Samaritan woman at the well, contravening social conventions. Those distinctions did not matter to Jesus.

Even today, norms erect powerful structures that welcome some and exclude others. Advocacy for building projects or policy changes is usually a public endeavor that requires organizing groups of people and moving public opinion on an issue. Advocacy work often moves from the public sphere to the private sphere. Perhaps advocacy occurs around the dinner table or with a friend group. This kind of advocacy interrupts racist jokes or sexist comments that turn people into objects. Advocacy at the level of norms is personal and can challenge the way people think and act. This private work is as important as the public work, and it is accessible to anyone who has the courage to do it. It is not easy to challenge friends and family members who make comments that attack the dignity of others. Standing in the gap and kindly speaking to challenge stereotypes and stigmas is a powerful and necessary form of advocacy.

Social structures include the built environments, policies, and norms of a given society. The effect that these structures have on society is contested, with some arguing that structures are only minimally related to outcomes such as educational attainment, housing, employment, and upward mobility. According to this argument, people use their strength and ingenuity to overcome obstacles and achieve their goals. Many people know someone who has overcome intense difficulties and found resounding success. These stories do not negate the importance of analyzing structures and advocating for equity. Structural analysis does not ask whether one single person within a particular group, or set of groups, is able to be successful. Instead, it asks why more people in those situations are not able to succeed. Identifying the barriers to success shows where advocates can begin working.

Practical Suggestions for Advocacy

In this chapter on advocacy in redemptive service we have discussed forms of advocacy and areas of society that require advocates. Since most of this discussion has been theoretical, we finish this chapter by proposing six practical steps to advocacy. These steps were developed by sociologist Michael Schwalbe, who suggested ways that advocacy can be accessible for everyone:

1. The foundation of advocacy comes from listening to those for whom you are advocating and learning from them.
2. Start the work in smaller social circles—friends and family.
3. Find commonalities and similar interests; build empathy for others from there.
4. Everybody makes mistakes: acknowledge them and learn from them.
5. Speak to members of your own broader group, moving beyond friends and family.
6. Amplify the voices of those who are marginalized.[18]

Conclusion

Advocacy is a vital aspect of redemptive service. Short-term interventions can provide treatment and help immediate concerns, but advocacy

18. Michael Schwalbe, *Making a Difference: Using Sociology to Create a Better World* (Oxford: Oxford University Press, 2020), 75.

can prevent others from experiencing the same difficulties. For example, imagine a community with contaminated water that is causing people to get sick. Helping those who are ill is an example of relief. Development might consist of building pumps and purifiers to clean the water so people stop getting sick. But it's possible that the community has contaminated water due to industrial waste dumping into water systems. Advocates can seek to pressure these industries to stop the dumping, which would solve the problem at its root.

The work of advocacy includes advocating for, advocating with, and making room for self-advocacy. Sometimes each of these will be necessary, and needs can change over time. Most of all, to advocate well within redemptive service, spend time with the people. Get to know them. Hear their voices and seek to amplify those perspectives.

DISCUSSION QUESTIONS

1. In the saying "Give a person a fish and feed them for a day. Teach a person to fish and feed them for a lifetime," this chapter has broadened the perspective to focus on attending to the conditions of the pond. Why might it be important to think about the conditions of the pond with redemptive service?

2. Have you ever had someone stand up for you? What happened? How did that make you feel?

3. Discuss the difference between advocating for, advocating with, and self-advocacy. How is people's dignity the key distinction in which type of advocacy to do?

4. Structures include built environments, policies, and norms. How does the work of advocacy change depending on which type of structure you are attempting to change?

5. In what ways is Jesus an advocate for you?

FOR FURTHER READING

Kenny, Amy. *My Body Is Not a Prayer Request: Disability Justice in the Church.* Grand Rapids: Brazos, 2022.

Krinks, Lindsey. *Praying with Our Feet: Pursuing Justice and Healing on the Streets.* Grand Rapids: Brazos, 2021.

Offutt, Stephen, F. David Bronkema, Robb Davis, Gregg Okesson, and Krisanne Vail-
lancourt Murphy. *Advocating for Justice: An Evangelical Vision for Transforming
Systems and Structures*. Grand Rapids: Baker Academic, 2016.

Pellow, David Naguib. *Garbage Wars: The Struggle for Environmental Justice in Chicago*. Cambridge, MA: MIT Press, 2004.

Rothstein, Richard. *The Color of Law: A Forgotten History of How Our Government Segregated America*. New York: Liveright, 2017.

Watson, Joanna. *Advocacy Toolkit*. 2nd ed. Teddington, UK: Tearfund, 2015.

10

Who's Invited?

Social Location and the Christian Worldview

In the first half of this book we introduced *why* Christians should engage in redemptive service. In the second half we have explored *how* a Christian should engage in redemptive service. In this chapter we briefly discuss *who* should be the focus of redemptive service. While everyone can benefit from service, we should pay special attention to those whom society tends to omit, modeling the redemptive service that we find in Scripture. While all people can be beneficiaries of redemptive service, both the Old and New Testaments instruct God's people to be especially attentive to those on the margins of society. The Torah gives special provision for the poor, widows, orphans, and sojourners. And Jesus brought the good news to the poor, the captive, the blind, and the oppressed. Unfortunately, in a fallen world not all of God's image bearers receive equal treatment and opportunity. It is our responsibility to look critically at society, discern how social factors may be at work to disadvantage some persons, and work to rectify that inequality. In this chapter we reflect on who is included or excluded from various communities. Just as Jesus had special solidarity with those who were marginalized, redemptive service can also look critically at society and see who is included or excluded.

Unnatural Disasters

On December 26, 2004, a tsunami swept across South Asia, killing over 220,000 people. Known as the Boxing Day Tsunami, it is widely regarded as one of the deadliest natural disasters in recent times. Subsequent analyses of the catastrophe show that the wave did not take lives equally across different demographics of the population. In Indonesia, across the Aceh Besar district, 70 to 80 percent of the lives that were lost were women. The pattern held stable in the affected areas of India as well, where three times the number of women died than men. And in the Pachayankuppam village, women were the only casualties.[1] Many overlapping reasons account for the increased toll on the lives of women. In some areas, women were more likely to be left at home while men were out fishing, relatively safe in boats. Women's clothing in these areas make it harder to swim, and women are less likely to learn how to swim or be able to climb a tree, and are more likely to be carrying babies or young children. Combined, these factors explain why more women died than men.

Further analysis into the Boxing Day Tsunami indicates that communities that were already suffering from lower socioeconomic status were hit harder than communities that had greater levels of wealth, largely because of the tsunami's impact on vulnerable housing. Structurally sound houses might have been damaged but were still habitable, while vulnerable houses were destroyed by the tsunami. Oxfam (a global organization that fights poverty and injustice) found that those people who were displaced and living in camps suffered a 94 percent drop in their income while those people who were able to return to their homes only suffered an 11 percent drop in income.[2]

Other axes of vulnerability in the Boxing Day Tsunami were ethnicity and caste. In some parts of Sri Lanka, twenty years of militarized conflict had destabilized the Tamil people before they were hit by the wall of water. Throughout the region, caste also played a role in initial vulnerability and affected relief and cleanup efforts.[3]

1. "The Tsunami's Impact on Women," Oxfam Briefing Note, March 25, 2005, https://policy -practice.oxfam.org/resources/the-tsunamis-impact-on-women-115038.
2. "Targeting Poor People: Rebuilding Lives after the Tsunami," Oxfam Briefing Note, June 26, 2005, https://policy-practice.oxfam.org/resources/targeting-poor-people-rebuilding-lives -after-the-tsunami-114609.
3. K. N. Ruwanpura, "Temporality of Disasters: The Politics of Women's Livelihoods 'After' the 2004 Tsunami in Sri Lanka," *Singapore Journal of Tropical Geography* 29, no. 3 (2008): 325–40.

There is very little that is "natural" about the effects of natural disasters. Tsunamis, earthquakes, hurricanes, and other catastrophes expose existing inequalities. Social location helps us understand the inequalities evident in the aftermath of natural disasters. It refers to the place that people have in society relative to their status and various roles. While some status and roles are achieved through hard work, others are ascribed to a person based on norms and structures. A person's identity in the context of the overall structure explains the person's social location. For example, Japan experienced a deadly earthquake and tsunami in 2011. Almost twenty thousand people went missing, but the losses in Japan were disproportionate not along lines of gender (as in the Boxing Day Tsunami) but by age: the vulnerable population in Japan were elderly people.[4] When natural disasters occur, those who are in more vulnerable social locations before the event are disproportionately exposed. Likewise, those who are already in stronger social locations are largely shielded from the worst effects of these events. With the Boxing Day Tsunami, the myriad social factors comprising a person's social location came together to influence outcomes. Women in general were less likely to survive, but those women who were living in poverty had compounding exposure to the tsunami. Even poor women who survived were thrust deeper into poverty than those who had more economic means before the event. Compounding factors of gender, ethnicity, caste, and poverty converged to worsen the tolls.

The Least of These

In mainstream Christianity in the US, social location is greatly debated. The idea that some people are disadvantaged, experiencing more obstacles in their path to success and well-being along with fewer opportunities to succeed, makes many uncomfortable. If it is true that some people have a marginalized status, then the converse must also be true: some social locations come with advantages. The idea of advantaged and marginalized social locations is difficult for many in mainstream Christianity to accept, yet the Bible directly addresses this.

In Matthew 25:40 Jesus tells a parable of sheep and goats. In this parable, the king says, "Truly I tell you, just as you did it to one of the least of these brothers and sisters of mine, you did it to me." In this parable, the

---

4. Shinji Nakahara and Masao Ichikawa, "Mortality in the 2011 Tsunami in Japan," *Journal of Epidemiology* 23, no. 1 (2013): 70–73, https://doi.org/10.2188/jea.je20120114.

"least of these" refers to foreigners, people who are poor, people who are in prison, and people who are ill. While these descriptions refer to the circumstances of people's lives, they can also be described as social locations. People who are ill take on a sick role, but that is not their identity. Migrants move from the familiar to the unfamiliar. Being hungry and without a home are circumstances of people's lives. These social locations influence people's opportunities. By calling these people "least," Jesus is not saying that they are inherently less. In fact, Jesus expresses solidarity with people who occupy marginalized social locations, calling them his "brothers and sisters." The designation "least of these" should be understood as a social location or status rather than deeper notions of personhood, being, or intrinsic value. If some people are on the margins, others are in the center. If some are disadvantaged, others are advantaged. Jesus speaks to people of advantaged social locations and directly states how they are to view and interact with those who occupy stigmatized social locations.

Social Location as a Methodological Lens

People's identities in specific contexts influence what happens throughout their lives, called "life chances." A person's chances in life are affected by their social location. Social science has demonstrated repeatedly that personal merit does not fully explain why one person is more likely to be offered an interview while another person's résumé will not garner any attention. In one study, with only the names on the résumés changed, and all other factors being equal, people with White-sounding names were more likely to be called for an interview than people whose names seemed to belong to racial or ethnic minorities.[5] Marginalized and advantaged social location helps us make sense of this pattern.

Using social location to make sense of the world is like wearing a pair of glasses that clarifies patterns and helps us focus. A person who is far-sighted can often see well enough to drive but might need to wear reading glasses to see text in a book. Similarly, social location brings into focus how some people are included while others are excluded. A person's social location can help us understand their life events. While some events in a person's life occur by their own choices or mindset, other factors are also

5. M. Bertrand and S. Mullainathan, "Are Emily and Greg More Employable than Lakisha and Jamal? A Field Experiment on Labor Market Discrimination," *American Economic Review* 94, no. 4 (2004): 991–1013.

at work. Social location is best understood as a set of theoretical glasses (a methodological lens) that helps interpret people, events, and places.

To illustrate how social location can act as a methodological lens (a set of questions that guide our thinking) and to help conceptualize how an event or situation affects people differently, let's again take the case of COVID. A person's health situation affected their vulnerability to the virus. Those with diabetes, respiratory illnesses, or heart disease were found to be at increased risk of mortality from the illness. Likewise, anyone with an autoimmune disorder was more vulnerable to hospitalization due to weakened self-defenses in attacking the virus. As a result, preexisting physiological conditions were one axis of vulnerability to this disease. These medical conditions alone, however, do not sufficiently explain how people were differently affected by COVID.

A person's age also affected their vulnerability to COVID. The virus had higher hospitalization and mortality rates for senior citizens than it did for younger people. Some of this can be explained by the preexisting conditions typical in older people, yet even seniors who did not have any conditions experienced higher levels of risk. And not all senior citizens experienced the virus similarly. Children, on the other hand, had a low risk of mortality, yet they lost important days of schooling and connection with peers due to the virus.

In addition to medical conditions and age, people in the labor sector experienced challenges with COVID in different ways. Many people lost their jobs when businesses closed. Unemployment rates spiked. Health care workers put themselves at risk every day. Many in the service industry who were fortunate enough to keep their jobs had to work in constant contact with the public, which came with increased risk.

Family structure also affected the impact of the disease. When schools went remote, parents had to navigate childcare and their own jobs in uncertain times. Those who have more people, such as multigenerational families, living in their homes had increased risk of exposure and vulnerability to the disease.

The list of different axes of vulnerability to the disease is long, and these few examples are not exhaustive. Gender also played a role, as did race, ethnicity, class, and other aspects of people's identities.[6] These identities directly affected how different groups experienced COVID. These axes

6. A racial analysis of COVID, though important, is best contextualized into the broader structures that disproportionately affect people of color in any catastrophe. People of color were not biologically more at risk of contracting the disease. Rather, they disproportionately

of identity relate to social location. People's social locations are variable, changing throughout a person's life. One person might also have a variety of social locations at once. Some of these locations compound to give people greater access to health care and other resources necessary for living a full and complete life, while other identities converge to put up greater barriers to a healthy and dignified life. Social location clarifies the barriers that our neighbors may face that are different from ours. Social location helps us recognize who is excluded and who is included.

Social Location and the Biblical Story

Using social location as a methodological lens to understand exclusion is not unique to the twenty-first century. Throughout both the Old and New Testaments, God is sensitive to people's identities. God chose Jacob, the younger brother, to receive the blessing. Leah—the sister who was not beautiful and whom Jacob was tricked into marrying—was chosen by God and blessed with many children, including the line that would bear Jesus. Ruth was a woman, a foreigner, a widow, and poor. Her story and the work of Boaz as her kinsman redeemer make no sense without understanding Ruth's social location. In the New Testament, God's solidarity with the marginalized is such that Jesus was born into a stigmatized city. Upon hearing about Jesus, Nathanael states, "Can anything good come out of Nazareth?" (John 1:46). Fortunately for Nathanael and us, his prejudice did not disqualify him from being one of the twelve apostles, and he likely did not hold such prejudice for long. Women, people who were poor, ethnic minorities, and other marginalized groups are systematically included in the biblical story, with their identities openly labeled. Numerous Bible stories actually rely on social location to understand the narrative. The fact that people embody different social locations and that we should be mindful of these realities is present in the biblical text long before social scientists came up with the theory of social location. "Social location" is a relatively new label, but the underlying ideas are clearly illustrated in the biblical narrative.

In Acts 6:1, the early church shows its sensitivity to social location. Social and material exclusion existed even within the early church. The identities and social locations that led to the women's hunger occurred

---

endured systematic exclusion from housing, jobs, health care, and other benefits that would have protected them from the virus and increased resiliency if COVID were contracted.

along lines of ethnicity and language, age, marital status, and gender. These women were Jewish, but they spoke Greek, not Aramaic, as their native language. The diversity of language indicates that ethnic communities had integrated into the wider Jewish community. The Hebraic Jewish widows were getting their portion, so ethnicity clearly played a role. In a patriarchal context, these women could no longer be supported by their husbands, nor had they remarried. Further, they were women in a society where women did not inherit property or have the same earning potential in the labor force. The social location of these women was determined by their age, ethnicity, language, marital status, economic position, and gender.

The story of the Hellenistic Jewish widows in Acts 6 highlights two important aspects of using social location as a methodological lens in redemptive service. First, being mindful of the potential for marginalization that comes with different social locations keeps us from perpetuating patterns of exclusion, even if unintentionally. Everyone is born into a social system and is socialized into ideas of who is worthy or unworthy. When someone attempts the work of redemptive service without mindfully looking for these patterns, patterns are considered natural and inequities are perpetuated, as happened with the Hellenistic Jewish widows. Those who were distributing the food probably did not realize they were being unjust in their service. By not being attentive to the marginalized social location of the Greek-speaking widows and their own biases, the food distributors were perpetuating inequalities and reinforcing biases. Second, seeing and bearing witness to the injustice of various social locations undermines them. Redemptive service must see "the least of these" as brothers and sisters of Jesus. In doing so, their marginalization becomes unpalatable to us and we seek to overturn it.

Social Location: Identity in Context

Social Location and Identity

Social location has two dimensions: the identities that people have and the context for those identities. A person's various identities intersect to influence that person's life course and experiences. *Essentialism* occurs when we limit a person to just one identity, which distorts the interaction between identity and experience. Essentialism is the misguided perspective that any one characteristic of a person explains all of a person's experience.

In the example from Acts 6, the women were denied food not just because they were women. Nor was it merely because they were widows. Their identity as Hellenistic Jews also does not fully explain their exclusion. Essentialism falls short. Their exclusion can be understood only through their combination of identities: being women, widows, and Hellenistic exponentially increased their vulnerability and exclusion.

Understanding identity is vital to understanding people. People carry a multitude of identities as defined by society, leading to social divisions and categories. The social divisions that most affect people are race, class, and gender. There is nothing innately negative about the identities that people inhabit.[7] There is nothing inherently less valuable about being a woman versus being a man. Valuing diversity entails celebrating the benefits that come with an integration of people across different racial and ethnic categories in churches, schools, neighborhoods, friend groups, families, and workplaces. With this benefit perspective of racial and ethnic categories, it would be illogical (and wrong!) to say that there is anything inherently negative about racial and ethnic identities. Identity alone cannot explain a person's social location. Broader society defines those identities and what meanings people are socialized to ascribe to them.

To say that the identities and categories that people carry are not innately negative is not to say that they are inconsequential. Regarding race and ethnicity, for example, White people often claim that they do not see color or racial categories. Such "colorblindness" creates problems for a variety of reasons.[8] For one, it denies the beauty, nuance, perspective, history, and experience that people of diverse racial, ethnic, and cultural backgrounds bring. People with diverse identities are beneficial to one another and add nuance, depth, and interest to institutions. Churches are

7. A more nuanced argument is important here with regard to class. Economic poverty brings inherent challenges and problems. Struggling to find housing or food, for example, deteriorates people's quality of life. While there are fundamental negativities involved with living in poverty, this is vastly different from stating that the people who are in poverty have innate cultural or personal deficits. To understand more about the experience of extreme poverty in the US, see Kathryn Edin and Luke Shaefer, *$2.00 a Day: Living on Almost Nothing in America* (Boston: Houghton Mifflin Harcourt, 2015).

8. Eduardo Bonilla-Silva uses the term "color-blind racism" to explain that color-blind ideology can never be benign. Instead, it promotes and perpetuates racist policies, beliefs, and structures. In the post-civil-rights era, the majority of racial discrimination seems, on the surface, to be nonracial. Color-blind language is used to support and preserve those discriminatory practices. A more thorough explanation of this argument can be found in Bonilla-Silva, *Racism without Racists: Color-Blind Racism and the Persistence of Racial Inequality in America*, 5th ed. (Lanham, MD: Rowman & Littlefield, 2017).

healthier when they are integrated. People's circles of friends are stronger when they better represent the beauty and diversity of God's creation.

Social Location and Context

A person's context determines how a person's identities will be received. Being a woman is a marginal category only if the context denies women equal access to opportunities and the freedom to live a full and dignified life. Likewise, certain racial categories are marginal only in a society that elevates some racial groups at the expense of others. In analyzing social location, people's identities are important in the context that those identities are defined. The context determines how people's various identities are viewed. Someone's social location is a combination of that person's identities in their context. The story of Ruth illustrates this point. Ruth and her mother-in-law Naomi went to Israel after their husbands died and left them destitute. Ruth's situation can be understood first through her identities: a woman, a widow, poor, and a Moabite (foreigner in Israel). But these identities alone do not explain Ruth's vulnerability. She was a woman in a patriarchal society that did not give her many options to make money and feed herself. The context that limited her choices is as important as her identity as a woman. She was also a foreigner in a context of long-standing enmity between the people of Moab and the people of Israel. Ruth was a childless widow in a society that did not have systems to care for women such as her. Ruth's vulnerability is evident when both Boaz and Naomi advise her to work only in Boaz's field to avoid being harmed (2:8, 22). Even within Israel, Ruth found relative safety in Boaz's field, as she would have been unsafe in a different field because of her identities. Understanding context is necessary for understanding social location in the work of redemptive service.

Context is an abstract way of describing the elements of people's lives that enable and constrain their activities. Most people have some goals, but their ability to achieve those goals varies by context. Even though some people overcome immensely difficult situations to achieve their goals, it is still important to describe and understand the difficulties that had to be overcome. Others are able to work assiduously and achieve their goals with few obstacles. While they still have to labor, they are able to enjoy the benefit of their work with relatively few setbacks. Contexts and their structures account for these two experiences. Sometimes people work hard and the context rewards their labor. Other times, people work hard but cannot seem to achieve positive outcomes. As with the story of Ruth, a positive outcome occurs from paying attention to the structural conditions of a person's life. When Boaz provided protection for Ruth, the structures that he put into place positively influenced her livelihood and dramatically improved her life chances.

Social structures are one aspect of the context that affect people's quality of life. A person's identity is often connected to the built environment in which they live. For instance, many towns in the southern United States have literal train tracks that border neighborhoods, marking the "other side of the tracks." This phrase, referring to socioeconomic status, often has classist overtones and stigmatizes people based on their income. This phrase illustrates how deeply ingrained context and identity are in contemporary society. Policies are another aspect of context that affects social location. Policies state where people go to school, how they can access health care, and other aspects of their lives. Norms are also part of the context, determining whom to befriend and whom to exclude in public high schools, for example, perpetuating inequalities.

Social location matters because it describes more than just a person's identity; it shows how broader forces come to bear on a person. Many arguments today revolve around whether problems are due to individual choices or structures. Viewing this question from just one side or the other is misguided. The question is not whether the problem is with the individual or structures. Instead, social location shows that people cannot be separated from the structures in which they reside. They influence one another.

Scripture and Social Location as Identity in Context

Galatians 3:28 states that in Christ there is neither Jew nor Greek (ethnic division), slave nor free (economic division), male nor female (gender division). In this verse we see the importance of social location and identity in the biblical text. If these identities were inconsequential, Paul would not have needed to make this statement. Paul acknowledges that these differences exist; he recognizes that there were distinctions based on ethnicity, economy, and gender (the book of Philemon is a tribute to how he does indeed see the importance of social location). He notes that the differences of social location are unimportant in the context of God's ideal. The phrase "in Christ" gives the context for the erasure of the divisions. In the perfection of Christ, people who are poor would not be living without basic sanitation or access to water. In the perfection of Christ, policies do not discriminate against women, people of color, those with disabilities, immigrants, or those who are economically isolated. In the perfection of Christ, there are no unspoken norms or hidden biases that perpetuate the exclusion of some at the benefit of others. But the perfection of Christ is not yet the full reality. Today, we live in a broken world in which divisions have consequences.

Using Social Location as a Methodological Lens in Redemptive Service

Social location identifies the many identities that people carry and questions how those identities are defined and treated in a context. This concept serves as a methodological lens, or a set of questions to ask, when looking at a particular situation. To engage in relief, development, and advocacy well, we must begin with the question of who might be excluded and how the context is excluding them, providing a path to a solution that promotes justice.

The story of the early church in Acts 6 illustrates practically how an analysis of social location is necessary in redemptive service. In this story, the church identified the axes of identities in the context and found an equitable solution. The Hellenistic widows were being excluded based on their identities. The context helps us understand this story. The apostles who were responsible for distributing the resources were Hebraic Jews who, until it was brought to their attention, did not realize that their normative patterns of viewing the world were causing them to withhold food from widows of a different ethnicity. With the exclusion identified, they proposed to find different people to govern food distribution. Biblical scholars note that the names of those in charge of this task were Hellenistic.[9] Those who shared the identity of exclusion (other Hellenists) became part of the solution to promoting equity. By giving the responsibility of food dispersal to Hellenistic Christians, the church found a way to share the food fairly. Those who were most sensitive to the exclusion were in the best location to govern the outcome.

The work of redemptive service seeks to promote justice in communities using relief, development, and advocacy. The vital question to ask

---

9. Willie James Jennings, *Acts: A Theological Commentary on the Bible* (Louisville: Westminster John Knox, 2017), 48–49.

is, Who might be missed in these efforts? And the best way to move forward is to centralize those perspectives and experiences when thinking of solutions.

A contemporary example of using social location as a way to analyze problems and find solutions in redemptive service comes from a story of gender development in Khartoum, Sudan. An organization in that region had established a women's center that provided services and development for Sudanese women. The center contained an educational center, computer lab, library, and fitness room. The target audience was the Sudanese women who were living in the surrounding neighborhoods. Yet over time, the clientele increasingly consisted of expatriate women more than Sudanese women. In one particular instance, one of the center's English classes consisted exclusively of Korean women. While the center was happy to offer these services to anyone, these Korean women had other opportunities for English classes. They did not necessarily need to go someplace that was exclusively for women. English was useful for them, but not in the same ways that it would have been useful for Sudanese women in Khartoum. To find out why the Sudanese women were not using the services or enrolling in the courses, the director spoke with various Sudanese women who were regulars at the center or living in the neighborhood.

By seeking out and centralizing the perspective of the Sudanese women, the center found simple solutions. The women identified gaps in the marketing. The center was not marketing the classes in Arabic, so the Sudanese women did not know about the courses. Many of the time slots for the classes were inconvenient given the typical meal preparation times of the Sudanese women. The leadership at the center—expatriate women with the mindsets and norms of Westerners—had failed to see the cause. The Korean women had networks that marketed the English classes, but the Sudanese women needed to see the class advertisements printed in Arabic. The class times also had to be conducive to the context of the target women. The only way to employ social location to understand why Sudanese women were being excluded was to deliberately ask them. In this case, the solution was simple. The start times and marketing materials were adjusted. The local women started coming. While they had not been intentionally excluded, the logistics of the classes and marketing excluded them. Social location as a tool of analysis centralizes the experience and viewpoint of those who are intended to be served.

The use of social location in this story led the leadership at the center to show humility about preconceived notions and to be intentional about who is included in social situations. Without intentional thought and consideration of people's social location, the work will never reach its fullest potential. People will be missed. Social location as a methodological tool helps workers be deliberate about who is and who is not being helped and then be accountable to those people. Service activities that do not adopt this perspective are limited and can even be harmful. Intentionality is necessary for development and redemptive service.

We see intentionality and humble introspection in the story in Acts 6, in which the disciples question their own personal biases. Though they certainly loved God, the disciples nonetheless had forgotten a group of people within their body because of their prejudices. Social location is a way of questioning our own norms and patterns of thinking. Everyone has biases and stereotypes about people and situations. Those who engage in redemptive service will have limited knowledge of the context in which they are serving. They must continually acknowledge and question these personal limitations. As with all personal growth, such work can be painful. But refining our worldview is necessary in the hard work of redemptive service. Those who are attempting to transform the world need to be willing to be transformed themselves.

Redemptive service focuses on bringing the justice of Jesus to a world that desperately needs the spiritual, social, and physical hope that he offers. Social location focuses the work on the people who are being served. It might be more comfortable to aid those who are similar to us or deserving in some way, but Jesus calls us to serve those whom we might not consider to be legitimate recipients. Reflecting on social location makes us ask hard questions about the structures and experiences of marginalization. How do people experience inclusion and exclusion differently in these communities? How can everyone in a community have access to goods and services? What needs to change so that these barriers are removed?

Christian redemptive service is not so simple as just loving our neighbors like Jesus told us to do. Christians today need to understand who is more likely to experience oppression and exclusion, not disregarding the social location of different people. Not every neighbor has equal representation in our lives and environments. Without thinking critically about who is excluded from these communities, we cannot effectively and justly love our neighbors.

DISCUSSION QUESTIONS

1. How did you experience COVID? Whom do you know that had an easier or harder time with the lockdown, unemployment rates, and physical vulnerability than you, and could different social locations explain the difference?

2. Can one aspect of a person's identity explain their life story? Why might it be important to think about the various identities that come together to influence experiences?

3. Discuss the connection between identity and context. Share some examples of how built environments, policies, and norms have marginalized some people while centralizing others.

4. This chapter presents social location as a practical tool rather than just a theory. In your context (school, church, club, etc.), how could you use social location to discuss who is being missed or excluded? What steps would you take to address the problem?

5. Thinking about social location requires us to see the world differently and intentionally listen to perspectives that would have otherwise been missed. What do you find personally challenging about seeing and listening differently? How might you overcome those challenges?

FOR FURTHER READING

Blum, Elizabeth D. *Love Canal Revisited: Race, Class, and Gender in Environmental Activism*. Lawrence: University Press of Kansas, 2008.

Klinenberg, Eric. *Heat Wave: A Social Autopsy of Disaster in Chicago*. 2nd ed. Chicago: University of Chicago Press, 2015.

Kozol, Jonathan. *Amazing Grace: The Lives of Children and the Conscience of a Nation*. New York: Crown, 1995.

Taylor, Dorceta E. *Toxic Communities: Environmental Racism, Industrial Pollution, and Residential Mobility*. New York: New York University Press, 2014.

CONCLUSION

Connecting Your Calling with Redemptive Service

We want to use this conclusion to reflect on the idea of calling. In some sense, this entire book has been about this topic. Recall from chapter 1 that humanity is created in the image of God and charged with serving as God's representatives and agents in this world. Because of the fall, humanity's service becomes *redemptive* service since our work must now participate in the restoration of God's creational intent (redemption) for the world. Christians intercede on the world's behalf until it is transformed to fulfill God's purposes for justice and shalom. This is our earthly vocation and our general calling. Part 1 further detailed why God has called us to this vocation, and part 2 offered some direction for how we can live out this calling.

We all have a general calling to redemptive service, but we also have a missional calling through which we use the gifts and talents that God has uniquely given us to contribute to making the world a better place. We are all called to participate in the work of redemptive service, but *how* we go about doing that will vary. In this conclusion we explore different types of calling, how to discern a missional calling, and ultimately how our missional calling connects with redemptive service. Further, we highlight some barriers that prevent us from living out our missional calling to redemptive service, and we note that no matter how small our contribution, our faithfulness to the call is not in vain. We are building *God's* kingdom of new creation and thus God will take our various efforts—however small and feeble—and incorporate them into the mission of redemption that has been at work since creation.

Calling

Discovering the Differences

What is a calling? Is it audible? Is it divine? Does everyone have a calling or does it only have to do with those going into formal or full-time ministry? Is vocation different from calling? Can I miss God's calling on my life? How do I find my calling? These are good questions that perhaps you have wrestled with at some point. The Christian tradition has long used the terms "calling" and "vocation" to address issues of direction, purpose, and meaning for our lives. The word "vocation" comes from the Latin *vocare*, which means "to call." Thus, "vocation" and "calling" can function interchangeably, and that is how we are using these terms. Nonetheless, though these words are synonymous, their usage within the Christian tradition has developed and changed over time. Consequently, it is especially important to delineate what we mean when we use the words "calling" or "vocation."[1]

We distinguish three types of calling: general calling, missional calling, and direct calling. While there are conceptual distinctions, these three are interrelated, as illustrated in figure C.1. General calling is the broadest, followed by missional calling and direct calling. As the arcs in the diagram become smaller and more focused, so do the callings. The callings are also situated within one another, as depicted in the diagram. There is no direct calling without a missional calling, and there is no missional calling without a general calling.

General calling refers to that which God calls all people to do; it is what God desires of everyone all the time. It is the broadest, most all-encompassing calling. We do not need to seek out or discern our general calling because Scripture is clear about what kind of life we should live. Texts such as Matthew 22:34–40—which calls us to love both God and neighbor—and Romans 12:9–21—which offers a list of instructions for how to live a godly life—point the way and offer guidance as to how we are to conduct ourselves. This general calling is lived out in the mundane details of everyday living. Whenever we are growing as a faithful disciple

1. William C. Placher, ed., *Callings: Twenty Centuries of Christian Wisdom on Vocation* (Grand Rapids: Eerdmans, 2005), 1–11.

Figure C.1 Three types of calling

of Christ and engaging in practices that form and shape us as such, we are living out our general calling.[2]

Missional calling is decidedly different from general calling. It refers to the contribution *your* life makes to God's kingdom. This type of calling is a sort of life mission statement: the direction toward which you aim to spend the majority of your time, gifts, and energy as they align with the way God has created you to serve. Missional calling is specific to each individual, like a set of fingerprints that is uniquely yours. While Scripture affirms that God intimately knows us (Ps. 139:13–16; Eph. 2:10) and has created us with certain gifts that place us in unique positions to contribute (Rom. 12:4–8; 1 Cor. 12), the biblical texts do not explicitly lay out what each person's missional calling will be. Rather, determining one's missional calling must be discerned individually. When someone comes to recognize their missional calling, they often see that they have already been moving in that direction for some time. Further, each person might live out their missional calling in a multitude of ways over their lifetime.[3]

Last, direct calling refers to a specific task that God instructs an individual to do. It might not even align with that person's giftings or passions, and it can vary in duration and scope. Many of the biblical stories that we associate with calling are illustrative of direct calling. God calls Abraham to leave his country, people, and father's household to go to the land God will show him (Gen. 12:1–3). God calls Moses from a fiery bush to return and lead the Israelites out of Egypt (Exod. 3:1–4:17). God calls Mary to bring forth Jesus, the Savior of the world (Luke 1:26–38). God calls Paul to be a witness to the Gentiles (Acts 9:1–16). Unlike with missional calling, we don't need to go looking for a direct calling. Rather, God will find

2. Doug Koskela, *Calling and Clarity: Discovering What God Wants for Your Life* (Grand Rapids: Eerdmans, 2015), 47–69.
3. Koskela, *Calling and Clarity*, 1–23.

us if there is a particular place to go or task to be done, and when God gives a direct call there is usually little doubt about what is being asked. While we still need confirmation that we have heard clearly from God, we usually do not need help interpreting the message. Moreover, unlike general and missional callings, not everyone will receive a direct calling, and one person might receive more than one direct calling in a lifetime.[4]

So, how do these callings come together? What do they look like in someone's life? Let us offer our own journeys as examples. I (Lisa) grew up in the church. Even from a young age I was aware of my *general calling* as a Christian and attempted to live my life accordingly. I faithfully went to church, read the Bible, prayed, served others, and largely tried to conduct myself in a way that marked me as a follower of Christ. While I was certainly no saint, I recognized early on that Christians are called to live their lives differently, and thus I strove to do so as best as I could. During my teenage years, I began to discern my *missional calling*. This did not happen overnight. This gradual process spanned over a decade of my life. I was always studious and fascinated with the Bible and theological ideas. I was constantly reading Christian discipleship books, listening to preachers, and learning as much about Christian spirituality as possible. I would spend hours doing biblical word studies with a concordance and putting together discipleship lessons for junior high students at my church. During my undergraduate years at college, I gained further clarity with respect to my missional calling. While I had always envisioned myself finding work in a traditional church setting pursuing ministry, during my first year I was captivated by my Bible and theology professors. Being in the college classroom with them opened my eyes to a new opportunity to live out what I had been sensing all along in my own life but in a manner I had not known until then. It quickly became clear to me that God had gifted me as a teacher with a heart for Christian discipleship. Following this path would bring together many of the strengths, desires, and joys that I had been experiencing for years, but I did not know precisely where they were leading or how they were merging together. While this missional calling could have been lived out in a myriad of ways, I was drawn to and pursued Christian higher education. After spending several more years earning various college degrees in religion, I found myself employed as a theology professor at a private Christian university. I heard a *direct call* from God that this was the particular institution and denomination that

4. Koskela, *Calling and Clarity*, 24–46.

I was to commit to—at least for a time—as I sought to live out my missional calling.

My (Ruthie's) journey to discover my calling is more indirect. My parents and grandparents were all pastors and missionaries. Growing up in a family where everyone had experienced a *missional call* into vocational ministry and a *direct call* into specific contexts, I simply believed that I had as well. I pursued an undergraduate degree in church ministry and Bible to become a pastor upon graduation. However, no ministerial doors opened after graduation, and my first job was in a professional setting—not ministerial. I felt like I must be missing God or missing my calling since I was not using my degree in this professional office. I decided to explore a master of divinity degree and seek credentialing with my denomination. During the process of becoming an ordained minister, I was required to meet with a regional supervisor for the denomination. In order to move to the next step of the ordination process, the regional supervisor asked me to write out my *missional call* to be a pastor. I tried for weeks, but sitting down and writing out my *missional call* to be a pastor was impossible. I could write about my grandparents' calling, my great-grandparents' calling, my parents' calling, and my training for my bachelor's degree. However, I could not find any words to articulate my personal, *missional call* into ministry. God seemed silent on the issue. This left me in a crisis. Since I could no longer pursue formal work in a church, I followed the *general call* to pursue the good things of God throughout my twenties and thirties. Opportunities opened for me to travel, teach, and love God more in order that my life would better reflect God's goodness. God stayed close, and I looked to serve him as I followed open doors, interests, and life's natural limitations. This led me to professional credentialing in Teaching English to Speakers of Other Languages (TESOL), teaching opportunities around the world, and a masters degree specializing in that field.

Throughout all of this, I spent seven years traveling and working abroad. While I wanted to continue working in other countries, life circumstances brought me back to the United States. Because of my experience and degree, I got a job developing and running a TESOL program for a state university. I loved working in the university system in the United States. As I spent more than a decade helping people improve their lives through English, I started to see how language fits into a bigger picture of social systems. This eventually led me to complete a doctorate in sociology. Through this process, I discovered that my *missional call* is to teach and engage students as well as actively work toward building the kingdom of God that looks like Revelation 7:9, one in which people from every nation, tribe, people, and language are included and treated with justice. When I found myself at Lee University (after I turned forty!), I finally was able to articulate a specific, *direct call* from God.[5] I was able to see how my experiences, skills, knowledge, and talents all converged with a deep love for my students and passion for justice. Even the undergraduate degree that I spent decades thinking would never be useful is now very helpful. Discovering both my *missional call* and my *direct call* has been a process that has taken almost twenty years, but it is one that has filled me with profound joy.

Redemptive Service and Calling

Let's further focus now on how redemptive service relates to two of these callings: general and missional.[6] Redemptive service constitutes part of one's general call as one of the practices that God desires us to be engaged in. Part 1 of this book focused on why God expects us to fulfill this general calling as Christians and how it is fundamentally connected to our Christian identity (people of God, body of Christ, and community of the Spirit). Part 2 focused on the different ways we can embody this general calling in the world today (relief, development, and advocacy).

But though this relationship between general calling and redemptive service is clear, we are still left with the question of how our *missional calling* is related to redemptive service. How can our unique gifts and talents be used in specific service to those around us to further God's kingdom work of making things whole? While redemptive service does not exhaust our missional calling, it certainly intersects with it. When we begin to discern our own missional calling, we must think intentionally about the ways in which God is calling us—uniquely and individually—to mend the brokenness in the world.

DISCERNING YOUR MISSIONAL CALLING

Before considering how our missional calling might intersect with redemptive service, we must first be able to identify our missional calling. However, though the biblical texts support the idea of missional calling, we

5. My experience here illustrates that our understanding of God's call in our life is not always linear. I felt a sense of pull to Lee University, but it wasn't until I started working with students that I realized how my work was a direct call from God. Sometimes the process of moving into our call requires steps of faith.

6. While direct calling certainly can focus on redemptive service (e.g., a direct call to start a nonprofit food co-op), it might not explicitly do so.

won't find the details of our specific missional calling there. And we should probably not look for miraculous signs and wonders to get our attention either. While burning bushes and voices from heaven are easier ways of hearing a call, these extraordinary accounts—especially in Scripture—are usually in connection with a direct calling, not a missional calling. So, where do we look for our missional calling? Or perhaps better stated, to what or whom do we listen to hear our missional calling? Rather than searching high and low for the answers, we can turn inward. We can begin to listen to our life and allow it to tell us who we are. It is in the ordinary, rather than the extraordinary, that we will hear God's voice speak to us and guide us into our missional calling. Parker Palmer describes this process as "letting your life speak." He says, "Before I can tell my life what I want to do with it, I must listen to my life telling me who I am. I must listen for the truths and values at the heart of my own identity, not the standards by which I *must* live—but the standards by which I cannot help but live if I am living my own life."[7]

As we get older, many of us will get better at letting our lives speak to us. However, even as young adults we must begin to discern our missional calling. While there are no simple steps or easy formulas that we can use in this process that will magically deliver our missional calling straight into our laps in one neatly wrapped package, there are several signs that we can look for to try to better discern our missional calling. These are best understood as signposts along our journey that can guide us in a particular direction. Through these signposts God speaks to us and directs us toward our missional calling.

The first signpost to consider is what motivates you and brings you joy. Where are your energies and passions focused? Do you like being with the elderly? Do you enjoy working with numbers? Do you take delight in being with people from other cultures and languages? Whatever it is that captures your interests and brings you happiness, begin to view these things as key indicators that God has made you with these particular loves. They are not accidental or arbitrary. Your missional calling usually corresponds with the desires God has created in you, so begin to pay attention to what those are. While we may have the fear that God will call us to do something we do not want to do (and God may), that type of calling is better understood as a direct calling, not a missional calling. We should expect

---

7. Parker Palmer, *Let Your Life Speak: Listening for the Voice of Vocation* (San Francisco: Jossey-Bass, 2000), 4–5 (emphasis original).

our missional calling to resonate with who we are created to be and what
motivates us into action.[8]

The second signpost to consider is the talents you possess. Are you
good at working with your hands? Do you have a beautiful voice? Are
you a gifted public speaker? Can you write in a clear and interesting way?
Good intentions or motivations are not enough when it comes to living
out our missional calling. Certain things in life might bring us joy, but we
must also have—or be willing to obtain—the sorts of skills necessary to
get the job done. God has created all of us with certain abilities and gifts.
Sometimes these talents need refining and strengthening over the course
of our lives, but their initial form is usually already present even when we
are young. Christians have been taught to value the supernatural, but God
is not less present when we exercise our natural abilities. If God created
us and gifted us, what better way could we glorify God than to put these
talents to good use?[9]

The third signpost to consider is what experiences—positive or
negative—have shaped you and are pushing you toward a particular missional calling. Positive experiences can make us more aware of our joys
and talents. For example, working with younger kids in the public school
system can validate one's desire to be an educator. Or taking a medical
missions trip can substantiate one's desire to be a nurse. Tragic experiences can also propel us to become more involved and point our lives in a
certain direction. For example, experiencing sexual abuse can make one
more aware and empathetic to other victims and lead to becoming an
advocate against sex trafficking. Or the loss of a loved one to substance
abuse can focus one's passion on preventing it from occurring in other
people's lives. While certain experiences can be very painful and might not
be ordained by God, they can still be used to bring healing and restoration
to a broken world.[10]

The fourth signpost to consider is what close friends and family members see in you. We are not left to discover our missional callings alone.
Participation in a community can help us in the discernment process as
well. We cannot always see what is right in front of us, but those closest to

8. Jerry Sittser, *The Will of God as a Way of Life: How to Make Every Decision with Peace
and Confidence* (Grand Rapids: Zondervan, 2004), 175, 182–83; and Koskela, *Calling and
Clarity*, 4.
9. Whether natural gifts or Spirit-endowed gifts, both are ultimately from God. Sittser, *Will
of God as a Way of Life*, 175–77; and Koskela, *Calling and Clarity*, 3–4.
10. Sittser, *Will of God as a Way of Life*, 177–78.

us have the healthy distance and clarity needed to help us hear God. This community could include a number of different people: parents, pastors, teachers, mentors, or friends. Because various people see a different part of you at different times of your life, it is best to seek a variety of perspectives for insight into your missional calling. While our friends and family are not the absolute authority, they do give us valued discernment as to what God may be calling us to do.[11]

The fifth signpost to consider is what opportunities (or lack thereof) are presented to you. Sometimes we refer to these opportunities as the proverbial open door, with the assumption that we should walk through any open door. God can and does use circumstances to guide us toward our missional calling. But closed doors can give us a clue to our calling as well. As painful as it may be, closed doors can have the same guiding effect. Yet we should be cautioned that an open or closed door is just *one* signpost that should be discerned in conjunction with the others mentioned above. An open door does not necessarily mean that any given opportunity is God's will for your life (especially if there are multiple open doors), just as a closed door does not necessarily mean the opportunity is completely closed off forever (maybe it's just not the right time). Thus, the process of discernment uses *all* the signposts to find a way forward.[12]

When you reflect on your life using these signposts, you might see a pattern begin to emerge that makes sense and points you in the right direction. From the beginning, our lives provide clues to our missional calling, and trying to interpret these clues can be profoundly worthwhile, even if messy and complicated! Discovering one's missional calling does not happen overnight; it is a gradual process. Even when we think we have discerned our missional calling, we still do not know exactly how we will live this out. Our missional calling is like a compass that points us in the right direction, but it does not provide a trail map for every step of the rest of our lives. Yet when we are living into our missional calling, it will feel as natural as breathing air. We will be content and fulfilled, knowing that we are engaged in the work for which we were created.

One final note about missional calling is that there is a difference between our missional calling and our career. Whereas missional calling is a theological construct that points to a specific vision of how God wants us to use our time, energy, and abilities, "career" is a secular word that indicates

11. Sittser, *Will of God as a Way of Life*, 181–82; and Koskela, *Calling and Clarity*, 5.
12. Sittser, *Will of God as a Way of Life*, 178–81.

a particular line of work we do to earn income. If we are lucky, our career will overlap with our missional calling. But this does not always happen (just recall some of the jobs you may have had as a teenager!), and missional calling is broader than career. Our missional calling is not fulfilled simply by having a particular job or working at the office. We might even have to work in places and positions that do not resonate strongly with our missional calling, but that does not mean we no longer have one. Throughout our lives, our missional calling will be realized and lived out in varying degrees in our career, but it should never be equated with our career.[13]

WHAT DO YOU SEE?

We return now to the question of how our missional calling intersects with redemptive service. What role is God calling you to fulfill in bringing healing to a hurting world? Though we may all be moved to compassion to meet the needs of those around us (recall the parable of the good Samaritan), *what* we see as most pressing and *how* we choose to meet those needs will vary. Jerry Sittser offers the following example that illustrates this well:

> Imagine ten people arriving at the scene of a terrible accident. Though they witness the same event, they all see something different and respond in different ways. One man sees confused motorists unsure of what to do, so he begins to direct traffic. A woman sees the details of the accident, immediately calls 911 on her cell phone, and describes the scene with astonishing accuracy. A retired teacher sees two traumatized children whose mother is lying lifeless on the side of the road; she wraps her arms around them to comfort them. A nurse sees catastrophic injury and immediately checks vital signs. A pastor sees a witness to the accident sobbing uncontrollably and tries to calm her down. A young woman, still in her teens, sees a spiritual battle unfolding and prays. Other people see chaos, so they get blankets, flares, and emergency supplies out of their cars and put them to good use. Everyone responds differently to the accident because they see differently. What they see is determined by something deep within them.[14]

God has created each of us to see the world in a particular way, and our vision is shaped by our missional calling. As citizens of the kingdom, we are all called to work toward the flourishing of life, to bring about the

13. Sittser, *Will of God as a Way of Life*, 157–68; and Koskela, *Calling and Clarity*, 5–6.
14. Sittser, *Will of God as a Way of Life*, 167.

healing and renewal of creation that God ultimately intends. But how we engage that work will be determined by who we are and by our missional calling. So, what do *you* see around you? What has moved *you*? How can *you* respond to the hurt and brokenness in the world based on who God has created you to be? Each of us has our own unique contribution to make. We are all called to situate our personal story within God's greater story of redemption. How we choose to live out redemptive service will ultimately be informed by our own missional calling.

Excuses, Excuses

Although we are all called to engage in the work of redemptive service, experience reveals that many of us fail from time to time for a host of reasons. Several decades ago, social scientists conducted a series of experiments to investigate a person's participation—or lack thereof—in emergency situations. Despite the various scenarios, the researchers identified three stages that individuals proceeded through when encountering a victim: *notice* the event, *interpret* the event as an emergency, and *decide* that it is one's personal responsibility to act. At each of these stages, participants could choose to remove themselves from the process and fail to help.[15] These experiments revealed that when individuals did not offer to help a victim, it was usually because of one of two failures.

The first failure was a participant's inability to notice and interpret a need when they encountered it (the first two stages noted above). In the experiment many individuals were preoccupied with another task and thus were hurried when they encountered the victim. While we might assume that these rushed people were uncaring, closer examination revealed that the issue was not callousness but perception. When those in a hurry were confronted with a victim who needed help, how they *noticed* and *interpreted* the event differed from other individuals who stopped to help. Their hurriedness caused them to neglect others' distress, and thus they believed assistance was unnecessary.[16] They did not see a need, and so they did not understand themselves to be refusing to help.

15. Bibb Latané and John M. Darley, "Group Inhibition of Bystander Intervention in Emergencies," *Journal of Personality and Social Psychology* 10, no. 3 (1968): 215–21; and Latané and Darley, *The Unresponsive Bystander: Why Doesn't He Help?* (New York: Meredith, 1970), 87–112, 121–28.

16. Researchers also note that some subjects found themselves conflicted over helping the experimenter who had assigned them to do a task versus helping the victim. Because they

We too can be guilty of the same failure. We find ourselves too busy and thus miss out on connecting our missional calling with redemptive service. The hurriedness of life impedes our vision so that we do not even *see* the brokenness; we do not *see* those hurting and needing us to reach out. We need to slow down and recognize that one of the greatest tasks God has given us is to live out our missional calling in redemptive service to others. To fail to do this is ultimately to fail the mission that directs our lives and the mission that God has been bringing about in the world since creation.

The second failure the experiments revealed was the participants' inability to decide that the need encountered necessitated their responsibility to act (the third stage noted above). The social scientists found that the more bystanders that were present to "witness" the situation and potentially respond, the less likely someone would be to intervene in an emergency situation. This phenomenon is now referred to as the *bystander effect*. A person's sense of responsibility dissolves when other onlookers are present. Hence, a person can rationalize their own inaction by convincing themselves that somebody else must be doing something about the problem.[17] Their inactivity results from their assumption that someone else will help.

A similar occurrence can take place with redemptive service. While we might see a need, we assume someone else will take care of it. As Rabbi Jonathan Sacks observes, "Often, we fail to act because we think someone else will, or should, or is better qualified than I am. More than evil or indifference, the fundamental moral problem is, 'Why me?' What connects me to this person in need? What gives me the right or duty to intervene?"[18] When we respond this way to the needs that confront us, we deny our own responsibility to be the image of God in this hurting world. Being the people of God, the body of Christ, and the community of the Spirit is to tend to the well-being of our neighbors. We cannot continue to look on the brokenness around us and assume someone else will take charge and respond. It is up to each one of us to intervene and to act. We are called to be a fragment of God's presence in other people's hurting lives.

---

knew someone was depending on them to get to a certain place quickly, they did not want to disappoint and thus failed to stop and help. See John M. Darley and C. Daniel Batson, "'From Jerusalem to Jericho': A Study of Situational and Dispositional Variables in Helping Behavior," *Journal of Personality and Social Psychology* 27, no. 1 (1973): 108.

17. Latané and Darley, "Group Inhibition of Bystander Intervention," 215–21; and Latané and Darley, *Unresponsive Bystander*, 87–112, 121–28.

18. Jonathan Sacks, *To Heal a Fractured World: The Ethics of Responsibility* (New York: Schocken, 2005), 253.

Mustard-Seed Wins

There is a popular story about a starfish thrower that beautifully illustrates the work we are called to do. A man walking along the beach noticed a boy hurriedly picking up and gently throwing things into the ocean. Approaching the boy, he asked, "Young man, what are you doing?" The boy replied, "Throwing starfish back into the ocean. The surf is up and the tide is going out. If I don't throw them back, they'll die." The man laughed to himself and said, "Don't you realize there are miles and miles of beach and hundreds of starfish? You can't make any difference!" After listening politely, the boy bent down, picked up another starfish, and threw it into the surf. Then, smiling at the man, he said, "I made a difference to that one."[19]

There are days when we might feel like our dreams and ambitions to change the world will never make a difference, but we must understand that transformation happens one starfish at a time. We can be overcome by the sheer number of people needing help that we can become frozen into inactivity. We may wonder "What does it matter?" or "Is it going to make any difference?" The simple answer is yes. It makes a difference for each and every person—however small or great the gift or gesture. The greatest accomplishment in our lives is to be an agent of hope for at least one other person, even for one moment. It only takes a little light to drive away the darkness, and every act of redemptive service lights a candle of hope in a dark world. Moreover, "when light is joined to light, mine to yours and yours to others, the dance of flames, each so small, yet together so intricately beautiful, begins to show that hope is not an illusion. Evil, injustice, oppression, cruelty do not have the final word."[20]

The Gospels liken the kingdom of God to a mustard seed (Luke 13:18–19) and to yeast (13:20–21). Both a mustard seed and yeast are tiny. Their potential power is underestimated because of their size. How could something so small really make such a big difference? Yet in the parables the tiny mustard seed grows into a large tree and the yeast permeates the dough and makes it rise. Our redemptive service is likewise not constituted by grand gestures and sweeping changes. Rather, our redemptive service happens in our daily choices and actions, small though they may feel, that ultimately transform the world. Rabbi Sacks says, "We mend the world one life at a time, one act at a time, one day at a time. . . . Every generous deed, each

19. This version of the story is adapted from Loren Eiseley, *The Star Thrower* (New York: Times Books, 1978), 169–85.
20. Sacks, *To Heal a Fractured World*, 270–71.

healing word, every embracing gesture brings redemption nearer. Each is a letter we write in the book of life."[21]

Victories gained for the kingdom are more like mustard-seed wins. They may seem insignificant, but the hope and promise of the Christian faith is that God will use these tiny wins to build the kingdom. When we partner with God, none of our efforts of redemptive service are meaningless or insignificant. They all contribute to the inbreaking of God's kingdom of new creation. Each of us must go and image God according to how we have been gifted; the world cannot afford for us to wait a minute longer to fulfill this calling. Go and serve! Be the people of God, the body of Christ, and the community of the Spirit to the hurting and the broken, joining with God's mission to redeem the world. When we do this, we will be loving our neighbors well!

DISCUSSION QUESTIONS

1. Think about how you have understood calling in the past. How does distinguishing between general, missional, and direct calling compare? Do you find this threefold distinction helpful?

2. Reflect on your life in light of the five signposts noted above. In light of these signposts, what do you think your life is saying concerning your missional calling?

3. Given what you know about your missional calling, what are some specific ways you feel drawn to engage in redemptive service?

4. Can you think of a time when you have been too busy to notice the needs around you? Have you ever found yourself guilty of the bystander effect?

5. How might having a mindset of mustard-seed wins change the way you approach or evaluate your engagement in redemptive service?

FOR FURTHER READING

Koskela, Doug. *Calling and Clarity: Discovering What God Wants for Your Life*. Grand Rapids: Eerdmans, 2015.

Palmer, Parker. *Let Your Life Speak: Listening for the Voice of Vocation*. San Francisco: Jossey-Bass, 2000.

21. Sacks, *To Heal a Fractured World*, 266.

Placher, William C., ed. *Callings: Twenty Centuries of Christian Wisdom on Vocation*. Grand Rapids: Eerdmans, 2005.

Schmidt, Len, and David Schmidt. "What's Wrong with Being Comfortable? In Praise of the Much-Maligned 'Comfort Zone.'" *Prism* (Spring 2014): 43–45.

Sittser, Jerry. *The Will of God as a Way of Life: How to Make Every Decision with Peace and Confidence*. Grand Rapids: Zondervan, 2004.

INDEX